AN INTRODUCTION TO
BUSINESS FINANCE

AN INTRODUCTION TO
BUSINESS FINANCE

G. S. HEMINGWAY, B.Sc.(Econ.)

Senior Lecturer, Department of Advanced Business Studies,
Hammersmith & West London College

HEINEMANN : LONDON

William Heinemann Ltd
15 Queen St, Mayfair, London W1X 8BE

LONDON MELBOURNE TORONTO
JOHANNESBURG AUCKLAND

Printed in Great Britain
by Cox & Wyman Ltd
London, Fakenham and Reading

To Ann

Preface

This book aims to promote understanding of the basic financial operations of businesses in general and of listed companies in particular.

After reviewing the legal forms in which they may be organized, it considers where and how firms may obtain the funds they require. This involves examination, against a background of inflation, of:

1 The role of the tax system in encouraging retention of profits.
2 The significance of depreciation.
3 The relative importance, benefits, costs, and gearing effects of the various external sources of funds.
4 The procedures (including Stock Exchange requirements) for new issues, and their main features – especially those by tender or involving rights or capitalization.

Since control of assets may be obtained without buying them, attention is also given to leasing and hire purchase facilities and, at greater length and within the context of the Take-over Code, to mergers.

Two major problems facing a business in using the funds at its disposal – the avoidance of overtrading and the selection of the most profitable assets to invest in – are then dealt with, and the importance of accurate cash flows and of d.c.f. appraisal techniques is emphasized.

Finally, the ways in which a firm may safeguard the assets which it has obtained are considered in a review of conventional insurance arrangements and a simplified presentation of hedging in commodity and foreign exchange markets.

The main theme is set out in the nineteen chapters, the four appendixes being used for the development of some of its related aspects.

The book was conceived to meet the requirements of those taking Business Finance on H.N.C./H.N.D. Business Studies courses, but it will also help candidates preparing for the Business Finance paper of the Institute of Chartered Secretaries and Administrators, the Financial Management paper of the Association of Certified Accountants, or other comparable examinations. To help such students, a selection of examination questions, arranged to follow the order in which topics are dealt with in the text, is given at the end of the book.

Having large interfaces with law, economics, and accountancy, business finance covers a vast field. It is likely, eventually, to be considerably influenced by U.K. membership of the European Economic Community, but even apart from this its content will probably change as much and as fast in the future as it has done in the past. No one book can span it all, and this one does not claim to do so.

The book has benefited, in both content and presentation, from helpful observations from several quarters, and I wish to thank in particular my esteemed colleague, Bob Horne, whose many valuable comments greatly improved an early draft. The faults that remain are mine, and I should welcome criticisms or suggestions for improvement.

G. S. HEMINGWAY

Acknowledgments

I gratefully acknowledge the co-operation of the following organizations in permitting reproduction of the material indicated:

Alex Lawrie Factors Ltd: restrictions on factoring (Ch. 5)

Bank of England: Table 10.1

Constable & Co. Ltd: extract from Slater's *The Growth of Modern England* (Ch. 15)

Council of the Stock Exchange: extracts from the Yellow Book (Ch. 10 and 11, Appendix to Ch. 10)

Her Majesty's Stationery Office: definition of partnership (Ch. 1) and of bill of exchange (Ch. 5); Companies Act 1948, section 79 (Ch. 7); extracts from Business Monitor Series M3, *Company Finance* (Tables 3.1, 5.1, 8.2, and 14.2); the *Report of the Committee of Inquiry on Small Firms*, Cmnd 4811 (Ch. 5 and 13); and the *Report on Shortages of Gas Supplies etc.* (the Wynn-Edwards Report) (Ch. 18)

International Chamber of Commerce (the world business organization): definition of documentary credits (Appendix to Ch. 5), contained in their publication, *Uniform Customs and Practice for Documentary Credits*

Lloyds Bank, *Review*: extract from Prof. Reddaway's article (Ch. 14)

Midland Bank, *Review*: Table 8.1

Panel on Take-overs and Mergers: extracts from the Take-over Code (Ch. 14)

Also, for examination questions:

Association of Certified Accountants

Institute of Bankers

Institute of Chartered Accountants in England and Wales

Institute of Chartered Secretaries and Administrators

G.S.H.

Contents

SECTION A

FORMS OF BUSINESS ORGANIZATION

1 Unincorporated Businesses

1.1 INTRODUCTION

This chapter reviews the three different organizational forms in which an unincorporated business may operate, starting with the simplest – the sole proprietorship – and going on to the more complex general and limited partnerships. Usually such a change in form will be paralleled by a change in size, but this is not always so.

1.2 SOLE PROPRIETORSHIP

1.21 INTRODUCTION

The easiest and most obvious way for a business to come into existence is for one person to start on his own, using just his personal resources or these supplemented by funds borrowed from sources dealt with in Chapters 5 and 6. A business of this kind is called a sole proprietorship or, sometimes and less accurately, a sole tradership. Whereas 'trading' means simply buying and selling, sole proprietors may engage in manufacturing and other activities too.

1.22 LEGAL CHARACTERISTICS

The legal position of a sole proprietor differs little from that of any other citizen. It is true that his income is taxed under Schedule D (profits from a trade or profession) instead of Schedule E (income from employment). In addition, there may well be health or other regulations which apply to his business and not to the population at large. But the latter will be due to the nature of the business he conducts, not to his status as a sole proprietor as such. In the eyes of the law (though not of his accountant), there is no difference between the proprietor and his business; the assets of the former are indistinguishable from those of the latter, and the debts of the business are the debts of the owner, without any limit to his liability for them.

The only legal requirement affecting a sole proprietor which does not apply to other individuals is that contained in the Registration of Business

Names Act 1916. This Act applies to any individual or firm having a place of business in the United Kingdom and operating under a name other than that of the true surname of the individual, or surnames of partners who are individuals, or corporate names of partners who are corporations. Anyone doing so must, within fourteen days of starting business, register with the Registrar of Business Names certain details: mainly the christian names and surname, nationality, residence, and other business occupation, if any, of the individual concerned, or of each of the partners if a partnership is involved. The Registers are kept in London and Edinburgh and are open to public inspection in normal business hours. Anyone convicted of failing to register is liable to a fine of up to £5 for each day that the offence continues, and also loses his rights under any contract he has made in relation to the business which should have been registered. Every business affected by the Act must show on all its stationery the present and former names, and nationality if not British, of the proprietor(s). After registering, the firm or individual concerned must exhibit the certificate of registration or a certified copy of it in a conspicuous position at its principal place of business – a requirement which seems to be honoured more in the breach than in the observance. The Registrar must be told, within three months of the event, if any registered business goes out of business, and he may himself remove names from the Register if he has reason to think that the enterprise concerned is dead.

1.23 NUMBERS

In economies like that of the United Kingdom, such one-man businesses (i.e. one proprietor, although there may be several employees) are constantly emerging – mainly in retail distribution, hotels and catering, and building – and equally constantly vanishing. However, there appear to be no precise figures for the total population, and changes in the population, of sole proprietorships. The Register of Business Names helps a little; by the beginning of 1975 nearly 2 million names had been recorded since it opened in January 1917, but active businesses are known to be considerably fewer than this. In any case the total is not a reliable guide to the number of sole proprietorships, partly because registration applies also to partnerships and, since 1948, to companies, but largely because it obviously does not include people carrying on businesses under their own names. The number of new registrations and deletions is published each year; those for 1973 totalled nearly 105,000 and 10,000 respectively [1].

The most up-to-date information on small businesses generally is to be found in the Bolton Report [2]. As to the total population of sole proprietorships, it says that about 1·5 million Schedule D assessments are raised on such businesses each year. As to their ability to survive, Table 2.X1 of the Report indicates mortality rates among small firms (a term covering much more than sole proprietorships). It shows that, of a sample of firms in existence in 1963, 19% of those in the motor trade, 23% of those in manufacturing and construction, 28% of those in retailing, and 33% of those in wholesaling had either ceased trading, gone into liquidation, or been taken over by 1970 – and the percentages exclude mortalities among firms established between 1963 and 1970.

1.3 PARTNERSHIP

1.31 INTRODUCTION

A sole proprietor whose business is capable of expansion and who wishes it to grow will probably, sooner or later, contemplate changing the formal nature of its organization. Problems of taxation, fund raising, management, or control, either singly or in combination, will lead him to consider turning it into either a partnership or a limited company.

1.32 LEGAL CHARACTERISTICS

Section 1 of the Partnership Act 1890 defines partnership as 'the relationship subsisting between persons carrying on business in common with a view to profit'. There must obviously be at least two members of a partnership, and section 120 of the Companies Act 1967 sets an upper limit of twenty members for all partnerships except those of solicitors, members of a recognized body of accountants or members of a recognized Stock Exchange. The government may make regulations exempting other professions or trades from that limit, and certain partnerships of patent agents, valuers, auctioneers, surveyors, estate agents and managers, actuaries, consulting engineers, and building designers have been freed from it (as have been certain limited partnerships – *see* below – of valuers, auctioneers, surveyors, and estate agents and managers) [3].

With two or more people running a business, problems might easily arise. To prevent, or cure where necessary, such problems there are other requirements over and above those applicable to a sole proprietorship. Thus, although a partnership may be established informally, even by oral agreement, the relationship between partners is usually set out formally in a partnership deed, and the legal framework within which this type of business operates is provided by the 1890 Act already mentioned or, in a few cases, by the Limited Partnership Act 1907.

Despite this, for all practical purposes the legal position of partners is no different from that of sole proprietors; the law recognizes no distinction between the partners as partners and as individual citizens. The assets of the partnership belong to the partners and are indistinguishable from their personal assets; the liabilities of the partnership are the joint and several liabilities of the individual partners; they are assessed for income tax under Schedule D; and they have the same responsibility to register under the Registration of Business Names Act 1916.

1.33 NUMBERS

As with sole proprietors, there is no exact figure for the total of partnerships at any one time, but the Bolton Report says that about 300,000 Schedule D tax assessments are raised on them each year [4].

1.4 LIMITED PARTNERSHIP

1.41 LEGAL CHARACTERISTICS

The only means by which the position of partners may be changed within the partnership framework is by the formation of a business under the Limited Partnership Act 1907. This enables people prepared to forego an active role in the running of a firm to join a partnership on a limited liability basis, by which their liability for the debts of the business is limited to the amount of capital they have undertaken to subscribe. However, in every limited partnership there must be at least one general partner whose liability for the business's debts is unlimited, and any 'limited' partner participating in the management of the partnership loses his limited status.

1.42 NUMBERS

The Private Companies Act 1909, now effectively replaced, removed much of the attraction of limited partnerships; the total number on the Registers in London and Edinburgh was only 2,401 at the end of 1973.

1.5 SUMMARY

The simplest forms of business organization, and collectively the most numerous, are those unincorporated firms in which the owners are legally indistinguishable from the businesses they run, i.e. either sole proprietorships or partnerships. Legal requirements are minimal and thousands of new firms are formed each month, but the failure rate is also very high.

2 Incorporated Businesses

2.1 INTRODUCTION

Incorporated businesses, called companies, are fundamentally different from unincorporated ones. This chapter explains the nature of the difference, reviews the essential features of the various forms of company, and considers the particular advantages and disadvantages of holding companies.

2.2 INCORPORATION

If a sole proprietor reorganizes his business as a company (after either exploiting to the full the extra resources potentially available through a partnership, or side-stepping this phase completely) he will make a critically important change. The formation of any company requires an act of incorporation, which is most commonly performed now by a relatively simple procedure of registration, as Figure 2.1 indicates. Once incorporated, the company is a legal entity with an existence and powers quite separate and distinct from those of its individual members, called shareholders. It is subject to a special body of law, set out for the most part in the Companies Acts 1948–67, and to those taxes which apply to companies but not to individuals, notably corporation tax.

2.21 ADVANTAGES OF INCORPORATION

There are considerable advantages in incorporating:

1 The new legal person so created has the very convenient attribute of perpetual succession, i.e. it does not die nor is it affected by the mortality of its members, unlike a partnership.
2 The company may sue and be sued in its own name, without necessarily involving any of its members.
3 Dealings between members are simplified, being always at arm's length and unaffected by that common membership. By contrast, members of a partnership are legally held to be in a special relationship with each other, and they may bring actions against each other only on a contract.
4 Although not all partnerships are subject to a membership limit (*see*

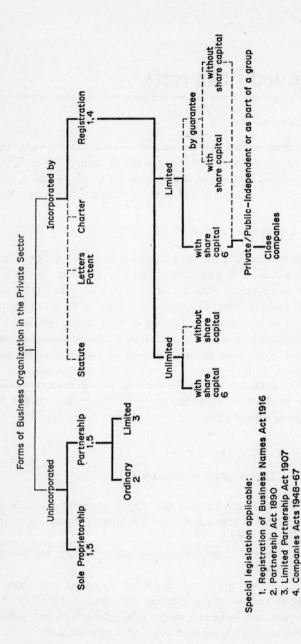

FIGURE 2.1   Forms of business organization in the private sector

p. 3), incorporation may – and in the case of public companies generally does – provide access to more members and thus, in principle, more capital.

5 The economically significant companies are those which have shares, and transfer of these is not impeded by the need to realize and split up the business's property, or rewrite the partnership deed, every time its membership changes.

6 Furthermore, the ability to issue shares provides an additional means of acquiring assets denied to unincorporated businesses (*see* Chapter 14).

7 An additional means of raising money is available in that a company may borrow on the security of a floating charge (*see* p. 76). Technically, unincorporated firms may do this too, but if the charge attaches to chattels it has to be registered as a bill of sale. The Register is checked by credit control agencies and details of new entries are regularly published in the appropriate trade journals. Readers interpret such registration as a sign of financial weakness and may withhold supplies, so that unincorporated businesses registering floating charges destroy their creditworthiness.

8 The profits of an incorporated business are subject to corporation tax, which is at a flat rate, apart from the abatement provisions for small companies [1]. By contrast, the profits of unincorporated firms are liable to income tax with some degree of progression.

(As will be seen later, the financial decisions of any undertaking, incorporated or not, will be influenced to a greater or lesser extent by the tax system currently in force. Both rates and forms of taxation are, however, liable to rapid change and those used in the text are by way of illustration only.)

Limited liability

The liability that the members of a company have for its debts is limited to the face value of the shares in it that they have agreed to buy. However, this protection is in essence available to members of limited partnerships, which are not incorporated, and is not available to members of unlimited companies, which are. Limited liability therefore is not an advantage of incorporation as such, although it is usually found with incorporated businesses.

2.22 DISADVANTAGES OF INCORPORATION

There are also certain disadvantages in being incorporated:

1 Privacy is lost because of the obligation to file an annual return, including a copy of the balance sheet and profit and loss account, with the Registrar

of Companies. Unlimited companies avoid this disadvantage (*see* p. 11).

2 Extra costs are incurred, partly in the registration procedure itself, partly in the 1% duty on capital raised, and partly in the maintenance of certain registers and accounts in a prescribed minimum form.

3 Capital withdrawal or reconstruction requires High Court sanction, whereas in a partnership it can be arranged much more informally and cheaply.

When an unincorporated business becomes incorporated, it is most likely to emerge as either a private or a public limited company, although unlimited ones also exist.

2.3 PRIVATE LIMITED COMPANIES

2.3 FORMATION

A private limited company is formed by filing with the Registrar of Companies certain documents specified in the Companies Acts: principally a Memorandum of Association and Articles of Association, setting out respectively (i) the basic nature and purpose of the company, and (ii) the rules for its internal regulation. Receipt of the Registrar's certificate of incorporation entitles the company to start operating. The procedure is relatively cheap and simple, designed with the needs of the small family-type business in mind.

2.32 LEGAL CHARACTERISTICS

Three legal features, now set out in section 28 of the Companies Act 1948, distinguish a private from a public company:

(a) Limitation on membership

Membership (member = shareholder) must number at least two and not more than fifty, excluding employees and ex-employees who became members while employed. Whatever the original purpose of this exception, it now serves to remove the discrimination which would otherwise exist between private and public companies in the development of profit-sharing schemes. Under such schemes, employees are helped to buy ordinary shares in their firm, so that as the enterprise prospers they may receive dividends and/or capital gains. Since ownership of just one ordinary share makes a person a member of the business concerned, the operation of a profit-sharing scheme could increase a company's membership quite quickly. No problem arises with a public company because there is no legal upper limit to the number of shareholders, but a private company could find itself unable to offer this benefit to its employees if its membership could not exceed fifty.

Of course, the exception also enables the controllers of a private company to ignore the upper limit on membership if they so wished; they could hire people (presumably just issuing them with clock cards would do), sell them shares in the company, and then fire them or accept their resignations. This might make for a record-breaking labour turnover, but it would also make it possible for the controllers legally to raise the membership of the organization to any level they wanted.

(b) Public investment ban

Appeals to the public for funds by offering securities for sale to them are completely banned.

(c) Directors control share transfer

The directors have the obligation and power to restrict or refuse the transfer of shares in the company. It is true that a public company, also, may provide itself with similar powers in its Articles of Association (providing it has not got or is not seeking a Stock Exchange listing), but what may be a matter of convenience for some public companies is a matter of critical concern for all private ones. With ownership in the hands of a small group, often just the directors, it is vital for shareholders to be personally acceptable to each other, and without control over the transfer of shares this could not be ensured. (Arithmetically, too, this power must be present if the legal limit on membership is to be maintained. Otherwise a situation could arise where one of, say, forty-nine members decided to sell his holding and it was bought by, say, four people not already members and not holding jointly. If such a transfer went through, the membership would rise to fifty-two and the enterprise would no longer qualify for private company status.)

Before 1967, the vast majority of private companies were exempted by the Companies Act 1948 from having to file with the Registrar of Companies a copy of their annual report and accounts. Largely because of the anomalies which had arisen, the Jenkins Committee [2] recommended the abolition of this exempt category and this was done by section 2 of the Companies Act 1967. However, that statute stopped short of implementing another of the Committee's recommendations: that the different statutory treatment of private and public companies also be abolished. Later proposals, indeed,

have pointed in the opposite direction, i.e. towards sharpening the overt
distinction between private and public companies by specifying (in line with
E.E.C. thinking) a minimum paid-up capital for the latter, requiring private
companies to state explicitly in their title that that is what they are, and then
adjusting the extent of disclosure required of a company to its size and
status [3].

2.33 NUMBERS

The private limited company may not now provide very much in the way of
privacy, but the figures show no signs of a decline in its popularity: 66, 756
new ones with share capital were registered in 1973 [4], and at the end of that
year registrations totalled 583,929 [5]. Not all of them would have been active,
but even so this type of company clearly still has great appeal.

2.34 ATTRACTIONS

Partly this is a matter of the ease and cheapness of establishing and operating
a private company as compared with a public one; the latter in fact usually
start life as private companies and are then converted [6]. Basically, however, as the figures for close companies indicate (see below), their attraction
for the family business is the potential tax advantage which any company
has over any unincorporated firm.

2.35 CLOSE COMPANIES

This designation derives from the Income and Corporation Taxes Act 1970
[7], and broadly applies to U.K. resident companies controlled by five or
fewer participators or by their directors. It is thus a form of private company
ideally suited to the needs of family concerns.

Close companies are regarded by the Inland Revenue authorities as a
form of business organization designed to promote tax avoidance, because
their owners would be able, if not prevented from doing so, to leave profits
in the business and thus avoid paying tax on them at all, or to pay tax on
them at a lower rate than would apply if they had been distributed as
dividends. Such companies (and similar ones since 1922 [8], are accordingly
liable to 'shortfall assessment' (previously called surtax direction). In
essence, this means that they are required to distribute as dividends each
year specified percentages of their investment and trading incomes (in 1974,
100% and 50% respectively), so that the resulting amounts may be taxed as
income in the hands of the recipients. The percentages stated are maxima;
less is required if it can be shown that distributing at these rates would

prejudice the maintenance and development of the company's business. Such shortfall assessments, incidentally, override any restraint on dividend distributions which may be temporarily imposed in connection with incomes policy.) Other rules applying to close companies limit the interest which may be paid to directors and associates and require loans from the company to participators to be treated as dividends – hence as income liable to tax.

Close companies are numerically very important. Of the 320,000 active companies charged to corporation tax at the time of the Bolton Committee's inquiries, about 220,000 (70%) were close companies [9], and there is no reason to suppose that the position has changed much since then.

2.4 UNLIMITED COMPANIES

Since 1967, all private companies have had to provide for public scrutiny as much information as public limited companies. Furthermore, the advantage of limited liability for family-type businesses has long been more apparent than real because, when borrowing, owners of such businesses have found themselves required to give personal guarantees of repayment which override any limit to their liability as shareholders. Accordingly, some private limited companies have changed their status to that of unlimited companies. (Public companies may do this too, but private companies have stronger reasons.)

2.41 LEGAL CHARACTERISTICS

Although the 'unlimited' in their title refers to the liability of the members for the business's debts, such organizations also have no limit to the number of their members. More important, however, is the fact that although they are corporate bodies, with all that this implies, section 47 of the Companies Act 1967 exempts them from filing the statutory documents mentioned earlier with their annual returns – providing they are neither a subsidiary nor a holding company of a limited company (*see* p. 14 for terms), nor engaged in promoting a trading stamp scheme. (These provisions are designed to ensure that the disclosure otherwise required of companies by the Companies Acts and the Stamp Trading Act 1964 is not avoided.)

2.42 NUMBERS

At the end of 1973 there were 4,525 unlimited companies on the British Registers. Although new registrations rose sharply after the change in the law in 1967, the vast majority of them existed before then [10].

2.43 ADVANTAGES

The main attraction of this form of organization is that it is able to avoid objectionable publicity – objectionable not just because of what competitors may learn from it but also because of what it may reveal to dominant customers [11].

2.5 PUBLIC LIMITED COMPANIES

2.51 FORMATION

If the existing or expected demand for funds outstrips the capacity of the private limited company to provide them, the next step may be to form a public limited company. Although this step may be taken by any of the forms of business organization previously mentioned, most public companies do in fact start as private ones. As indicated below, the reason for their change in status is not always financial.

A public limited company is formed in the same way and is subject to the same body of law as a private one, but it may not begin operations until it has received from the Registrar of Companies a specific authorization to do so, commonly called a trading certificate.

2.52 LEGAL CHARACTERISTICS

(a) Membership number

It has a minimum membership of seven, and no maximum.

(b) Public investment

It may appeal to the public for funds, by offering to sell them its shares of different types or to borrow from them. However, although a public company is entitled to solicit funds from the public, it does not have to do so – many, indeed, do not have the Stock Exchange listing without which any such appeal is likely to be unsuccessful. Thus, at the end of 1973 the Stock Exchange listed the securities of 3,429 companies registered in the United Kingdom [12], but public companies with share capital probably then totalled two or three times that number (*see* 2.53 below). An appeal for public subscriptions made by an unlisted company is not necessarily doomed to failure, e.g. in 1972 two companies tried it – the Commercial Bank of Wales (successfully) and the British Bangladesh Trust Ltd (rather less so) – though neither had a listing then.

A business may reach the stage of being a public company without applying for such a listing for more than one reason. It may become a public company inadvertently by failing to meet one or more of the statutory requirements set out in 2.32 above. Or, if by accident or design it becomes public, the directors may be unwilling to apply for a listing because of the rigorous scrutiny of the business's performance by the Stock Exchange that this would entail [13]. They may feel unwilling to do so either because – as with the Commercial Bank of Wales and the British Bangladesh Trust – there simply has been no performance, or because they consider it has been too short. (It need not, in fact, be very long. Northern Songs Ltd – the company set up to exploit some of the Beatles' music – was registered as a private company on 22 February 1963, became a public company on 11 February 1965, and made a public issue one week later, for which Stock Exchange listing was given.) On the other hand, they may be able to show a perfectly satisfactory performance, but may consider the benefits that would result from a listing to be not worth the trouble and expense involved.

However, the simplest explanation is that the directors wish to keep the shares within a selected group and are therefore unwilling to permit their unrestricted transfer. This points to the third difference between the public and the private company:

(c) Unrestricted share transfer

If it has, or is applying for, a Stock Exchange listing (but not necessarily otherwise), a public company's Articles must allow unrestricted transfer of its shares – providing they are fully paid [14]. By implication, despite the Stock Exchange's concern to ensure a free market, even a listed company may restrict the transfer of partly paid shares. This is to protect it from the loss which could otherwise arise if it sought to raise funds by making a call on such partly paid shares. A member wishing to evade his obligation to meet such a call (e.g. he might think that the company was in trouble and be naturally averse to throwing good money after bad) could do so by making over his holding to a 'man of straw' – someone of no financial substance, unable to pay anything – thus depriving the company of the funds it was entitled to obtain.

2.53 NUMBERS

New registrations roughly offset removals due to mergers, liquidations, and conversions to private status, so that the total of 15,576 on the British Registers at the end of 1973 was practically unchanged from ten years earlier [15]. How many of these have share capital is not now known, but probably not more than two-thirds [16].

2.54 ADVANTAGES

Apart from those already mentioned, the public company's great potential advantage – often realized – is that of sheer size. It offers directly or indirectly a massive outlet for investment funds, and the means of financing the acquisition of assets on any scale. It is thus not surprising that the public listed company has become the dominant form of business organization in the private sector of the United Kingdom – as its counterpart has done in similar economies. This is indicated in the analysis of company accounts referred to on p. 28.

2.6 HOLDING COMPANIES

2.61 FORMATION

The final stage in the development of a business may be the formation of a holding company. Section 154 of the Companies Act 1948 defines this as one which holds more than half of the equity share capital, or is a member and controls the composition of the board of directors, of one or more other companies, called its subsidiaries. A holding company is often called a parent company; parent plus subsidiary/ies are referred to as a group. The parent may itself engage in productive operations, or it may be a holding company pure and simple.

2.62 COMPARISON WITH OTHER ORGANIZATIONS

Like any other company, holding companies may be either private or public and are bound by the relevant requirements set out earlier. As a form of business organization, however, they do have peculiar advantages and disadvantages, which are most conveniently dealt with here. Three things must be borne in mind at the outset:

1 Whatever these advantages and disadvantages may be, they are potential only; they may not be realized in practice.
2 Although the group may well be a large organization, the benefits and costs of sheer size are irrelevant to the assessment of holding companies as such. What follows is a brief consideration of those which are claimed to be peculiar to holding companies by virtue of their being a particular form of organization.
3 Comparison must be of like with like, e.g. not of what may happen in a well-run group with what may happen in a badly-run company without subsidiaries.

63 ADVANTAGES

) *Preservation of goodwill*

his benefits both the owners of the holding company and the public at
rge. A comparison of business expansion via the complete integration of
mpanies and via the use of a holding company will show how it arises.
'ith integration, at least one company ceases to exist. Its name is removed
om the Register of Companies and no longer appears on stationery,
lvertisements, or any assets, and those who have previously traded with it
） longer have any opportunity to do so.

When a holding company adds a company to its group, however, the
osition is quite different. The parent acquires all or most of the ordinary
ares involved and is then in unchallengeable control of the subsidiary's
isiness. But, apart from any publicity at the time (and this is most likely to
： stimulated by disputed acquisitions of and by quoted companies – many
xpansions occur outside such limits) or any deliberate action by the
arent itself, there is no open indication of this change in ownership.
he subsidiary remains registered as a distinct company; the composition
' its share register will have changed but, since there does not have to be
y change of name or of any other readily visible detail, neither suppliers
or customers need know what has happened. With nothing to disturb
tablished trading patterns, the subsidiary – and hence the parent – will
ntinue to benefit from any previously existing goodwill, and since this is an
dication of the customers' satisfaction, they will benefit too.

Two points may be made here.

Keeping alive the name of a subsidiary is not the only way of preserving
any goodwill associated with it; if it has any registered trademarks or
brand names, these may be used by the holding company.

Although the parent may leave its subsidiary completely alone, it is more
likely to make some alteration to the latter's procedures. Such changes,
even in what may appear to be exclusively internal matters like accounting
arrangements and location of stocks, will sooner or later be noticed by
customers and suppliers. If they consider themselves adversely affected by
them, goodwill will be reduced even though the firm's identity seems unchanged.

) *Preservation of tax benefits*

reservation of a subsidiary's identity also safeguards any tax allowances
nd reliefs accruing to it. Since such reliefs apply to specific named businesses

and may not be claimed by any other, they would be lost in a merger in which one firm completely absorbed another.

(c) Better monitoring of performance

This gain may also emerge – an advantage primarily to shareholders of the parent, but conceivably also to the public at large. It hinges on the fact that since the subsidiary is by definition a separate legal entity, it must continue to produce at least the basic information which has to be filed each year with the Registrar of Companies. The group's management will thus automatically receive at least some of the data they need for policy making. In a unified organization the various operating divisions have no similar externally imposed obligations to report, and some of this detail will therefore be available only if special efforts are made to get it. However, merely producing the information is no guarantee that it will be used, or used properly.

(d) Better use of managerial talent

It may be claimed that the holding company provides a unique means of making the best use of managerial talent. Assuming that this is scarce, that it is in everyone's material interest to put what there is to the best possible use, and that the control of resources requires some degree, however small, of ownership of them, the holding company offers greater possibilities for controlling large quantities of assets with a small initial capital stake from an entrepreneur than any other type of business organization. It does this through the scope it offers for what is called 'pyramiding' (not to be confused with pyramid selling, with which it has only a name in common).

Pyramiding means constructing a group in which some subsidiaries are themselves holding companies, so that the whole organization is a series of tiers. Figure 2.2 shows a highly simplified three-tier pyramid.

In this pyramid, the parent company A is capitalized at £20,002 – the odd £2 being needed to make the arithmetic of control absolutely certain in normal circumstances – and this sum has been used to buy 50% + 1 of the ordinary shares of each of companies B and C. (An equity holding of 50% + 1 share guarantees a voting majority of two on all issues except the special resolutions required when any important constitutional change is proposed, for which section 141 of the Companies Act 1947 prescribes a three-quarter majority of those entitled to vote and actually voting). Companies B and C have, in turn, used their resources to buy 50% + 1 share of the equity of subsidiaries D and E, and F and G, respectively. Companies A, B, and C are holding companies only; the profits or losses are made on the bottom tier. In each subsidiary, outside subscribers hold the minority share capital

(50% − 1 share) and all the debt. The important point about the whole arrangement is that whoever controls company A (and doing so calls for the control of only 5,001 shares) controls companies with capital of £320,000, and assets perhaps considerably greater than this.

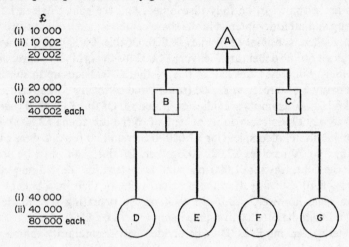

```
        £
 (i)  10 000
 (ii) 10 002
     ─────────
      20 002


 (i)  20 000
 (ii) 20 002
     ─────────
      40 002 each


 (i)  40 000
 (ii) 40 000
     ─────────
      80 000 each
```

FIGURE 2.2   A group organized as a pyramid

Note Capital (i); fully-paid £1 ordinary shares (ii) 10% debenture

Obviously, an arrangement of this kind depends on there being buyers for the minority share interests and debentures at each stage. Equally obviously, it would be unrealistic to suppose that even such a simple pyramid would emerge complete in a short space of time. The fact remains that it would be possible to arrange for assets to be organized in some such way as this and, bearing in mind the assumptions made earlier, it follows that the holding company offers advantages in financial organization not found in other types of business unit. Whether anyone has the talent effectively to direct organizations of the size made possible by such arrangements is doubtful; the record of recent mergers in the United Kingdom is not particularly encouraging (*see* p. 151).

2.64 DISADVANTAGES

(a) *Excessive concentration of profits*

This disadvantage may arise from the pyramidal structure illustrated in Figure 2.2 because of the mixture of share and loan capital with which the whole group is financed. The disadvantage is a social one – the beneficiaries are unlikely to complain!

How it works can be seen by supposing that in a given year each of the operating companies makes a profit of, say, £8,000 before deducting debenture interest and that this is doubled the following year. (In the interests of simplicity, tax and the odd £2-worth of debt at each stage are ignored, profits are assumed to be fully distributed, and the split between holding company and minority interest in the share capital is taken as exactly equal.) In year 1, then, subsidiary D makes £8,000. Of this, £4,000 must be used to pay interest on the debentures, leaving £4,000 for the ordinary shareholders. The minority interest takes half of this, so that £2,000 goes up to subsidiary B. Company B also receives £2,000 from E, and company C likewise receives a total of £4,000 from its subsidiaries, F and G. Of this £4,000, B must use £2,000 to pay the interest on its debt; half of the remaining £2,000 goes to the outside shareholders, leaving £1,000 to be remitted to A. C does exactly the same, so A receives £2,000 altogether. Of this, half must be used to service the debt, leaving £1,000 available as reward for the ordinary shareholders – a 10% dividend on the nominal value of their investment.

Next year, however, profits in each of the operating subsidiaries are £16,000. From the £16,000 available in company D, £4,000 goes as before in debt interest, leaving £12,000 to be divided between minority shareholders and company B. £6,000 thus passes from D to B, and a similar sum comes to B from E. Company C likewise receives £6,000 from each of its subsidiaries, F and G. Company B, after paying debt interest of £2,000 and £5,000 to its minority shareholders, sends on the balance to A. The latter thus receives £5,000 from B and, by a similar process, another £5,000 from C. From this £10,000, A has to pay, as before, £1,000 in interest on its debt, leaving £9,000 for distribution to its shareholders. Thus, a doubling of profits at the base of the pyramid, which leads to a trebling (from 10% to 30%) of the reward to shareholders at that level, causes a nine-fold increase (from 10% to 90%) in reward to shareholders in the apex company. Naturally, this accelerator also works in reverse; a fall in profits of the operating companies produces a disproportionately large fall in the reward available at the top of the pyramid – but, within the context of any argument about the connection between effort and reward, this phenomenon attracts unfavourable comment.

(b) Unfairness to minority shareholders

Another potential disadvantage of holding companies, which could emerge in a pyramid but does not depend on the existence of such a structure, is that they may penalize minority shareholders. (Clearly the disadvantage, if it arises, is to such shareholders. With wholly owned subsidiaries, therefore, there is no problem.)

Again illustrating with a simple and exaggerated example, what may happen is this. The directors of B may notice that D, which broke even last year, looks set for a profit after interest but before tax of, say, £10,000 this year while company E, which made a loss of £10,000 last year, looks like breaking even this year. If B does nothing and what is foreseen actually happens, D's profit of £10,000 will involve a payment of, say, £5,200 in corporation tax and the receipt by B of a dividend of £2,400. If, however, D's forecast profit could be made to appear in E instead, there would be no tax to pay – D would have no taxable income, while E's loss last year would be offset against this year's taxable profits. Even though, on the assumption of full distribution, half of this saving would go to E's minority shareholders, B would still gain £2,600 from the manoeuvre since, instead of the £2,400 it would otherwise have been paid from D's post-tax income, it would receive £5,000 as its half share of E's (tax-free) £10,000 profit. (Actually arranging this result should present no difficulties; if D and E trade together, prices could be adjusted so that E benefits to the required extent; if they do not, D could be required to hire something from E.)

The important thing is that, although the group as a whole is better off to the extent of its share of the tax saved, D's minority shareholders have been deprived of a dividend which was properly theirs. They will suffer no penalty only if they are also shareholders in E – each holding, in this particular case, at least twelve E shares for every twenty-five in D. Even if they were the entire minority membership of B, they would still be worse off. Since neither of these is likely to be the case, they would be made to suffer as a result of the transfer of earnings.

What, if anything, they would be able to do about such a situation is uncertain, and not very encouraging. Seeing what had happened might be hard enough, but proving that it had been done deliberately to their detriment would be much more so. The problem is to some extent taken care of by the Take-over Code (*see* Chapter 14), but it is not always easy to enforce this, even against quoted companies. A solution might have emerged from the recommendations concerning minority shareholders in the 1973 proposals to reform company law [17], but the bill based on them was killed by the spring 1974 dissolution of Parliament.

(c) Secret market control

This objection is a corollary of the 'preservation of identity' argument mentioned earlier; it is that they provide a means of acquiring market power secretly. As already indicated, a group may be established and extended without anyone's being very much the wiser; although holding companies are obliged to disclose all their subsidiaries and associated companies, they do not have to say what percentage of a product or a market they supply. Thus, hitherto competing firms may cease to compete as they come under the control of the same parent, and a sector of the economy outwardly well served with independent producers may become, to a greater or lesser extent, dominated by one or two companies. For example, people buying footwear in Britain may feel free to choose between the products and facilities of Curtess, Dolcis, Freeman Hardy & Willis, Lilley & Skinner, Manfield, Saxone, and True Form, but these are all subsidiaries of B.S.C. Footwear Ltd, which is a wholly owned subsidiary of British Shoe Corporation Ltd, which in turn is a wholly owned subsidiary of Sir Charles Clore's Sears Holdings Ltd [18].

The disadvantage here is not necessarily that a holding company may extend its influence over a wider and wider section of the market; doing so may enable it – and conceivably the general public – to benefit from scale economies and rationalization measures. The snag is simply the secrecy in which this influence is gained. With no overt change to attract attention and stimulate comment, the risk that the increasing market power may be used to the profit of the holding company alone seems likely to grow.

In the past, a similar result might have been achieved by different means. A company aiming at national market dominance and finding its plans thwarted by a locally powerful independent, might establish a so-called 'fighting' company. Such a company – a wholly owned subsidiary of the aggressor – would operate only in the area served by the independent and would simply cut prices until the latter was driven out of business. The parent could then wind up the fighting company and continue to supply the market, on its terms, either through the one-time independent, through another subsidiary, or directly. The Monopolies Commission – the establishment of which, as the Monopolies and Restrictive Practices Commission in 1948, indicated rising public concern over abuses of market power – drew attention to the questionable ways in which powerful firms sought to achieve and maintain market supremacy. In 1956 it criticized the British Oxygen Company for, among other things, its use of fighting companies [19]. This particular ploy is presumably no longer open to holding companies.

2.65 NUMBERS

The published statistics of company registrations do not distinguish between holding companies and others. Probably the best guide to the extent of this form of organization, and to the constituents of any one group, is to be found in the relevant edition of *Who Owns Whom* [20].

2.7 SIZE VERSUS COMPLEXITY

Before going on to the next chapter, a word of caution may be necessary. Although this outline of the organizational changes which a business may go through as it expands has started with sole proprietorships and ended with public limited companies, it does not follow that all businesses at any one stage or in any one form are necessarily larger – in labour force, assets, turnover, profits, or anything else – than those at an earlier, simpler stage. Not all large firms are public companies, nor are all public companies large firms. Not all private companies are small firms, nor are all small firms private companies. The largest sole proprietor could easily be bigger than the smallest public company.

2.8 SUMMARY

The most important distinction between forms of business organization is that between incorporated and unincorporated concerns. Incorporation confers great legal and financial advantages, usually including limited liability for members, but there is no necessary connection between these two concepts. Within the incorporated sector, the main distinction is between the private limited company – characterized by membership limits, a complete ban on public appeals for funds, and overt restriction on the transfer of its shares – and the much less numerous but economically much more important public company, to which in general these restraints do not apply. Although private companies no longer have privacy (corporations prizing this enough register as unlimited companies) the number of close companies emphasizes their tax attractions. Holding companies, although not a distinct form of business organization, are increasingly important as a means of concentrating economic power – with the potential costs and benefits that this entails. Figure 2.1 sets out the framework of business organizations.

3 Internal Sources

3.1 INTRODUCTION

Both the establishment and the expansion of a business, in whatever form it is organized, will call for finance. The sources from which a business obtains the funds it needs are commonly divided into those which are internal and those which are external to it, and although this division has its difficulties it will be followed here. This chapter is concerned with the internal source: retained earnings. It reviews the case for and against them, and the changing role of the corporate tax system.

3.2 RETAINED EARNINGS

For unincorporated businesses, and for them only, the pockets of the owners may be an important internal source of funds – internal because, as already indicated, the owners *are* the business. In general, however, the internal sources which matter are those producing funds directly as a result of a business's profitable handling of its existing assets. They do include such profits as may arise from the sale of fixed assets, i.e. those not sold and replaced in the normal course of activities each year, but the sums involved are usually relatively small and are not dealt with further here. (Capitalization issues based on them are explained in the Appendix to Chapter 11.)

What really count as an internal source of funds for all forms of business are retained earnings, also called undistributed or ploughed-back profits. These are that part of net-of-tax income arising from everyday operations which is not drawn out by the proprietor(s) or paid out as dividends, but kept in the business. Traditionally, businessmen are said to have relied on three kinds of money: patrimony, matrimony, or parsimony. Since they, in common with other mortals, were unable to pick their fathers, and since the law generally allowed them only one wife at a time, they could not often be sure of finding much support from the first two of these. Parsimony, however, was something much more under their control, and today as in the past the savings it produces are an important source of funds for all forms of business – for unincorporated firms, perhaps a vital one [1].

To the latter it means, as mentioned above, that the owners deliberately deny themselves current income – extracting from the business a smaller amount of cash than has been earned by the enterprise – in order to help finance its growth. Applied to a company with shareholders it means that, ostensibly for the same reason, the directors deliberately deprive the owners of current income in the form of dividends. Directors may, of course, be shareholders too, but they do not have to be unless the Articles of Association require it, and even then their holdings are often minuscule where listed companies are concerned.

3.3 ARGUMENT AGAINST RETENTION

Saving out of one's own income is one thing, but saving out of someone else's is quite another. It is thus not surprising that there has been considerable criticism of both the corporate practice of retaining earnings and, even more, of measures to encourage it.

The basic objection has been that retentions hinder the free working of the capital market and thus give rise to misallocation of economic resources. The fact that a business makes profits is not proof that it is efficient; it may do so by virtue of its size, or through patent protection, or via government policy towards its products. Simultaneously there may well be other, better-run and potentially more attractive firms which are unable to expand because they cannot obtain the resources they require, either at all or on acceptable terms.

To remedy this situation, it is argued that all companies should have to distribute to their shareholders each year all their genuinely available earnings, i.e. everything which is left over after deducting from net-of-tax earnings any extra sums needed to cover replacement of assets in periods of inflation and any sums required to redeem maturing debt. After all, whether distributed or not, those earnings do belong to the shareholders. Companies would then have to bid, at the going market rates, for whatever funds they needed to finance developments. As a result, not only would shareholders have more say in the spending of their own money, but managements would be kept on their toes because funds, and hence real resources, would flow to the firms offering the highest returns – by inference, to those which society most wished to promote. Instead of there being, as now, a disintegrated capital market made up of many separate pools of investible funds each under the control of a particular company, there would be one integrated market into which all such funds would flow and from which all demand would be satisfied. Reasoning such as this may well account for the taxation of retained earnings at 52·53% and of distributed earnings at 15·45% in West Germany.

3.4 ARGUMENTS FOR RETENTION

There are naturally objections to this view – objections not based solely on the discomfort which its implementation would cause to those now cushioned from competitive pressures by their own captive funds.

3.41 STABLE DIVIDENDS

It is claimed that shareholders like some degree of stability in their incomes; certainly they do not like them to fall. Since earnings fluctuate year by year, they would lose this advantage if no retentions were allowed because a stable dividend, based on smoothing out the shortfall of a bad year with the surplus of a good one, would be impossible.

3.42 COST

Significant cost is incurred in raising fresh capital from the market, however efficient the market may be, and this is avoided if retention is permitted. The exercise of sending people dividend cheques and then immediately asking for some or all of their value to be returned and exchanged for share certificates certainly sounds a prime candidate for rationalization.

3.43 SAVINGS PROMOTION

Retentions may also be thought desirable because they are a form of saving, and saving is a good thing. Support for this view may depend on a complex of attitudes – e.g. that it is wrong to satisfy one's own material desires instead of smoothing life's path for one's offspring, or that it is imprudent not to prepare for a dignified retirement or the inevitable misfortunes of life. It may be that these values are carried over unquestioningly from the personal to the business sphere, so that conduct approved for an individual becomes equally approved for a company.

Some weight may appear to be added to this by the seeming desirability, in periods of demand inflation, of holding dividend distributions down as a means of reducing spending. Doing so may indeed cut the expenditure of shareholders, though even this is uncertain because they may borrow more against the security of their shares, the value of which will have risen because of the retentions, other things being equal. But the anti-inflationary argument requires that the companies retaining profits should not spend them either, and that no bank should lend, for spending by others, any of the enlarged balances of their non-dividend-distributing customers. These conditions appear unlikely to be met.

3.44 INVESTMENT PROMOTION

However, the argument which seems to have made the biggest impact, at least on official thinking in postwar Britain, has been that retentions stimulate investment. The country's economic performance in this period has been poor compared with that of many of its competitors, and this is thought to have been largely due to its relatively low level of investment.[2] Corporations account for most of the investment in the economy and, assuming that they would have done more if they had had the money, it has seemed reasonable to encourage retention of earnings and thus help to mobilize the necessary funds. The means chosen to achieve this end has been the tax system, as outlined below.

3.5 RETENTIONS, INVESTMENT, AND CORPORATE TAXATION

3.51 BACKGROUND

Before the introduction of corporation tax in 1965, corporate profits were subject to income tax at the going standard rate plus profits tax. Although the percentage rate of the latter varied quite often, between 1947 and 1958 that on distributed profits was always higher than that on retained profits; the peak discrimination came in the few months after October 1955, when distributions suffered profits tax at a rate eleven times that on retentions. Not until 1958 did the corporate tax system become neutral in the sense that company earnings were taxed at the same rate irrespective of what was done with them.

With the replacement of profits tax plus income tax by corporation tax, bias was again introduced in favour of retentions. This was because the introduction of corporation tax made possible a distinction between companies and their shareholders which the previous arrangements had not permitted. This in turn allowed different treatment of the income tax which a company has always had to deduct from any dividend it pays. Before 1965, a company did not have to hand over the amount so deducted to the revenue authorities; it could instead offset it against the income tax which would be charged on its profits. Obviously, since the company and its shareholders were not regarded as totally distinct, it would have been inequitable to subject the latter's income to the same tax twice.

After 1965, however, income tax deducted from dividends could not be offset against that falling on profits, for the simple reason that income tax no longer applied to the latter. The amount deducted had to be paid to the tax collector; dividends accordingly cost the paying company their full gross amount. Presumably it was intended that companies should react to this higher cost of dividends by paying out less and retaining more of their disposable income. This, plus the fact that corporation tax (initially at 40%) was well below the combined rate of standard-rate income tax $(41\frac{1}{4}\%)$ plus profits tax (15%), would mean that they would then have more funds to finance more investment.

3.52 CRITICISMS OF THE TAX ARGUMENT

There were at least four reasons for doubting that this tax change would increase either retentions or investment:

(a) Relationship of distributions to tax

There was no certainty that the size of distributions varied inversely with the amount of tax on them. It had been claimed that the main influence on the amount of dividends paid was the apprehension felt by the directors of the paying company that it might be taken over; if it were, the existing board might well be sacked. In order to protect their positions therefore, directors began to sanction higher dividends. These helped to keep the shareholders happy and made the shares affected seem less attractive to the potential bidder by raising their market price. The highest level of tax on distributed, as distinct from retained, profits coincided with an increase in distributions – not a decrease [3].

(b) Relationship of investment to funds' availability

It had never been clearly demonstrated that business investment had been held back by lack of funds alone. If expectations made investment desirable, money to pay for it would be found; if they made it unattractive, money would not be spent no matter how plentiful and cheap it was.

(c) Use of extra funds

Even if corporate retentions rose, the extra funds might be spent on plusher offices or government securities, i.e. 'investments' making little direct impact on the stock of productive assets.

(d) Reactions to tax changes

Finally, it would be critically important to the investment-stimulation argument for corporation tax that businessmen should understand the tax system and react in the intended way to changes in it. Arguments about taxes tend to be long on opinion and short on fact, but such evidence as that of the survey in the Richardson Report, showing that the majority of the large firms questioned looked at the return on investment before, not after, tax[4], did not seem very encouraging on this score. (However, the fact that businessmen do not react in the intended way to tax changes does not mean that they do not understand them. They may understand them too well. Experience may have shown that rates of tax and depreciation allowances (*see* p. 39) are so unpredictable and unreliable that it is best to exclude them from any investment calculations. Constancy has not been a marked feature of the treatment of corporate profits in Britain.)

3.53 THE EVIDENCE

Whatever the validity of these objections, the available evidence of the discriminatory power of corporation tax seems to offer little support for its protagonists. The relevant aspects of companies' operations are summarized in Table 3.1. Since the avowed object of the introduction of corporation tax was to encourage retention of earnings, to discourage the distribution of dividends, and thus to provide the financial means which would enable companies to invest more, the record under these three headings must be considered.

(a) Retentions

If the percentages shown in column 4 for 1965 and 1966 are regarded as reflecting abnormal and non-recurring action by companies adjusting to the new tax arrangements, the overall tendency can hardly be called markedly rising. Nor is there support for any claim that the new tax helped or enabled companies to maintain retentions at a level above that which would otherwise have been achieved, since published figures indicate that retentions in 1964 were not an exceptionally high proportion of total income compared with previous years [5].

(b) Distributions

Similarly, the percentages in column 6, showing what part of total income was paid out each year in ordinary dividends, do not indicate any

Table 3.1. Retention and distribution of income, and investment by companies covered by the Department of Trade analysis (£m)

Year	Total income from trading and other activities (a)	Retained profits and other capital receipts (b)	3 as % of 2	Ordinary dividends payments (c)	5 as % of 2	5 as % of 3	Expenditure on tangible fixed assets and increase in current assets etc. (d)	3 as % of 8	Total sources of funds (e)	3 as % of 10	Year
1	2	3	4	5	6	7	8	9	10	11	12
1964	3,807	746	19·6	671	17·6	90	3,079	24·2	5,155	14·5	1964
1965	3,912	1,029	26·3	714	18·3	69	3,222	31·9	5,473	18·8	1965
1966	3,812	530	13·9	648	17·0	122	2,883	18·4	5,032	10·5	1966
1967	4,270	812	19·0	956	22·4	118	3,207	25·3	5,589	14·5	1967
1968	4,954	984	19·9	1,028	20·8	104	3,900	25·2	6,588	14·9	1968
1969	5,021	869	17·3	1,038	20·7	119	4,605	18·9	7,426	11·7	1969
Revision of Cover											
1970	5,196	1,035	19·9	1,041	20·0	101	4,672	22·2	7,744	13·4	1970
1971	5,707	1,150	20·2	1,088	19·1	95	3,389	33·9	6,505	17·7	1971

Source: Based on Business Monitor Series M3, *Company Finance,* 5th edn., published by the Business Statistics Office of the Department of Industry (London: H.M.S.O., 1974) Tables 3, 5, and 6; values rounded to the nearest £m. The figures in M3 'are derived from the accounts of companies engaged mainly in the United Kingdom in manufacturing, distribution, construction, transport . . . and certain other services. Companies whose main interests are in agriculture, mining, shipping, insurance, banking and finance and those operating wholly or mainly overseas are not included. The figures for 1970, 1971 . . . relate to companies with net assets of £2·0 million or more, or gross income of £200,000 or more, in 1968 . . . The companies in the current analysis are thought to account for between three-fifths and two-thirds of the net assets of all industrial and commercial companies' (M3, p. 58). The revision of cover does not significantly affect the series.

Notes:
(a) Gross trading profit has never been less than 85% of the total shown.
(b) Exclusion of these, which are in any case small, would make retentions an even smaller proportion of total income.
(c) Calculated by deducting the amount appropriated for preference dividends (which do not lend themselves to retention) from the amount actually paid in dividends each year.
(d) Current assets include portfolio investment, but the amounts involved are not large enough to affect the results.
(e) Equals total sources of funds minus acquisitions of subsidiaries by issuing shares or loan stock.

pronounced reduction. It is true that, if the net payments in 1964–6 were ad-justed on the assumption that income tax at $41\frac{1}{4}$% had already been deducted from them, the percentages in column 6 would be 31, 32, and 30 respectively – showing, apparently, that here at least the figures have moved in the way that the corporation tax's proponents intended. But since it is actual cash flows out of businesses which the tax was intended to influence, such an adjustment is scarcely relevant.

However, linking retentions and distributions through 'Total income etc.' (column 2) is open to the criticism that this total is calculated before deducting depreciation, long-term debt interest, and tax. It hardly qualifies therefore as discretionary income which directors of the companies con-cerned are free to allocate as they choose. A more accurate picture of the relationship between retentions and distributions may be given by directly expressing one as a percentage of the other (column 7). Again, if 1965 and 1966 are regarded as exceptional, subsequent years show no pronounced tendency for companies to spend less on ordinary dividends and to plough back correspondingly more. Even if the 1970–1 decrease is maintained, it will still be above the proportion in 1964 – before corporation tax was effective.

(c) Investment

The position here is shown in columns 3, 8, 9, 10, and 11. These give reten-tions in relation both to the amounts spent on acquiring productive assets and to the total funds available to the companies analysed. Presumably they were meant to become more important in both respects. Here too there is no conclusive evidence that corporation tax has had the hoped-for effect; the importance of retentions under both headings, even in 1970, was still less than it had been in 1964, and the change in 1971 reflects not an increase in them but a large-scale contraction in the use of trade and other credit that year.

3.54 THE 1973 REVISION

Whether because of this sort of information or not, modified corporation-tax arrangements came into force in 1973, working roughly like the system in operation before 1965. Companies are now liable to pay corporation tax at a single rate on all their profits, whether distributed or not. If they distri-bute dividends, within three months of issuing the dividend warrants they have to make an advance payment of corporation tax equal to the basic income-tax rate times the gross amount of the dividend. (This advance corporation tax – ACT – was increased by 50% in 1974, but as this rise broke the link between corporate and personal tax which the change had restored, and aggravated corporate liquidity problems which were already serious, it could prove temporary and so is ignored here.) Such advance payments are set off against the tax liability for the accounting period concerned; the balance, called the 'mainstream' liability, is payable on the appropriate date. (Companies incorporated before April 1965 pay any corporation tax due on 1 January of the year following the end of the tax year in which the taxable profits were made. The interval between earning profits and paying tax on them thus ranges for such companies from a minimum of nine months to a maximum of twenty-one. All companies incorporated after April 1965, however, pay corporation tax nine months after the end of their financial year. Of the quoted companies in the analysis drawn on above, about 40% had accounting periods ending in the fourth quarter of the calendar year and about 30% had them in the first quarter.)

Shareholders receive, with their dividend cheques, a tax credit which serves to discharge their tax liability at the basic personal-tax rate on that dividend. If they are not liable to income tax at this rate, they are able – as they always have been – to claim a refund; if they are liable to tax at some higher rate, this is calculated on the total income represented by dividend plus tax credit.

Table 3.2 illustrates the effect of these arrangements on a company with a

Table 3.2. Effect of corporation tax, 1973+

		£	
(i)	Pre-tax profits		300,000	
(ii)	*Less* corporation tax @ 52%		156,000	=Total liability, for discharge on the
(iii)	Post-tax profits (i−ii)		144,000	appropriate 1 January.
(iv)	Dividend @ 20%	200,000		
(v)	*Less* ACT*	66,000		Paid to the tax collector within three months of the distribution, and offset against (ii).
(vi)	Paid to shareholders (iv−v)		134,000	
(vii)	To reserves (iii−vi)		10,000	

*Calculated at the rate of thirty-three sixty-sevenths of the dividend paid: (33/67) × 134,000 = 66,000. It also equals 33% (the basic income-tax rate) of the total dividend declared: (33/100) × 200,000 = 66,000.

paid-up ordinary share capital of £1 million, pre-tax profits of £300,000, and a 20% dividend declared. On the appropriate 1 January the company would pay the tax collector £90,000; this sum, added to the £66,000 paid within three months of the dividend distribution, would discharge its total liability of £156,000.

Examination of this example shows that the 1973 change has approximately restored neutrality to the corporate tax system. If all the profits are retained, the shareholders have an increase of £144,000 in the assets attributable to them. If some are retained and some distributed, their position is the same – in the example, they receive £134,000 in cash and have another £10,000 in the form of extra assets in the company they own. If they so wished, the whole £144,000 of post-tax profits could be paid to them as dividend; a rate of about $21\frac{1}{2}\%$ would do this. The corporate tax system, in other words, no longer discriminates in favour of retaining profits and against distributing them.

Note that the position is slightly different seen through the eyes of the company. Since any distribution will involve an advance payment of corporation tax, and since any earlier outflow of funds is worse than any later outflow of the same size (*see* Chapter 17), the company will be better off from the cash point of view if no distributions are made.

3.6 SUMMARY

The most important internal source of funds is retained earnings – and any form of business may generate them. Because of the aims of national economic policy and the importance of corporate investment to those aims, the tax system has for long periods been used to encourage companies to retain rather than distribute their earnings. Such efforts have had uncertain theoretical justification and, as Table 3.1 shows, little observable effect. Since 1973 they have been in abeyance.

4 The Significance of Depreciation

4.1 INTRODUCTION

Chapter 3 looked at the use of the tax system to induce companies to retain rather than distribute their profits. But it is not just the allocation of such profits which matters; their sheer size and timing are important too. In these respects the arrangements for taxing profits – all profits, not just those of companies – may also be an important influence. They will exercise this influence through the way in which they enable depreciation to be dealt with.

This chapter accordingly looks at the nature of depreciation, the impact on it of inflation, and the connection between depreciation, retained earnings and taxation.

4.2 DEFINITION

Depreciation is the loss of value suffered by an asset as a result of wear and tear, obsolescence, or simply passage of time. The first two causes affect such things as tools, vehicles, plant, and machinery; the third affects assets such as copyrights, patents, and leasehold property. Permanent buildings generally depreciate at a very much slower rate than other assets, and the financial arrangements referred to below do not therefore apply to them – still less to land, which has gained in value (at least in money terms) over much of the country in recent years.

4.3 DEPRECIATION AS A PRODUCTION COST

The loss of value which an asset suffers may properly be regarded by the business owning it as part of the cost of producing output; it represents the value of the capital which has been used up in a given production period, in just the same way that outlays on raw materials, fuel, power, and people's time and effort represent the value of these inputs which has been consumed in the productive process. All such costs may, in principle, be set off against the total receipts of a business, so that the true size of the net income of that business may be properly established – not least for tax purposes. This is so irrespective of the size or form of the business; it applies to the smallest sole proprietorship just as much as to the largest company.

4.4 DISTINCTION FROM OTHER PRODUCTION COSTS, AND THE PROBLEM OF INFLATION

Depreciation differs from other production costs in several important respects:

4.41 ABSENCE OF CONTRACTUAL OBLIGATION

Provision for depreciation is not usually made under any contractual obligation. It is so only in those rare cases where it takes the form of premiums due under an insurance policy designed to produce at maturity a capital sum equal to the cost of the asset concerned.

Failure to pay for the transport, power, labour, or any other goods and services used in production, sooner or later results in legal action by the supplier for breach of contract. So, also, does failure to pay interest on funds borrowed to buy assets. But failure to pay for the using up of the capital assets themselves does not; machines etc. do not sue their owners if their book value is not properly written off. In other words, depreciation may be a moral or technical obligation, but it is scarcely a legal one.

It may be objected that section 14 of the Companies Act 1967 requires a company's auditors to state whether the accounts have been prepared properly and whether, in their opinion, they give a true and fair view of the company's financial condition and performance. As the auditors cannot do this if they consider the depreciation provision to be in any way unsatisfactory there is, in fact, a legal obligation involved. The weakness of this objection is that a 'true and fair view' is so much a matter of opinion that the 'obligation' boils down to not doing anything the auditors might not like. In any case, it applies only to companies' accounts – although the books of unincorporated firms do have to be kept in such a way as to satisfy the tax officers.

4.42 IMPRECISE NATURE

Depreciation is not precisely known – nor, indeed, knowable. It is bad enough trying to decide how much to set against a business's total income for the materials etc. used in generating that income; at least the items concerned are often susceptible to forms of measurement which enable a physical basis for their cost to be calculated [1]. For much capital equipment, however, this is just not possible; trying to establish, by weighing or measuring it, how much of a machine has been used up in producing the output of a given period is as futile as trying to do so by interrogating it. Since there is as yet no acceptably precise way in which depreciation can be calculated, it is fixed arbitrarily, by accounting conventions, and by tax law.

The problem of inflation

The difficulty of not knowing exactly how much of an asset's value to charge to current receipts as a production cost must not be confused with the difficulty arising from the more pressing problem of inflation. In principle, the setting aside from current earnings of provision for depreciation is intended to ensure (i) that the cost of the asset concerned is spread properly over its working life, and (ii), that the business will be able to finance its replacement when this becomes necessary. (It may not; the intention may be that the operation should end when the assets are worn out, as in, perhaps, a mining venture.) Not knowing exactly how much of an asset's value has been consumed each year may be irritating, but given stable prices, as long as it has been fully written off by the time it is due for replacement, its owners will not inadvertently have treated as income any of their capital stake.

However, if asset prices are rising, replacing assets when they are worn out will require greater monetary – though not necessarily real – outlay than when they were first bought. Since depreciation is traditionally based on historic cost, i.e. on the monetary outlay actually incurred at the time of purchase, the provision made in the accounts to replace them will inevitably be less than that required. Not only that; failure to make adequate provision for the replacement of assets means that the business concerned will have been thinking itself generally more profitable than it is and also paying more tax than it should. Moreover, the increase in sales revenues likely to occur during inflation may serve merely to blind it to the true position.

How these dangers may arise is illustrated in Table 4.1. Suppose a company buys some new machinery for £3,000 at a time when the price of this type of asset is rising by 10% a year compound. The machinery has an expected life of six years and its cost is to be completely written off, for both tax and internal purposes, by the straight line method over this period.

(The annual depreciation charge under the latter is a fixed amount found by dividing the cost of the asset concerned, i.e. outlay minus expected scrap value, by its expected life in years. Under the common alternative – the reducing balance method – it is a fixed percentage of the asset's current book value as reduced by earlier depreciation; the inevitable final balance outstanding is adjusted at the end of the asset's life. Although, at the time of writing, the straight-line method was not allowed for tax purposes in the United Kingdom, its use here instead of the approved reducing balance method enables the principle to be illustrated with simpler calculations.)

Suppose also that the business's total income is £4,500 a year and that corporation tax is at 52%.

With depreciation on a conventional historic-cost basis, Table 4.1(a) indicates how the relevant accounts will look at the end of the first year.

Table 4.1. Inflation Accounting

(a) Not allowing for replacement of assets
Profit & Loss A/c for y/e . . .

	£		£
Depreciation ($\frac{1}{6}$ × 3,000)	500	Gross revenue	4,500
Other expenses	1,500		
Net revenue	2,500		
	4,500		4,500

Appropriation A/c for y/e . . .

Corporation tax @ 52%	1,300	Net revenue	2,500
Disposable income	1,200		
	2,500		2,500

Provision for Depreciation A/c

	Profit & Loss A/c	500

If nothing disturbs this pattern, after six years the provision for depreciation will amount to £3,000 – the original cost of the asset concerned. But by then its replacement cost will be £5,315 (£3,000 compounded at 10% for six years) and mobilizing this larger sum may well put considerable strain on the business's resources.

Although the drain involved seems to occur when replacement becomes necessary, it will in fact have been spread over the preceding six years in the form of capital consumption linked with excessive tax payments and exaggerated disposable income. Thus, at the end of the first year the cost of replacing the machinery will have risen to £3,300, and depreciation at the rate of one-sixth of this should be £550. Charging the year's revenue with depreciation of this amount reduces the tax payment and the amount of disposable income, as shown in Table 4.1(b). Charging to taxable income one-sixth of the current cost of the asset concerned cuts the tax payment by £26 and the amount available for shareholders by £24 – but the item called disposable income is really income, not partly capital.

By the end of the second year, one-third of the value of the machinery will have been used up in production, so that the depreciation provision should by then equal one-third of its current cost of £3,630. Of the £1,210 required, £550 will already have been provided, so the depreciation charge for year 2 will be £1,210−£550 = £660. Net revenue will then fall to £2,340, tax to £1,217, and disposable income to £1,123. Similar adjustments in each of the

remaining four years will enable the depreciation provision to be built up to
the £5,315 needed, with corresponding reductions in the tax charges and
disposable income. By year 6, tax payable will be down to £890 and income
available to members to £821.

(b) *Allowing for replacement of assets*
Profit & Loss A/c for y/e ...

	£		£
Depreciation ($\frac{1}{6} \times 3,300$)	550	Gross revenue	4,500
Other expenses	1,500		
Net revenue	2,450		
	4,500		4,500

Appropriation A/c for y/e ...

Corporation tax @ 52%	1,274	Net revenue	2,450
Disposable income	1,176		
	2,450		2,450

Provision for Depreciation A/c

Profit & Loss A/c	550

Inflation affects all costs and prices, not just depreciation provisions, and
pressure to deal with the accounting and tax problems it presents has been
rising. The Bolton Committee urged – and not solely for small firms – that
only true profits be taxed, after the effects of inflation had been allowed for
and the real capital of businesses safeguarded [2]. In 1974 the Institute of
Chartered Accountants in Statement 7 of its Standard Accounting Practice
recommended that basic, i.e. historic cost, accounts be accompanied by
supplementary statements converting them to current values on the basis of
movements in the Consumer Price Index or the Retail Price Index. 'Indexing' accounts like this – that is, showing in them the effects of changes in the
purchasing power of money so that the current real value of money claims
and liabilities, the true increase or decrease in value of fixed assets, and the
genuine profit, are revealed – would certainly tell investors more about the
real, as distinct from the monetary, performance of a business. However, in
view of the government's appointment of the Sandilands Committee on
Inflation Accounting at the end of 1973, this I.C.A. standard is provisional,
and the Stock Exchange has not yet made it mandatory for listed companies.
Meanwhile, the November 1974 budget provided a remedy for the over-
statement of profits – and resulting overpayment of tax – due to increases in
prices of stocks of raw materials etc. Such stocks may be included in final
accounts at their value at the beginning of the relevant financial year,
although, as an adjustment for normal stock growth, 10% of any profits are
excluded from the tax relief so provided.

In any case, indexing accounts for greater accuracy is one thing; doing
so as a basis for calculating tax-allowable depreciation and other expenses is

quite another. Apart from the purely practical difficulties of compiling a suitable price index, and the inequity of giving owners of depreciable assets a degree of protection against inflation not conceded to owners of other types of assets, the official attitude had for long been that the acceptance of any kind of indexing of capital values would imply that the government was unable to control inflation. (Adjustment of incomes, e.g. public sector employees' incomes and National Insurance retirement pensions, apparently implied less impotence.) This view had changed enough by August 1974 for the government, following a recommendation of the Page Committee [3], to announce a small-scale experiment in inflation-proof savings bonds. Nevertheless, as noted earlier, the potential disturbance of the flow of tax revenue arising from any widespread capital indexing makes the whole issue still a very sensitive one as far as the tax authorities are concerned.

4.43 EFFECT OF DEPRECIATION ON TAX REVENUE

The third way, indeed, in which depreciation differs from other operating expenses is that its calculation is a matter of great interest to the Treasury. The latter, in order to safeguard the public revenue, specifies the rates at which different types of asset may be written off for tax purposes by profitable enterprises. Normally (*pace* any prices and incomes policy which happens to be in force), charges against the taxable income of a business for the supplies of goods and services which it uses are no concern of the tax authorities; the outlays involved are readily verifiable and there is no arguing about them. However, with the particular charge 'depreciation' the situation is different – and not because of the problems of inflation accounting outlined above.

The reason for the Treasury's concern can be seen by referring back to the company in Table 4.1(*a*). Suppose the data are as given there, except that machinery prices are stable and the government has not yet made any rules on how depreciation is to be treated for tax purposes. The directors of the business (and this would be true of any form of business organization) would then be perfectly entitled to charge to the first year's revenue the full cost of the machinery, even though it had five years' earning life left. The Profit & Loss A/c – assuming that the auditors thought that this asset should be written off over six years, to give a true and fair view – would show a depreciation entry of £500, but the Tax Computation A/c, in which the business calculated its tax liability for the current year, would show a depreciation entry of £3,000. This with other expenses of £1,500 would exactly equal the total revenue for the year of £4,500. Thus, income liable to tax would be nil, and the tax paid in that year also nil. The Profit & Loss A/c for the year would show net revenue of £2,500; the tax due on this, but not payable straightaway because there was no immediate liability, would be credited to a Tax Provision A/c and the position would be as shown in Table 4.2. For tax purposes only, the machinery would have been completely written off; for Profit & Loss A/c and balance sheet purposes, however, the book value of the asset at the end of its first year would be £2,500. If the trading

Table 4.2. Effect on tax payments of 100% depreciation in asset's 1st year

Tax Computation A/c for y/e . . .

	£		£
Depreciation (100% × 3,000)	3,000	Gross revenue	4,500
Other expenses	1,500		
Taxable income	—		
	4,500		4,500

Profit & Loss A/c for y/e . . .

	£		£
Depreciation ($\frac{1}{6}$ × 3,000)	500	Gross revenue	4,500
Other expenses	1,500		
Net revenue	2,500		
	4,500		4,500

Appropriation A/c for y/e . . .

	£		£
Corporation tax provision		Net revenue	2,500
(@ 52%)	1,300		
Disposable income	1,200		
	2,500		2,500

Tax Provision A/c

		Appropriation A/c	1,300

position did not alter, in each of the remaining five years of the asset's life taxable income would be £3,000, since there would be no more depreciation to be charged to the Tax Computation A/c. Tax on this income would be £1,560 – made up, each year, by £1,300 from the Appropriation A/c and £260 from the Tax Provision A/c; the latter account would be closed at the end of the asset's life.

Now suppose that the directors, instead of charging the whole cost of the machinery to the first year's revenue, decided to spread that cost by the straight line method over its working life. The Tax Computation A/c and the Profit & Loss A/c would then look alike, since each would show the same entry for depreciation (*see* Table 4.3). The tax due on the net revenue

Table 4.3. Effect on tax payments of spreading depreciation by straight line method

Tax Computation A/c for y/e . . .
Profit & Loss A/c for y/e . . .

	£		£
Depreciation ($\frac{1}{6}$ × 3,000)	500	Gross revenue	4,500
Other expenses	1,500		
Taxable income/Net revenue	2,500		
	4,500		4,500

would be £1,300 and this sum would be payable in each of the six years of the life of the machinery, provided the trading pattern did not change. The tax collector would thus receive:

	Year 1	Year 2	Year 3	Year 4	Year 5	Year 6
Either under Table 4.2	—	1,560	1,560	1,560	1,560	1,560
or under Table 4.3	1,300	1,300	1,300	1,300	1,300	1,300

In other words, in exchange for £1,300 now, he would be getting £260 in each of the next five years. For reasons set out in Chapter 17, no one in his right mind, least of all a tax collector, would willingly accept such an exchange, and it is basically for this reason – to ensure a satisfactory flow of revenue from business profits – that depreciation charges have not been left entirely to the whim of businessmen. (The latter can, of course, for their own internal accounting purposes use any rate of depreciation which they like and their auditors will accept. To establish taxable income, the tax authorities will simply add back whatever depreciation has been deducted and reduce the resulting figure by the currently-approved depreciation allowances.)

In fact the revenue authorities *do* accept unfavourable tax flows like the one above – not because of some mental aberration on their part, but because of the demands of economic policy. The desire to stimulate investment has widened the use of so-called 'free depreciation'. This offers the owner of eligible assets the choice of depreciating them for tax purposes at the rate of either 100% in the first year of their life or, for machinery, 25% a year on the reducing balance of their cost – but nothing in between. The more usual pattern, however, has been for the Board of Inland Revenue to lay down the percentage annual rate of depreciation which may be applied to assets of different kinds. To these annual rates have been added other rates at different times – specifically the initial allowance and the investment allowance. The former accelerates the writing-off process by enabling a business to claim a higher proportion of the total cost of an asset in the first year of its life; the latter, when in force, enables more than 100% of the cost of the asset concerned to be written off against taxable profits, with the benefit again coming in the first year of its life. Such allowances, which are available to all forms of business, aim at maintaining and expanding investment as a means of strengthening the economy. Whatever their intention, they have an important impact on the amount of its earnings that an enterprise may retain, and on the equally vital question of the timing of those retentions.

4.44 NO CASH PAYMENTS

Finally, depreciation differs from other production costs in that it does not involve any cash outlay on the factor input concerned (even if paid as described on p. 33. This is not to say that depreciation has no effect on the cash outlays of a business. It can be seen from Table 4.3 that, if no depreciation were deducted from the annual profits, tax payments and post-tax profits would certainly be higher than would otherwise be the case, and dividend distributions would probably increase too.

But *influencing* something is not the same as *being* that something. The depreciation charge certainly influences the cash outlays that a business makes, but it is not itself directly any part of those outlays. It is this aspect of depreciation which needs to be emphasized here, because of its impact on the resources which an enterprise may have available internally.

Depreciation may be thought of initially as a setting aside, within a business, of a part of the revenue received by that business as a result of its trading and other activities. In other words, before the owners can claim that revenue for their own use, they must first reckon to meet all the costs incurred in generating it; one of these costs, as has been seen, is the true cost of the capital used up in production. It is important to grasp what this 'setting aside' means; like the concept of 'reserves' which a business may establish, the underlying reality is not always clearly understood. Funds flow into a business mainly as a result of its sales (other sources are dealt with later in this section). These funds are used to defray expenses and, all being well, pay incomes to the owners. In all cases except that of depreciation, these expenses and incomes involve actual outflows of cash from the business. With depreciation, however, the appropriate part of the cash flow is kept. It is not held in a hoard of notes and coin – either in the office safe, under the boardroom floor, or (one hopes) behind a loose fireplace brick in the chairman's study – earmarked for ultimate expenditure on a particular asset or assets generally. Nor is it held in some more sophisticated form, such as on deposit in a special 'depreciation' account at the firm's bank. (Currency, remember, has negative earnings, as costs are incurred in keeping it safely. Bank deposits produce income, but only because someone else can afford to borrow them; if bank interest proves attractive on a long-term basis, the entrepreneur concerned should ask himself if he is in the right line of business!) Instead, the value represented by the depreciation provision is ploughed back into the organization. It is used to finance the acquisition of additional productive resources, and thus helps at least to maintain the original earning power and probably to raise it (*see* 16.4 below).

Inspection of the balance sheet of any public company will make this point clear. For example, that of Reed International Ltd [4] shows fixed assets at cost or valuation as approximately £363 million, and the accumulated depreciation on them as £180 million. Bank balances, however, total only £5 million. It is true that in the current assets there are short-term deposits of £52 million – but current liabilities include bank overdrafts of £38 million. The depreciation provision is clearly not being held in the form of cash or bank balances! Instead it is inextricably mixed up in all the asset values.

The position may be clarified by the following simple example, illustrated in Table 4.4. Suppose a business is capitalized at £1,000, this sum initially

Table 4.4. Nature of depreciation

(a) *Opening balance sheet*

Liabilities		*Assets*		
	£		£	£
Capital	1,000	Various (i)		1,000

being all in cash. Almost at once the money is turned into earning assets with a life of ten years, and these are then depreciated by the straight line method over this period. The balance sheet at first looks like Table 4.4(a).

Then assuming that all the profits are distributed and that only the depreciation is shown, the balance sheets after one year's profitable operations, and again after ten years' such operations, might look like those in table 4.4, either *(b)* or *(c)*.

EITHER   (b) *Balance sheet at end of year 1*

Capital	1,000	Various (i)	1,000	
		Less Depreciation	100	
				900
		Assets (ii)		100
	1,000			1,000

Balance sheet at end of year 10

Capital	1,000	Various (i)	1,000	
		Less Depreciation	1,000	—
		Assets (ii)		1,000
	1,000			1,000

OR   (c) *Balance sheet at end of year 1*

Capital	1,000	Assets (i)	1,000
Depreciation provision	100	Assets (ii)	100
	1,100		1,100

Balance sheet at end of year 10

Capital	1,000	Assets (i)	1,000
Depreciation provision	1,000	Assets (ii)	1,000
	2,000		2,000

After ten years, assets (ii) are liquefied (turned into cash) and the money is used to pay for the assets which replace the original assets (i), which by then are worn out and completely written off. In (b), assets (ii) disappear, assets (i) reappear, and the whole cycle starts again. In (c), the cost of the new assets is charged to the depreciation provision account, thus closing the account and restoring the position in the business's books to what it was ten years earlier. Either presentation shows, as is the case, that the proprietors' capital has been maintained intact by the proper depreciation of the assets, and that while it was going on this has involved outlays on assets other than those being depreciated.

4.5 CASH FLOWS

The combination of depreciation provisions and retained earnings in a business is called its 'cash flow' – a term not without ambiguity. When this cash flow falls short of the published plans or known capital commitments of a business (a company is obliged by law to indicate on its balance sheet the size of such commitments for the coming year), extra funds have to be raised and an issue of securities may be in prospect.

4.6 SUMMARY

No description of internal sources of funds is complete without some consideration of depreciation. Although in principle a production cost, it differs significantly from other such costs in several important ways. Its tax treatment has been designed to benefit profitable businesses by improving the amount and the availability of the earnings at their disposal. Depreciation itself is *not* a source of funds, internal or otherwise; if there are no profits, depreciation allowances – no matter how generous – will benefit a business nothing. But if enough profits are available (and their true size can be arrived at only after eliminating the effects of inflation), these allowances may make a big difference to both the size and the timing of tax payments on them, and thus to the resources which the business concerned may deploy.

5 External Sources: Short-term Lenders

5.1 INTRODUCTION

External sources must comprise all those not covered in Chapters 3 and 4. They fall into two broad categories:

1 Members of the organizations concerned. In the case of companies, such members may be existing ones or new; in the case of partnerships, to be classified as an external source they must be new only.
2 A whole range of outside individuals and financial institutions, both specialized and otherwise.

Funds raised from members as such will, of course, be contributions to share capital; those derived from non-members will be in the form of loans of one kind or another, conferring on their providers the rights of creditors.

Loans may be classified in several ways, e.g. by source, purpose, or nature of the security required, if any. The usual method, however, is to group them by duration into short (up to one year), medium (one to five years), and long (over five years). These distinctions are not hard and fast. Different lenders interpret them in different ways; the London capital market, for example, treats U.K. government loans as 'shorts' when they have five years or less to run to maturity. Furthermore, the passage of time may move a loan from one class to another. Borrowing originally undertaken on a long-term basis for repayment in, say, twenty-five years becomes a medium-term commitment after twenty years have elapsed and a short-term one after twenty-four; similarly, borrowing which (like overdrafts) starts as short-term not infrequently turns into medium- and sometimes long-term. In any case, institutions do not necessarily restrict themselves to providing funds on only one type of term. Nevertheless, the time classification is convenient and will be followed here.

This chapter reviews the importance and attractions of the main sources of short-term funds. Trade suppliers, the various specialist financial agencies (principally banks and discount houses), and the Inland Revenue are open to any form of business; intercompany loans, if negotiable, are of course available only to incorporated businesses.

5.2 TRADE SUPPLIERS

5.21 NATURE AND IMPORTANCE

The suppliers of the goods and services a business uses in the course of its operations are not likely to insist on cash on delivery; the accepted practice in most trades is for the customer to be allowed to pay for what he obtains some time after actually receiving it. This may mean, for example, that while a firm is invoiced for goods it has had in one month, it is not expected to pay for them until it receives the supplier's statement which comes out at the end of the following month. The buyer will thus have had supplies at least one and at most two months before having to pay for them, and this constitutes an apparently interest-free loan from the supplier to him. Somewhere along the line, of course, the supplier is paying for the credit he extends. If he seeks to recover such costs in the prices he charges, the latter will include a hidden lending cost.

For the companies covered by the Department of Industry analysis in Table 5.1, such trade credit was by far the most important source of short-term credit, consistently providing about three times as much as banks. Furthermore, not only were the sums involved large, but in the period covered they were of growing importance; by 1971, well over 40% of their current assets and 20% of their total gross assets were represented by trade credit. Figure 5.1 shows the main changes in the make-up of the three most important sources.

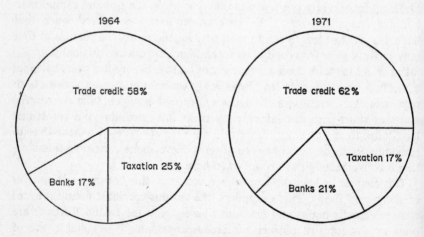

FIGURE 5.1   Sources of short-term funds: the changing pattern

Table 5.1. Sources of short-term funds* (£m)

Year	Trade and other credit (a)	2 as % of 11	2 as % of 12	Bank overdrafts and loans (b)	5 as % of 11	5 as % of 12	Taxation (c)	8 as % of 11	8 as % of 12	Total current assets (d)	Total assets (e)	Year
1	2	3	4	5	6	7	8	9	10	11	12	13
1964	5,312	33·8	19·0	1,610	10·2	5·8	2,249	14·3	8·0	15,716	27,993	1964
1965	5,943	35·1	19·5	2,044	12·1	6·7	2,018	11·9	6·6	16,917	30,481	1965
1966	6,371	35·4	19·7	2,337	13·0	7·2	2,050	11·4	6·3	18,005	32,365	1966
1967	6,742	35·3	20·1	2,333	12·2	7·0	2,141	11·2	6·4	19,080	33,489	1967
1968	7,640	36·2	20·8	2,608	12·4	7·1	2,516	11·9	6·9	21,104	36,724	1968
1969	9,097	39·1	22·7	3,230	13·9	8·1	2,325	10·0	5·8	23,254	40,060	1969
							Revision of Cover					
1970	10,404	41·6	24·2	3,760	15·0	8·7	2,709	10·8	6·3	25,018	42,986	1970
1971	10,822	41·8	23·8	3,641	14·1	8·0	2,849	11·0	6·3	25,896	45,530	1971

Source: Based on M3, *Company Finance*, 5th edn., Tables 3, 5, and 6; values rounded to the nearest £m.
* For the companies covered, see Table 3.1.

Notes:

(a) 'Other credit' covers a range of items, including such things as intercompany borrowing and debts to directors. When last shown separately from trade credit, such 'other' credit represented about 9 % of the total.

(b) There seems to be no published information showing these as separate items.

(c) The figures shown have been arrived at by summing the current and deferred taxation liabilities for each year.

(d) Total current assets is the gross figure – before deduction of current liabilities.

(e) Total assets equals tangible fixed assets (net of depreciation), goodwill and investments in unconsolidated subsidiaries plus total current assets (including 'other investments').

5.22 COST OF TRADE CREDIT

Obviously, properly run trade suppliers do not want to make free credit available any longer than is necessary, and the statements which they issue to their customers, generally each month, reflect their concern. Such statements may call for immediate settlement; they will say on them that their terms are net cash, meaning that the full amount due is to be paid straightaway. It is just as likely, however, that they will offer a discount as an inducement to customers to pay promptly. Such discounts are called cash discounts and are specifically a reward for prompt payment of debt (not to be confused with trade discounts, which represent traders' gross margins). Cash discounts vary a great deal from industry to industry, and from supplier to supplier within an industry. They may be flat-rate or tapering, i.e. higher at the start than at the end of the specified payment period. They may look so small as to be insignificant, but within the context of borrowed resources they may be very important and need to be carefully appraised.

Suppose a firm, having obtained goods from a supplier to the invoiced value of £500, receives a statement saying that this sum is due and offering a discount of $2\frac{1}{2}\%$ if it is paid within thirty days. By paying before this period is up, the buyer will save $2\frac{1}{2}\%$ of £500, which is £12·50; by delaying settlement beyond it, he will become liable for the full amount. If this arrangement were strictly enforced (in practice, a delay of a few days is likely to be tolerated even by a well-organized supplier) and the buyer were so ill-advised as to pay the day after the discount had lapsed, it would mean that he had paid £12.50 for borrowing £487·50 from the supplier for one day – an annual rate of interest of approximately 934%! However, since the capital sum (£487·50) and the charge on it (£12·50) do not alter, the effective rate of interest falls the longer payment is delayed. If the buyer does not settle until one month after the end of the discount period, he will be paying interest at an annual rate of approximately 30%; and if he manages to delay payment for a year, the rate will have fallen to practically $2\frac{1}{2}\%$ (strictly, about 2·56%, since the calculation is always on the sum borrowed, i.e. £487·50).

The significance of this is, of course, the great gains to be obtained by paying early enough to qualify for the cash discounts offered and, conversely, the potentially very high costs of borrowing from trade sources. In deciding what his policy should be in connection with these very attractive cash discounts, the buyer must consider what choices he has and what their relative costs are. The most likely substitute for reliance on trade credit is a bank overdraft. The rate of interest on overdrafts varies in line with altera-

tions in the relevant base rate (the nominal rate each clearing bank introduced as the basis of its lending charges when Bank Rate was abandoned for
this purpose in 1971) and according to the credit status of the applicant.
Suppose, for example, that an overdraft would cost the borrower 14% a
year. Borrowing £487·50 at this rate would cost him £68·25 for a year; since
overdraft charges are calculated on the daily balance outstanding, they
would have reached £12·50 by the sixty-seventh day. If, therefore, the
borrower expected that, having used his overdraft facility to the full, he
would not be able to reduce it for at least sixty-seven days, he would be
better off not to do so but to let the supplier's bill run on. (However, he must
bear in mind that suppliers have financial problems too, and may charge
interest on overdue accounts or simply refuse to trade on credit terms with
slow payers.) On the other hand, if he expected to be able to repay the overdraft before sixty-seven days had elapsed, he would gain by borrowing
from the bank rather than from the supplier; any reduction he could make
in the overdraft, short of wiping it out completely, would lengthen the
period for which it would be advantageous for him to substitute bank credit
for supplier credit.

Bearing in mind the vast sums involved and the potential cost of this
source of funds, trade credit obviously requires proper attention from
management. It seems not to have had it. The Bolton Committee thought
that the standard of credit management in much of British industry was very
poor, whether considered from the viewpoint of the giver or of the receiver,
and this applied not only to small firms [1].

5.3 BANK OVERDRAFTS

5.31 NATURE AND IMPORTANCE

Banks are the next most important source of short-term funds and the
largest of the specialist agencies which try, as all or part of their business,
to match the requirements of short-term borrowers with those of short-term
lenders. Table 5.1 shows their significance to the companies in the 1974
Department of Industry analysis, and the extent to which they are expanding in relation to trade credit. The general rise in costs since 1971, the
restrictions on price increases, and the collapse of the new-issue market in
1973/4 must have made bank lending even more important.

The picture is less clear with regard to the rest of the corporate sector and
to the whole of the unincorporated sector. The Statistical Annexes of the
Quarterly Bulletins of the Bank of England give a broad sectoral breakdown
of aggregate advances by the London clearing banks (i.e. of overdrafts plus
loans; as indicated on p. 64/5, these differ in important respects but

published information does not enable them to be shown separately). However, the proportion of the total advanced say, to construction, to retail distribution, and to professional, scientific, and miscellaneous services – all fields in which unincorporated businesses are probably numerous – is not shown.

The overdraft is basically a very simple way of borrowing. No additional account is opened for the borrower; after putting up whatever security is required, he is entitled to draw his current account down to the agreed debit limit. In principle, British banks, unlike their counterparts in some other countries, have preferred to lend in this way rather than to make long-term investments in their customers. Since much of their funds has come from customers' current-account balances, financial prudence has led them to favour short-term, so-called self-liquidating, loans. In other words, they have traditionally been inclined to provide working capital, i.e. the sums needed to cover day-to-day running costs. Such lending – e.g. to finance the acquisition of the larger stocks of raw materials called for by a proposed increase in output – is called self-liquidating because in the normal course of events the higher sales revenues from the extra output so financed will automatically generate, in a reasonably short and predictable time, enough funds to enable the loan to be repaid. The bank will easily be able to see that this is in fact happening, just by looking at the customer's account.

In practice, overdraft facilities are not created and extinguished as frequently as this – even after excluding those occasions when things go wrong and the bank decides to nurse the account in the hope that the situation will improve and the debt not prove entirely bad. A successful business is not likely to need an overdraft for a certain amount just once in its life; the very expansion which caused the first approach to the bank will probably lead to an even bigger request before long. And banks do not exist to withhold – and make money by withholding – funds from their clients. Therefore it is not unreasonable for a request for an overdraft of, say, £10,000 for six months to lead, before the repayment period has expired, to a request for an extension both in time and amount. Since the bank has an obvious interest in meeting such requests where it is satisfied that the business concerned is thriving and that incomings are keeping pace with larger outgoings, the limit may quickly be raised and the original repayment term waived in order to meet the growing needs of the borrower. In fact, the bank becomes a supplier, not of self-liquidating loans which it can recall whenever it likes, but of constantly rising and permanent additions to the capital which the business regards as an integral part of its financial structure, and which could not be withdrawn at short notice without grave, perhaps fatal, consequences. When this situation is reached (or, better, some time before), the bank will ask the borrower to engage in a 'funding' operation.

5.32 FUNDING

Although this word is sometimes used to mean substituting any long-term commitment (including one in the form of shares) for any short-term one, strictly speaking it means turning short-term debt into long-term debt. The reverse operation of converting long-term obligations into short-term ones is called 'liquefying', or 'unfunding' debt.

Thus, in response to the request from his bank manager, the customer sets about raising funds on a long-term basis. The method adopted depends on the form of business organization involved and the nature of its activities, and may cover anything from taking on a partner (or an additional partner) at one extreme to making an issue of securities to the public at the other. The funds so raised are used, wholly or in part, to eliminate the overdraft or bring it down to a level acceptable to the bank. Then the whole cycle repeats itself, with the overdraft creeping up until it again reaches a size and permanence which makes the bank feel unhappy, when another funding operation will be called for.

5.33 COST

Since the ending of the clearing banks' cartel in 1971, interest rates have become more competitive, but their absolute levels have risen considerably. Overdrafts may bear interest at up to four percentage points above the lending banks' base rate. However, although the overdraft rate is higher than that on term loans for customers of equal creditworthiness, and although it may be increased by the commitment fee charged by the bank to compensate it for risking loss of income because the facility may not be fully used, an overdraft may still be a relatively cheap way of borrowing. This is because the absolute amount the borrower pays depends on the use he makes of the facility, and this is to some extent under his control. However, when considering the merits of different forms of borrowing he must remember that overdrafts have tended to bear the brunt of credit restrictions in the past and have been subject to reduction or withdrawal at very short notice.

5.4 DISCOUNT HOUSES AND BILL BROKERS

5.41 ROLE

Discount houses, and to a lesser extent bill brokers (the distinction between them is mainly one of size), form another source of short-term funds and are open to all forms of enterprise. As far as the business world is concerned (and their involvement in public finance is not relevant here) the job of these specialists is to bridge the gap between (i) suppliers who, quite reasonably, do not wish to part with their goods until they have been paid for them, and (ii) buyers of those goods who, equally reasonably, do not wish to pay for them at least until they have got possession of them and preferably until they have had the time to sell at least part of them. (This gap will appear in all transactions which are not on a cash basis, but because of differences of language, law, currency, and business custom it is potentially a much bigger barrier to overseas than to domestic trade. The special facilities which have been developed to surmount it are dealt with in the Appendix to this chapter.)

5.42 DEFINITION AND USE OF BILLS OF EXCHANGE

The instrument used in the bridging exercise is the bill of exchange. Section 3 of the Bills of Exchange Act 1882 defines this as 'an unconditional order in writing, addressed by one person to another, signed by the person giving it, requiring the person to whom it is addressed to pay, at a fixed or determinable future time, a sum certain in money to, or to the order of, a specified person or to bearer'. It looks something like Figure 5.2 and works like this:

Serial No: £500   London, (date)

Ninety days after sight pay to (name of seller or payee designated by him) or order five hundred pounds, value received:

(Name of Buyer)
(Location)   (Signature of seller)

FIGURE 5.2   Specimen bill of exchange

The seller (S) undertakes to supply the buyer (B), whom he may never have seen, with goods worth £500. B undertakes to pay for them, not as soon as S parts with them nor even when he (B) receives them, but at some stated time in the future – often ninety days after the date of the bill of exchange which is drawn in connection with them, or after he has 'sight' of that bill. S despatches the goods and at the same time draws a bill of exchange on B – i.e. he makes out a document like the one in Figure 5.2 and sends it to B either directly or (more likely) through his bank. When the bill of exchange is presented to him, B signifies his willingness to pay the amount stated on it on the due date by signing his name across the bill, with or without the word 'accepted'; if B is a company, acceptance is made by an authorized signatory on its behalf. B then returns the bill, now called an 'acceptance', to S. At this stage of the proceedings S has B's undertaking to pay, but this will not produce any funds from B until the agreed settlement date. S therefore still has no money from B to cover the production costs he has incurred in meeting B's order. S solves this problem by taking the acceptance to a discount house or bill broker (or very often to his bank, since banks also engage in such business) and discounting it with them, i.e. selling it for less than its face value.

5.43 IMPORTANCE OF BILLS OF EXCHANGE

Bills of exchange are sometimes presented as archaic financial instruments, of declining contemporary use. The evidence does not support this view. The total value of U.K. commercial bills in the banking sector rose from £695 million in December 1963 [2] to £1,921 million in December 1973 [3]. Of this increase of approximately 177%, inflation seems to account for about a quarter on the basis of wholesale price changes [4], which are probably more relevant in this context than retail ones; it accordingly reflects mainly a rise in the volume of transactions financed in this way. A small part of the explanation of this is doubtless that bills of exchange were not specifically covered by credit squeezes until 1965, but their continued use since then must be based on more durable attractions to both lenders and borrowers (e.g. convenience, flexibility, and security).

5.44 COST OF DISCOUNTING

How much below face value S receives for the bill he discounts depends on three factors:

1 The current rate of interest charged by those who lend against this sort of paper.
2 The risk element associated with a particular bill.
3 The lender's administrative expenses.

Thus, if the rate of interest were 12% a year and the bill had exactly three months to run to maturity, the charge under the first heading would be 3% of the bill's face value. The risk element would be assessed by the discount house on the basis of what, if anything, it knew about B; if it thought there was some chance that B might not pay when the time came, it might assess this risk element at, say, 2% a year. The administrative charges (if levied separately) would probably be some relatively small fixed sum to cover the costs of maintaining a bill diary, to ensure that acceptances were presented for payment at the right time and place – say £0·50 a bill. Thus, in exchange for his claim on B with a face value of £500, S would receive now that sum minus:

$$
\begin{array}{ll}
& £ \\
3\% \times £500 = & 15·00 \text{ (3 months' interest @ 12\% per year)} \\
\tfrac{1}{2}\% \times £500 = & 2·50 \text{ (3 months' risk premium @ 2\% per year)} \\
& 0·50 \text{ (administrative charges)} \\
\cline{2-2}
& 18·00
\end{array}
$$

or £482, which he would then be able to use straightaway to finance his activities. (The discount house, or the bank to which it may in turn sell the acceptance, will eventually present the acceptance to B and collect its full face value. In effect – using funds it has obtained from its own shareholders and depositors – it lends the discounted sum for the period between the day S discounts the bill and the day B finally pays it. If for any reason B does not honour the bill, the presenting institution usually has a right to claim back from S the sum advanced.)

This basic transaction is often modified in two ways:

1 S may arrange with B (if the latter is an overseas customer) for B to have the bill accepted on his behalf by an internationally-known accepting house which, in exchange for a small fee ($\tfrac{1}{8}\%$ of the bill's value), will put its name on the bill as acceptor, instead of B's. (Refinements of this are dealt with in the Appendix.) Then, when S discounts the acceptance the lender sees that it bears the name of a firm which is certain to meet its obligations, and thus needs to charge no risk premium. (In the above example, B would pay £0·625 and so save S £2.50; they sort out the balance of advantage between them.)
2 S may well adjust the face value of the bill to include all the subsequent deductions, so that he finishes up with the net amount he requires.

5.45 BORROWING AGAINST BILLS

Discounting bills of exchange is not the only way for the drawer to obtain immediate financial benefit from them, nor necessarily the best way from his point of view. As has been shown, discounting means that he receives a lump sum at once – the present value of the future payment. But it is conceivable that he does not need or want all that money at once and that having to take the whole amount (since he cannot discount only a part of the bill's value) involves him in higher borrowing costs than he would really like. It might therefore be more satisfactory from his point of view to borrow against such bills, rather than discount them. In that case, the seller assigns his rights under the bills to his bank as security for an overdraft. He can then use this, up to the agreed limit, as and when he wants to, thus keeping his borrowing and its related charges much more under his own control.

Incidentally, treating bills of exchange in this manner would make the balance sheet totals of the borrower larger than they otherwise would be – by the size of the overdraft, initially. Use of a discounting facility, however, does not have this effect; it enables the composition of assets to be changed, rather than their total value.

5.5 INVOICE DISCOUNTING

5.51 ROLE OF INVOICE DISCOUNTERS

Traders have been able to discount bills of exchange for centuries. In recent years a somewhat similar facility has been developed in connection with invoices. A supplier, having made goods or services available to a customer and raised an invoice in the usual way, normally waits for his money until the appropriate statement has been sent and settled – on average, six weeks later. If the supplier's activities are being hampered by lack of cash, and if he is really anxious to get paid, he does not have to wait all this time; he may approach one or other of the firms which specialize in discounting invoices. It buys his invoices from him at less than their face value, and pays for them at once. (Such firms may be part of a larger financial organization. In the United Kingdom, for example, Credit Factoring Ltd belongs to the National Westminster Group and Griffin Factors is owned by the Midland Bank Finance Corporation Ltd and the Anglo African Shipping Co. (S.A.) Ltd. The use of the word 'factor' in their titles is a little misleading (*see* p. 56).)

A typical arrangement would be for the invoice-discounting firm, on being approached by a potential client, to investigate the applicant and establish, among other things, what his trade debtors were like as far as speed and reliability of payment were concerned; at least one year's audited figures would be required for this purpose. After satisfying itself on these points, the invoice discounter would agree either to pay the client at some agreed convenient interval (e.g. every week or ten days), or to allow him to draw up to, a specified percentage of the face value of the invoices raised in that period. It would receive copies of these invoices (and any relevant credit notes), together with some security for the money it had advanced on them.

(This might be in the form of the client's acceptance (*see* p. 51) or repayment guarantee for the amount involved, or his undertaking to pay all the sums received from his customers into an account from which only the invoice discounter might draw.) The originals of the invoices would go in the normal way to the client's customers, who might know nothing of the arrangement with the invoice discounter. The client would receive payment from them as before, then repay the advance by honouring its acceptance or guarantee as it was presented, or by lodging these payments in the special account described above.

5.52 BENEFITS

The advantage a firm gains by discounting its invoices is a quicker inflow of cash. As with bills of exchange, no increase in assets results immediately and directly from the operation; all it does is turn an asset which is already quite liquid into the most liquid one of all – cash. (A liquid asset, other than cash itself, is one capable of passing two tests: it must be readily convertible into cash, and this conversion must be possible without significant capital loss. Speed of conversion alone is not enough. The owner of a house would doubtless be able to turn it into cash quite quickly by offering it to passers-by for £1 – there might be some delay while he fought off the men with the straitjackets – but that would not make him regard his house as a liquid asset, because the capital loss would be unacceptably high. What constitutes a 'significant' capital loss can quickly be established empirically.)

This cash may then be used to pay suppliers early enough to qualify for cash discounts (*see* p. 46), to finance more stocks and hence a higher turnover, or to ease the strain of contractual outlays falling due at inconvenient times, e.g. hire charges.

5.53 AVAILABILITY

The Bolton Committee noted that:

'The size of client is largely immaterial: a small client with a few large, sound customers is more acceptable than a large client with many small customers. However . . . the factor will generally require that a client should channel through him a minimum turnover of £100,000 a year, that there should be an average annual turnover per customer of at least £1,000 and an average invoice value of at least £100. For these reasons very small and retail firms cannot effectively make use of factors and the service is in fact mainly confined in this country to manufacturing industry.' [5]

They quoted an estimate of £150–200 million for the total value of factoring turnover [6]; in money terms, this figure – like the minima above – may well have risen since their Report was written.

5.54 COST

The invoice-discounting firm would charge for the money it advanced, probably at least two percentage points above the clearing banks' base rate. It is not a particularly cheap way of raising money, but it may be well worthwhile for those firms which have acute liquidity problems (e.g. because they are new or have grown up in periods of credit or price restraint and have been unable to arrange the finance they required from banks).

In comparing the attractiveness of different invoice-discounting companies, a potential client should bear in mind not just the lending charges but also the choosiness of the lender in accepting his invoices. The latter would probably lend only against those invoices which it approved on the basis of its own ideas about eliminating bad debts, and even then perhaps not more than 80% of the face values involved. Such limits could make a considerable difference to the borrower – as might any efforts by the lender to influence him in his choice of customers, either present or future.

5.55 INSURANCE OF TRADE DEBTS

It is reasonable to suppose that the business wishing to use an invoice-discounting facility will obtain better terms if it can reduce the risk of bad debts among its customers, and show that this has been done. Even the most carefully run firm cannot entirely avoid bad debts, however, and the only satisfactory solution to the problem is credit insurance, i.e. the insurance of the whole of the trade debtors figure against the possibility of default.

The Export Credits Guarantee Department of the Department of Trade has, as explained in Chapter 18, for long provided a cheap and comprehensive system of cover against default by overseas buyers, whether due to commercial or political causes. In the domestic field, probably the most important institution offering this type of cover in the United Kingdom is the Trade Indemnity Company Ltd – a company managed (and in 1974 about 55% owned) by insurance companies, and specializing in the insurance of trade debts. Holding a policy from such an insurer, a client dealing with an invoice-discounting firm would be able to show that the bad debt risk had been taken care of, and thus be able to negotiate better terms. The savings so made would be reduced by the premiums due under the policy, but there should still be a margin in the client's favour.

Credit insurance, incidentally, appeals to a far wider range of businesses than just those interested in discounting invoices. It is increasingly used by large, well-established firms which have access to all the funds they normally need via traditional channels. Such firms would never dream of discounting their invoices – but like everyone else they still have to reckon with bad debts. Continuing industrial concentration means that firms deal with fewer and larger customers, and that fewer but larger trade debts emerge. Suppliers increasingly recognize that a single business failure can now jeopardize working capital to the tune of hundreds of thousands of pounds at one blow. The £5,143 million-worth of business insured by Trade Indemnity at the end of 1973 [7] must have come largely from such firms; certainly the invoice discounters' business would have accounted for only a tiny fraction of that total, even if all of it were insured.

Credit insurance is thus not just a development to enable certain types of business to sell their invoices on better terms; it also has an important role as an economic stabilizer. The collapse of a major business has, in the past, not infrequently been associated with a spreading failure among its suppliers; if the initial shock is absorbed by the vast resources of the insurance industry, the damage is confined. It is perhaps not without significance that the failure of Rolls Royce in 1971 was not followed by a string of liquidations among its suppliers and subcontractors. Trade Indemnity's gross commitment in that case was about £2 million, but the eventual disturbance to its profits proved minimal [8].

5.56 FACTORING OF DEBTS

Firms offering to buy at a discount the trade debts of others often call themselves factors (see p. 53). This is a little misleading because (i) a factor is a special kind of agent (in the common-law sense, 'an agent entrusted with the possession of goods for the purposes of sale' [9], and (ii) offering to factor someone's debts is quite different from offering to discount them. On a strict interpretation of the word, the 'goods' with which a factor in the financial world is entrusted are the accounts of the client firm's customers. In other words, the factor undertakes, for a fee, to run the whole of the client's sales-accounting operation.

What happens then is that the client, on selling to a customer, issues an invoice to him in the usual way and sends a copy of it to the factor. This invoice, or the statement which follows it if that is the accepted trigger for payment, tells the customer to remit the sum due not to the supplier but to the factor, whose name and address are shown on it. The latter has already entered the amount due on the customer's account and simply credits this with payments as they are received (and any returns recorded). On an agreed date, found by calculating the value-weighted average of the due settlement dates of the outstanding accounts, the factor pays the client the money it has received, minus its fee. Thus, instead of a large number of relatively small payments from its customers, spread over time, the client gets a lump sum at regular intervals from the factoring organization. (Various refinements may be made; for example, instead of being paid by the factor the client may have the right to draw on it up to an agreed limit – but the principle remains the same.) The factor takes on all the sales-accounting work – keeping accounts posted, maintaining credit limits, following up bad debts, and, in consultation with the client, pressing for their recovery – in exchange for a fee of $\frac{3}{4}$–$2\frac{1}{2}$% of gross turnover.

Although it is not hard to see how factoring and invoice-discounting facilities might be linked and offered as a package to potential clients, factoring as such is clearly a completely different type of job from invoice discounting (and if both services are offered by the same firm, each will be charged for separately). The client using factoring does not receive payment for his trade debts any earlier than he otherwise would do, but there are three other important benefits to him:

1 He saves all the outlays on management and clerical time, office space, machinery, and stationery which he would otherwise incur in running the sales-accounting side of his business, and is able to devote himself more fully to his chosen activities.
2 His gross revenue may also rise, if the greater debt-collecting efficiency of the factor enables him to dispense with the cash discounts he has previously offered his customers.
3 The overall efficiency of his undertaking may be improved if he decides to buy, as an optional extra, the sales analyses which the factor's computerized procedures make possible.

Factoring pure and simple thus obviously has important financial repercussions on the firms using it, but it remains essentially an exercise in specialization – not fund raising.

Factors indicate that the type of business for which their service is most suited is a U.K. registered company with an annual turnover of at least £100,000, selling goods in common use to trade customers [10]. Alex Lawrie Factors Ltd lists the types of business for which factoring is difficult to arrange as:

'Businesses selling only to individuals, such as retail businesses. The credit control problems are very great . . . Building contractors . . . because of the special nature of the standard form of contract under which work is

normally done in this country . . . Businesses with unusual terms of trade
. . . Businesses where customers are mostly "one-off", and companies
which make extensive use of Credit Notes, and/or payment by contra.' [11]

5.57 UNDISCLOSED FACTORING

In the early days of factoring, some potential clients thought that an
instruction to pay a third party might upset their relationships with their
customers – if it were regarded either as a breach of confidence or as an
indication that they were in some kind of financial trouble. In an attempt to
avoid such difficulties, rather complicated arrangements were made for the
factor to remain in the background. As factoring has become more widely
accepted, however, these original misgivings have been largely dispelled and
such 'undisclosed' factoring does not now seem to be commercially significant.

5.6 LOAN BROKERS

5.61 ROLE OF LOAN BROKERS

These specialists developed in the 1960s and early 1970s, acting as a link
between non-financial businesses having temporary surpluses of funds and
those other businesses, or local authorities, having temporary shortages. (It
may be argued that such specialists were unlike other short-term lenders in
that they did not own the funds they lent, but this is not a serious objection as
most of the money lent by banks, for example, is not theirs but their
depositors'. However, it is true that the brokers differed from other sources
in not *holding* the funds they employed.) Working on a commission basis,
they arranged loans for periods from 3 months to 5 years.

5.62 AVAILABILITY OF FUNDS

Market volume was reported to total £200–300 million in 1970 [12], but it is
since thought to have practically collapsed. This was partly because of the
strains felt by package holiday companies, whose customers' deposits and
other advance payments made up an important part of the supply of funds,
but even more because of the failure of one or two large borrowers, e.g.
Metal Traders Ltd which went down in 1972 with unsecured loans from
three companies totalling about £3·5 million [13].

Accordingly, the intercompany loan-broking business was not active by
the end of 1974, but if and when happier economic conditions return it
could regain its former significance.

5.7 TAX AUTHORITIES

5.71 THEIR ROLE

The tax authorities provide one other source of funds which may be tapped by any form of (profitable) business. This is so because, although a firm's taxable income and the tax to be paid on that income are established fairly shortly after the end of its financial year, the date for the actual handing over of the money to discharge this tax liability may not come until some time later. Companies incorporated before April 1965 have between nine and twenty-one months before they must pay any corporation tax due, while those incorporated after April 1965 must settle their tax bill within nine months of the end of their financial year (*see* p. 30). (Any company making a dividend distribution, no matter when incorporated, must make an advance payment of corporation tax within three months of that distribution.) Somewhat similar delays apply also to unincorporated businesses.

By being enabled to retain funds in this way, firms are in effect given interest-free loans by the government. (There is nothing new in this; some of the earliest rural banks in England were started by tax collectors [14]. They were empowered to collect some or all of the revenue from an area and remit it to London by a certain date. By gathering the amounts due well in advance, they were able to lend them at short-term and pocket the interest.) Given a reasonably stable level of earnings and of tax on them, the amounts so 'borrowed' may have an almost permanent appearance – but it would be imprudent to use them for financing anything other than self-liquidating assets, e.g. for trade debtors or stock. It would certainly be rank bad financial planning to have to sell fixed assets to meet a known tax charge! With this proviso, the source may be fully used.

5.72 AVAILABILITY

Table 5.1 shows the extent to which companies have taken advantage of this facility. Apart from 1964, the amounts set aside to pay tax due (sooner or later) have always financed a smaller proportion both of total current assets and total assets than bank borrowings; they have, nevertheless, been an important source of funds over the whole of the 1964–71 period, covering roughly 11% and 6% respectively of these asset categories.

Companies could thus be vulnerable to changes in the availability of this credit from the Revenue authorities – just as they are to changes in the availability of bank credit. They could be in financial trouble, not because of an alteration in the rate of tax applied to their profits (as seen on p. 38, tax allowances make tax rates a poor guide to disposable income), but because of a reduction in the allowed interval between establishing how much tax is to be paid and actually paying it.

5.8 SUMMARY

Probably for all forms of business – and certainly for those covered by the Department of Industry analysis – suppliers' credit is by far the biggest source of short-term funds (i.e. of funds available for up to a year); its importance does not, unfortunately, mean that it is well used. Next come banks, with total lending about two-fifths as large as trade credit, but expanding fast; traditionally they provide working capital via overdrafts. Discount houses and bill brokers have for long specialized in liquefying bills of exchange on a considerable scale, especially for exporters, while, more recently, invoice discounters have offered a similar facility for trade debts as well as the separate non-lending service of factoring. Finally, the customary interval between agreeing the amount of tax to be paid on profits and actually paying that amount enables funds to be borrowed, short-term and interest-free, from the government.

APPENDIX: DOCUMENTARY CREDITS

5.A1 DEFINITION

A significant influence on the use of bills of exchange in exporting has been the development of different forms of documentary credit. The Banking Commission of the International Chamber of Commerce defines this as:

'. . . any arrangement, however named or described, whereby a bank (the issuing bank), acting at the request and in accordance with the instructions of a customer (the applicant for the credit), is to make a payment to or to the order of a third party (the beneficiary) or is to pay, accept, or negotiate bills of exchange (drafts) drawn by the beneficiary, or authorise such payments to be made or such drafts to be paid, accepted or negotiated by another bank, against stipulated documents and compliance with stipulated terms and conditions.' [1]

5.A2 PURPOSE

This definition is rather a mouthful, but the purposes of such credits are more simply stated. They are:

1 To reduce the interval between the seller's parting with goods and actually getting money for them.
2 To reduce his risk of not being paid at all.

These two matters are of considerable importance to any business, exporting or not.

The first of these is a problem in any export sale where a bill of exchange is the means of payment, because before the seller can discount the eventual acceptance he must first obtain it – which means sending the bill of exchange to the overseas buyer and waiting for it to come back. The exporter cannot short-circuit this procedure by sending the bill before shipping the goods; the buyer will not accept it unless he has evidence that the consignment is on its way to him. Nor is the exporter likely to be much attracted by the idea of discounting the bill before it has been accepted. Such unaccepted bills – called 'one-name paper' because the only signature on them is that of the drawer – may be discounted, but since the drawee has not signified his consent to pay anything they are more risky, therefore less appealing to lenders, and therefore of lower present value for borrowers.

The second point arises because a buyer's acceptance of a bill of exchange signifies his willingness to pay a stated amount at a specified time, assuming no fraudulent intent. This is not the same as guaranteeing his ability to pay when that time comes. His business may have failed through no fault of his own; his government may have revoked his import licence; the necessary foreign exchange may not be released – any of a variety of factors may jeopardize the seller's chances of getting his money.

5.A3 USE

As the definition above makes clear, documentary credits overcome the first of these problems, because they entitle the seller to payment on presentation of 'stipulated documents' to a bank (these are, essentially, bills of lading, invoices, evidence of insurance, and whatever certificates of origin and quality the buyer calls for in connection with any particular shipment). There is no waiting for the bill of exchange drawn on the overseas customer to be accepted by him and returned; the bank to which the exporter presents the specified documents will probably be in his home town, so he collects payment at once.

Unfortunately, not all documentary credits are equally good for overcoming the second problem – that of uncertainty of payment. This is because there is more than one type of them, each with different features.

5.A4 TYPES

(a) Revocable

All documentary credits are revocable, unless otherwise stated [2]. A revocable credit is one which is subject to alteration or cancellation at any time by the buyer alone, without the seller's being able to do anything about it. Thus, the latter may ship goods under a contract covered by a revocable documentary credit, only to find, when he presents the relevant documents to the issuing bank, that the whole arrangement has been cancelled and that no money is forthcoming. (On top of this he will have the trouble and expense of disposing of the shipment when it reaches its destination.)

(b) Irrevocable

Any exporter will, naturally, seek to avoid such experiences by getting his customers to open irrevocable credits. Such credits cannot be cancelled nor may their terms and conditions be altered, without the prior approval of the beneficiary. Accordingly, a seller drawing bills of exchange on an overseas customer under the terms of such a credit will not find them suddenly and unpredictably made worthless by some decision of the customer.

Nevertheless, his money is not completely assured; he is still vulnerable on two counts.

1 The bank to which, under the terms of the credit, he is required to present bills of exchange and the relevant documents of shipment, may not be a branch of the overseas customer's bank but merely a 'correspondent' bank, i.e. one acting as an agent for the customer's bank. As such, it is not a party to the credit and is not bound by it in any way; it may therefore refuse to handle any bills of exchange presented under that credit, even though all the supporting documents are in order.
2 No credit can be any better than the bank behind it – and the customer's bank may just fold up.

(c) Confirmed irrevocable credits

Both these difficulties are overcome by the opening of a confirmed irrevocable credit. To confirm a credit a bank in the exporter's country adds its name to the arrangement (for a fee), so that it becomes committed to accepting or negotiating (as the case may be) bills which are properly drawn under it. 'Confirming', a credit to a beneficiary is quite different from 'advising' him of it. If an exporter stipulates that a confirmed irrevocable credit be opened in his favour and is eventually informed by one of his local banks that an irrevocable credit has been opened by an overseas bank, he will not have got what he asked for – the bank which passes on this information to him is in no way bound by the terms of the credit.) Once the credit is confirmed the exporter knows that it cannot alter in any way to his disadvantage without his consent, and that his bills will be honoured by a local organization in which he has confidence. (The risk does remain of those bills' not being honoured by the overseas buyer. Insurance against this risk is a common-sense precaution which the bank concerned will insist on; the main institution in this field is the Export Credits Guarantee Department (*see* p. 201).)

6 External Sources: Corporate Medium- and Long-term Lenders

6.1 INTRODUCTION

As already mentioned, medium-term lending is a rather indeterminate category, shading off at each end into lending for some more clearly defined period. Apart from the specialist bodies reviewed in the Appendix, the main sources are two already referred to as providers of short-term funds:

1 Banks, which may be tapped by any form of business.
2 Non-financial companies whose surpluses, lent through the intercompany loan market, are naturally available only to other incorporated firms.

Long-term corporate lending comes largely from the institutional investors, i.e. insurance companies, pension funds, investment and unit trusts, and building societies, from which, in principle, any form of business may borrow. The development of much of their activity in this field into sale and lease-back operations is considered here, the more general aspects of long-term lending being dealt with in the next chapter.

6.2 MEDIUM-TERM LENDERS: BANKS

6.21 NATURE AND IMPORTANCE

In addition to supplying short-term funds via overdraft facilities, banks also lend on a 'term' basis. The borrower opens a separate loan account for the amount and period of the loan, securing it, like an overdraft, perhaps by depositing signed, undated share or stock transfer forms together with the relevant certificates of ownership. Unfortunately it is impossible to say, from the published information, what proportion of banks' advances falls under each heading.

However, if the quantity of funds lent on this basis is not known, the purpose of such borrowings may be inferred. Given that the overdraft is reckoned to be an appropriate means of financing working capital for which any one day's cash requirement will be uncertain, the loan is likely to be the chosen instrument to enable some other kind of asset, with more predictable outlays, to be acquired. Since U.K. banks are traditionally reluctant to invest long-term in their customers' businesses, loans must be intended to help buy the shorter-lived types of plant, equipment, etc. from which it is not reasonable to expect quick recovery of the whole amount advanced, but from which earnings over a few years should pay off the debt comfortably.

6.22 COST

With interest rates at unprecedently high levels and liable to large and rapid changes, and with the spread between the rates charged to high- and low-risk customers exceptionally wide, statements about costs become hazardous. However, for customers of equal creditworthiness the rate charged on a loan will be lower than that on an overdraft, although the actual interest cost may be higher for a loan than for an overdraft of the same limit, since the rate will be applied to the initial sum borrowed. At least the advance will carry no risk of recall before the agreed time – usually a minimum of twelve months; however, the agreement may specify repayment by instalments.

6.3 INTERCOMPANY LOANS

6.31 LOAN BROKERS

When these were considered on p. 58, it was mentioned that they handled sums for periods varying up to five years; the mechanics of the operation do not call for further comment.

6.32 LENDING BY PENSION FUNDS

One aspect of intercompany lending which does merit attention, however, is the relationship between firms and their ostensibly separate and independent pension funds.

When a firm operates a pension scheme which does not require payment of contributions to any organization outside itself, it is obviously able to use those contributions to finance its activities more or less as it chooses. But even when the contributions are paid to some separate corporate body, this does not mean that the firm is denied access to them; common directors, for example, may give it effective control over the use of the pension fund without necessarily compromising the role of the directors as trustees of that fund. The resources provided may then constitute medium- or even long-term loans.

There seems to be no way of establishing how prevalent this sort of action is, nor the magnitude of the flow of funds attributable to it. The practice may be quite widespread, given the number of private pension schemes in operation. (There were about 65,000, with over 11 million members, at the end of 1971 [1], and they were being vigorously promoted in 1973.) Many such schemes, of course, involve contractual payments to insurance companies or pension funds and thus are outside the scope of this section.

Whatever the benefits of the practice, it is open to two objections.

(a) Danger to employees

If anything goes seriously wrong with the firm which is borrowing from its own pension fund, its employees stand to lose both job and pension simultaneously. The same objection would arise if the pension fund used a significant part of its income to buy shares in the firm concerned. For example, the manager of the Rolls Royce scheme was the blue-eyed boy of the pension world because he did neither of these two – and his choice seems to have been regarded as a most fortunate exception to a general practice [2].

(b) Misuse of funds

Of greater relevance here is the point that, if the pension fund makes financial resources available to the 'parent' firm at a time when the latter finds it inconvenient (or perhaps impossible) to raise funds in the open competitive market, the suspicion arises that the funds are being misused in the sense that the investing public would not have provided them given a free choice.

A corollary of this point is that the income of the pension fund – and hence the benefits it will be able to pay – will be lower than they otherwise would be. For example, Mr Robert Evans, a T.G.W.U. shop steward previously employed by the London Co-operative Society, was given leave in 1973 to proceed in the High Court with the case he was bringing against his one-time employer, alleging that the Society as trustee acted in breach of trust by lending superannuation fund money to the L.C.S. at rates of interest lower than it could have got elsewhere. The rate paid was reported to be $3\frac{3}{4}\%$ from 1933 to 1969, when it was raised to $4\frac{1}{4}\%$, and the interest 'lost' to be more than £10 million [3].

6.4 LONG-TERM LENDERS: INSTITUTIONS

6.41 MORTGAGES

Apart from contributing to the publicly issued loans considered on p. 100, the institutions may lend against the security of mortgages.

A mortgage is essentially a fixed charge (this term is explained on p. 74) on property in the form, generally, of land and buildings, and as such it is commonly thought of in connection with house purchase. It may thus tend to be linked with the one-man or other small business, where the largest asset of the proprietor is likely to be his own house. Building societies exist to lend money on the security of domestic property – but the money so raised does not have to be used to buy the premises concerned from their last owner; it may be used instead to finance the business activities of the existing owner. In other words, it is possible to borrow money from a building society to buy a house, and it is equally possible, having bought a house, to borrow on the security of it and use the funds for business purposes.

However, although building societies exist primarily to promote home ownership, and are established and operate under a body of law distinct from that applying to ordinary commercial undertakings, it does not follow that they may lend only against residential property or only to individuals. Section 21 of the Building Societies Act 1962 provides for 'special' advances (not to exceed 10% of the total advances in any one year), comprising loans of over £13,000 to owner-occupiers and of any amount to bodies corporate. Most corporations borrowing from building societies are in fact either housing associations or building firms engaged almost entirely in house construction, but inspection of the annual returns of building societies shows that they also lend money against the security (and for the construction) of shops, offices, warehouses, schools, factories, hotels, clubs, and university premises. They should therefore be considered a routine, though perhaps indirect, source of funds for incorporated as well as unincorporated businesses. Since the interest rate is usually $1\frac{1}{2}$–2 percentage points above that charged to owner-occupiers (i.e. $12\frac{1}{2}$–13% in mid 1974), from the cost angle they are also competitive.

Furthermore, there is nothing to stop any other institutional lender which has the necessary legal power from making a mortgage agreement with another commercial body. As a result of this the borrower would obtain a lump sum at once – to redeploy in its business as it wished – in exchange for repayments of capital and payments of interest at some agreed rate over the next, say, twenty or twenty-five years. The objections to this, from the borrower's viewpoint, are considered on p. 71.

6.42 SALE AND LEASE-BACK TRANSACTIONS

These are another major way in which insurance companies and pension funds, in particular, help to provide funds. Although they are not strictly a form of lending, it is convenient to look at them here.

(a) Description

A sale and lease-back transaction is based on (i) the possession by a business of valuable freehold property, and (ii) a desire by that business either to bring the composition of its assets more closely into line with the requirements of its particular activities or, more simply, to get some ready cash. It may gratify that desire by selling some or all of its real estate to, for example, an insurance company, and simultaneously leasing it back from the buyer at an agreed annual rental. By such an arrangement the seller receives in cash the capital value of the property sold, and after deducting tax is then free to use this cash to develop its undertaking in any way it wishes. Meanwhile it will have safeguarded for itself the continued use – as distinct from ownership – of the asset concerned. (The lease is likely to be for a long term – 99 and 120 years have been quoted – but to protect itself against being deprived of the use of the asset when the original lease expires, the selling firm may have a renewal option included in the lease.)

For example, Powell Duffryn, the engineering, shipbuilding, and building supplies group, sold its freehold London headquarters to the Legal and General Assurance Co. Ltd for £6·1 million in 1970, and leased them back for 99 years. In principle, 30% of the difference between the sale price and the 1965 value of the property would have gone in capital gains tax (since the proceeds of the sale would obviously not have been used to acquire another asset of the same kind), but the rest would have been available for redeployment in the group. In Powell Duffryn's case, the net amount realized (about £4·8 million) helped to reduce debt, promote the development of one of the subsidiaries, and provide the cash needed for two acquisisitions [4]. Such transactions are constantly going on; for example, even in the depressed condition of the property market in 1974, the Debenhams stores group arranged a sale and lease-back of its London headquarters, also for about £6 million gross, largely to cut its interest bill by repaying short-term debt [5].

(b) Advantages for the seller

A firm's balance sheet may show that its most important single asset is land and buildings. If the main purpose of the firm is to own and manage real estate such as hotels, blocks of flats, or holiday camps, this allocation of resources is as it should be – but examination of the reports of what the firm actually does may well reveal that it is not in the least interested in any of these things. (It is often instructive to compare what a company's spokesmen claim it is engaged in with what the composition of its assets indicates it is primarily concerned with.) It may instead be dedicated to producing electric light bulbs, fishing tackle, or any of the million and one other artefacts and services of modern life, for which it is necessary to have the use of property but generally unnecessary to have the ownership of it. (There may be exceptions to this principle in the case of things like patents and copyrights; the considerations on p. 139 should also be borne in mind.)

By selling the property and leasing it back, the business can free resources from the assets in which they were locked up and concentrate them on that activity in which it claims to be able to use them best. Then, on the not unreasonable assumption that the gain from the ensuing larger volume of business in its chosen field exceeds the rent it must pay for the premises it no longer owns, the seller will profit from the deal.

It is true, of course, that by selling some or all of its real estate the business denies itself the benefit of any future capital appreciation – and this has generally been big enough comfortably to outweigh the gain from increased output, even without price controls to limit profit margins. This penalty is not quite as heavy as it looks, however. In the first place, as the events of 1974 showed, there is no certainty that the real value of land and buildings will rise in the future – either as fast as in the past, or at all. The seller takes a realized gain now instead of a potentially greater but unrealized gain in the future. That is not an inherently wrong decision. Secondly, it seems an ineluctable fact that many businesses are interested, professionally, in all sorts of productive activities other than property ownership and management. For them, a major and recurring problem is, not how best to allocate the increased resources they may have at hand in, say, ten years' time, but how to make the best use of the assets they control now. For such firms, selling and leasing back may be a required action. A third aspect of the manoeuvre emerges if the problem facing the business concerned is one of finding cash for survival rather than expansion. Sale and lease-back may provide a partial or even total solution to this difficulty and enable the firm to buy time to continue the struggle.

(c) Advantages for the buyer

Naturally, a sale and lease-back transaction cannot go through just because the seller wishes to benefit from it; the buyer must be willing too. The advantages to the latter may be considerable. First, it provides a safe bulk outlet for some of the investment funds which pour in each day. The size of this flow is indicated by the fact that the cash value of the net acquisition of assets by insurance companies in 1973 was £1,550 million [6], and by superannuation funds was £1,346 million [7]. Faced with the need to find acceptable uses for an inflow of funds on this scale, it is not surprising that such institutions have a minimum investment stake (it was £25,000 (for loans) at the time of the Bolton Committee inquiries [8]) and that they are attracted by sale and lease-back deals under which a few big high-quality firms, offering negligible risk of default under their agreements, absorb large sums.

Profitability is also high. This is partly because commercial and industrial property, not being subject to rent control to the same extent as domestic property, produces satisfactorily rising income which is not eroded by inflation, providing reversions are frequent enough; and partly because such investments entail relatively low administrative costs. Investing a similar sum in a collection of smaller properties would be possible, but it would involve dealing with a correspondingly larger number of tenants, perhaps not all of equal financial standing. With the usual sale and lease-back there is just one large first-class cheque to be collected at the agreed interval from one large first-class tenant. Finally, if the buyer is an insurance company it should not be overlooked that it is in business to sell insurance; one of the strings attached to the contract may be that it collects all the seller's insurance business, and is thus doubly blessed.

(d) Advantage to the economy

Sale and lease-back also has a macro-economic attraction. The capital appreciation of the land and buildings adds nothing to real national income, whereas to the extent that greater output is achieved by the use of the value freed from the real estate, more goods and services become available from a sale and lease-back transaction.

6.43 MORTGAGES AND SALE AND LEASE-BACK COMPARED

At first sight it might appear that there was not much to choose between raising money on a mortgage and doing so via a sale and lease-back transaction. They have the same object, involve the same assets, and may have comparable gearing effects (see Chapter 12), since both rent and mortgage interest plus capital repayments are commitments which must be met irrespective of the level of profits, and since they may not be dissimilar in amount.

But there are other important considerations to be borne in mind, apart from those already indicated. First, a lease contract ties the selling business to a particular building, whereas mortgaged premises may be sold and the outstanding debt repaid if a shift of location is desired. Furthermore, a sale and lease-back is a once-and-for-all transaction; having done it the erstwhile owners have permanently reduced their borrowing power, because they have one less class of asset to offer as security. On the other hand, a business is likely to obtain more cash from a sale and lease-back than from a mortgage. The former is based on full market value, which even after capital gains tax is deducted will produce more than the 50–60 % of market value customarily advanced under a mortgage.

The really crucial distinction, however, is summed up in the word 'specialization'. The whole point of the sale and lease-back is to free resources, locked up in property, for concentration in some use indicated by the particular skills or interests of the owners and managers – and to free them permanently. The essence of a mortgage arrangement is that, although funds are provided against the security of real estate, this real estate eventually finishes up unencumbered in the same hands as before. The payments periodically made under a mortage agreement by the borrower to the lender are, as indicated above, partly interest and partly capital – so the initial transfusion of fresh funds is followed by a slow and deliberate haemorrhage. This does not make sense.

For this reason and the others set out above, selling and leasing back may well have almost completely replaced mortgaging as a means of raising money on commercial and, perhaps to a smaller extent, industrial property.

6.5 SUMMARY

Medium-term lending comes mainly from two sources already considered: banks, via term loans as distinct from overdrafts, and intercompany transfers, which may be economically and socially objectionable. Institutional lenders are major providers of long-term funds, not least as asset liquefiers through sale and lease-back arrangements. The latter, because of their considerable attractions to both lenders and borrowers, seem largely to have replaced mortgages as a means of raising money on freehold business premises.

7 External Sources: Lending by the Investing Public

7.1 INTRODUCTION

The term 'investing public' means all the individual persons who may sub-scribe when a fund-raising organization makes a public issue of securities. (Unfortunately, 'securities' is rather a misleading word; not only do many shares turn out to be worthless but, even more confusing, many loans are explicitly 'unsecured'. This is considered more fully on p. 77.) This defini-tion does not mean that subscriptions on such occasions come only from individuals; they also come from banks, companies, and the whole range of institutional investors – to the extent that it is legal for them so to subscribe.

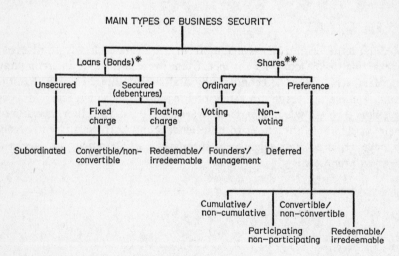

* Holders are creditors of the organization concerned.
** Holders are members of the organization concerned.

FIGURE 7.1   Main types of business security

Such institutional investors, however, are not included in the expression 'the investing public'. Furthermore, the institutions collectively allocate their investment funds over the whole range of forms of business organization, though in some cases their contribution may be very small. (Thus, the 'other' U.K. investment of investment trust companies referred to in Table 17 of the Statistical Annex of the Bank of England's *Quarterly Bulletin*, was not thought to include more than £1 million in loans to unincorporated firms at the end of 1972 [1].)

In contrast, the public, lacking the professional skill and knowledge of the institutions, channel their subscriptions directly or indirectly almost exclusively to one form of enterprise: the listed company. Accordingly, this chapter considers the types of debt which such companies may issue. Shares – the other pieces of paper sold by companies as a means of raising permanent capital – confer on buyers rights as members, not creditors, and are dealt with in Chapter 8. The main types of business security are set out in Figure 7.1.

7.2 DEBENTURES

When a company borrows on a long-term basis from one or other of the sources mentioned earlier, the details of the loan (i.e. amount, rate of interest, repayment arrangements, and security) are set out in a document which the borrower signs and gives to the lender as evidence of its debt to the latter. This document is a debenture (from the Latin *debeo*: I owe) and is defined as 'documentary evidence of debt of a permanent kind' [2]. Although governments also incur such debt, the word 'debenture' now conventionally applies only to the long-term debt of companies and other trading organizations. Thus, while all debentures are loans, not all loans are debentures.

If all the money is raised from one source, this document will consist of only one piece of paper, which will be held by the lender concerned. Such a lender is nearly always a corporate body like one of the institutions mentioned above, but large-scale lending by an individual to a company is not unknown. For instance, Mr Leopold Muller, together with Mr Leonard Jackson (a fellow director of De Vere Hotels and Restaurants Ltd), lent that business up to £1.75 million interest-free between 1963 and 1965, and smaller amounts subsequently. Mr Muller, with over 5 million ordinary shares, owns nearly half the equity in De Vere's, and has waived his right to dividends too [3]. But few concerns can rely on a fairy godfather with such wealth and dedication!

If, however, the money is raised from the public at large, the debenture will be in the form of many separate pieces of paper – each one a printed certificate in the hands of the lender to the effect that he has lent a specified amount to the borrower at the stated rate of interest. (As will be seen in Chapter 10, the borrower receives less than the sum nominally lent because of the costs of the issue and any discount allowed on the issue price.) In

principle, such a debenture may be 'simple' or 'naked', meaning that it is
unsecured by any charge on the issuing company's property. In practice,
debt of this kind is called unsecured loan stock; debentures are almost always that type of loan which is secured in one way or another and an unsecured debenture is becoming a contradiction in terms.

7.3 SECURED LOANS

7.31 DEFINITION

A secured lender is one who has some legally acknowledged claim on one or
more of the assets of the business to which he has lent, so that if it becomes
bankrupt (in the case of an unincorporated firm) or goes into liquidation (in
the case of an incorporated one) he is able to claim and realize the particular
asset(s) as a means of recouping his money, before the unsecured lenders get
anything at all. Secured creditors may claim only the assets which constitute
their security. If, on being sold, these assets realize too little to settle their
claims, the secured creditors join the unsecured claimants for the balance
due; if there is any excess on realization, that goes to the unsecured claimants. The latter must, in the event of the debtor's failure, recover what they
can from whatever is left over after the secured creditors have been satisfied
as far as is possible; there is no guarantee that there will be enough for all, or
even for the latter. The 'security' provided for a secured creditor comes
from a 'charge' on the borrower's assets; a charged asset is one which is
pledged to a lender to cover the eventual repayment of the money he has
lent. Such a charge may be either fixed or floating (or general).

7.32 FIXED CHARGES

(a) Essential features

There are two essential features of a fixed charge:

1 A physical identification of some specific asset.
2 A ban on any disposal of this asset without the lender's consent.

Probably the commonest illustration of the first feature is the scrappy
little drawing or section of local street map which accompanies the mortgage
deed familiar to every house buyer; it serves to identify, by a geographical
reference, a particular plot of land (together with any buildings which may
be on it).

The second feature is essential, because without it the lender has no genuine security at all – no matter how accurately the pledged asset is described. If anything goes wrong he has the right to claim a particular piece of property and no other. If that particular piece were no longer in the debtor's possession, it would not matter what else was; the creditor would have no claim on it and would be effectively unsecured.

(b) Supporting assets

Consideration of a business's assets will reveal which assets are suitable to support a fixed charge. The most liquid assets are debtors and stock – ignoring, for obvious reasons, any cash. Now it might be physically possible to identify each individual debtor and to record what he owed at the time the charge became effective; indeed, compared with this the potential lender's physical identification of all the stock would be child's play. (He could, for example, scratch his initials on any partly finished and finished goods and parcel up, under his seal, all raw materials and work in progress.) Such Herculean labours would, however, be quite pointless because of the second feature stated above: the ban on the disposal of such charged assets without the lender's consent. Disposing of debtors (by accepting payment from them) and selling stock are vital to the continued operation of the borrowing business – and, of course, to the lender's repayment prospects. But as soon as the creditor authorizes the 'disposal' of these assets, he loses his security; if he seeks to regain it by identifying stocks and debtors again, the whole exercise becomes even more absurd than it was to start with. Debtors and stock, therefore, are not suitable assets to support a fixed charge.

Plant, machinery, and vehicles may come next for review; what applies to them applies also to furniture and fittings, if these have significant value. Here the creditor's problem is a different one. It is not that the assets concerned do not lend themselves readily to physical identification – quite clearly they do. Nor is it that restricting disposal of them raises insuperable difficulties in the day-to-day running of the borrowing business – equally clearly it does not. Their major disadvantage as security for a potential lender is simply that, in periods when production techniques and consumers' tastes change so frequently, their second-hand value may not be much more than they are worth as scrap (and this value is all that the creditor will be able to count on, if he has to realize them). Therefore these assets also are unsuitable for use in connection with a fixed charge.

That leaves land and buildings – either freehold or, if the unexpired term is long enough, leasehold. As already mentioned, the physical identification of such assets is a routine matter presenting no problems at all. In addition, the legal procedure for transferring rights in these assets (e.g. the investigation and registration of land titles) is likely to be more formal and time-consuming than in the case of other assets, so that even if the borrower sought to alienate them without the lender's consent it would be much harder for him to do so. Accordingly, when a business raises funds on the security of a fixed charge, the assets pledged will almost certainly be land and buildings. (However, the British Oxygen Company's borrowing (*see* p. 77) provides an example of some assets that were not.)

7.33 FLOATING OR GENERAL CHARGES

Many businesses, although creditworthy and anxious to borrow, may find themselves unable to do so on a fixed-charge basis. Their resources may not include enough assets of the appropriate kind, as in the fields of publishing, road transport, and professional services, or their directors may already have borrowed to the hilt on them, or may have already read and profited by p. 68. This does not mean that such firms may offer prospective lenders only unsecured loans; they may borrow on the security of a floating or general charge, i.e. one attaching to all their assets, including any which might otherwise be the subject of a fixed charge.

This points to one of the features distinguishing a floating charge from a fixed charge: the former attaches, not to specific physically identifiable assets but to general classes of assets. Thus a lender would have the security, not of certain named customers or certain items of stock of the borrower (it has already been seen that such apparent precision is useless), but of the whole value of trade debtors and/or stock. The components of these two totals would be constantly changing, but their value at any one time could be reliably established, and this would provide the security the lender is looking for.

The other distinguishing feature of a floating charge, which follows from the first, is that the pledged assets may be freely disposed of by the debtor without the lender's consent, providing the disposal is in the ordinary course of business. This type of charge thus leaves the borrower free to deal normally with stock and debtors, replacement of equipment, etc., without weakening the lender's control over any land and buildings which may be pledged to him.

7.34 REGISTRATION OF CHARGES

All such charges given by a company over its assets must be recorded separately in a register of charges, a copy of which must be filed each year at Companies House, together with the other documents required by law. This registration of charges is a common and perfectly normal step for incorporated businesses to take, and no one thinks any the worse of them for doing so. With unincorporated concerns, however, the position is rather different; although borrowing on the security of a fixed charge presents no difficulties, trying to do so on a floating charge is likely to be counter-productive (*see* Chapter 2).

7.35 THE MEANING OF 'SECURED' LOANS

How significant the security is which a lender gets with a 'secured' loan depends on such factors as the size and type of asset pledged, the nature of the business involved, and the quality of its management. Lending to a holiday-camp operator on the security of a fixed charge over land and buildings may sound safe enough. But if the borrower is unable to make a success of the business and proves unable to service and repay the loan, how well-placed are secured creditors? They may find themselves in possession of a site and buildings which a professional management has been unable to run profitably and which may well have no ready alternative use. Finding another set of managers may not be easy either, and the lenders may not be too keen on the idea of running the place themselves. The apparent solidity of land and buildings may then prove ephemeral.

On the other hand, for example, the British Oxygen Co. Ltd has raised £23 million via its so-called 'Tonnage Debentures', the first issue of £6 million in 1966 setting the pattern for two later ones. The money was borrowed on the security of tonnage industrial gas contracts – fifteen of them, mainly for fifteen years, made with eleven steel companies. B.O.C.'s Chairman, in a letter to share- and debenture-holders dated 22 August 1966, said:

'The basic formula under which we propose to borrow will provide that the minimum payments accruing under the pledged contracts will be at least equal to one and a quarter times the cost of servicing the amount borrowed. . . . The minimum payment obligations of customers of such strength and repute as these provide a security of a special nature for the new Debenture stock.'

Here the lenders' rights under their contract with the borrower are secured by the borrower's rights under its contracts with customers. Putting it in another way, the security which lenders were offered was the sales proceeds of gas yet to be produced from plant yet to be built.

It seems clear that, from the point of view of their security, the main factor influencing lenders is the reputation of the borrower. If this is not established they start looking for all sorts of material support; if it is they look no further. Certainly firms like Imperial Chemical Industries Ltd, for example, have had no bother borrowing without security; at the end of

1973 the parent company had £292 million nominal of unsecured borrow-ings in the United Kingdom and overseas, not to mention unsecured bank overdrafts of £27 million [4].

7.36 TRUSTEES AND OTHER BORROWING RESTRAINTS

In any case, however, loan stocks (however described) sold by public companies are not a simple transfer of funds from the lenders to the borrowers. Since many of the former may be small-scale individual investors, unable easily to enforce their rights as creditors (even if they knew what they were), it is not unnatural that a third party appears on the scene, to safe-guard the lenders' interests. This third party is a trustee – usually a bank or insurance company – which, in principle, sees that the funds borrowed are used in conformity with the terms of a trust deed signed by the borrower, and that the lenders' security is always there in case of need. The terms of a trust deed of this kind may restrict the borrowing which may subsequently be undertaken. A definite restriction is normally also imposed by the com-pany's Articles of Association, and borrowers must ensure that they do not exceed any such limits; for example, when the shares of Rolls Royce Motors Holdings Ltd were offered for sale in 1973, the company's borrowing powers were limited to one and a half times its capital and reserves [5]. Where a company's Articles are silent on this point, clause 79 of Table A of the Companies Act 1948 requires 'the amount outstanding not to exceed, with-out previous sanction of the company in general meeting, the nominal amount of the issued share capital'.

7.4 REDEEMABLE LOANS

Borrowings by commercial organizations are nearly always for a fixed term, by or at the end of which they are repaid. Redemption may be by annual instalments; for example, after ten years of a twenty-year loan have elapsed, one-tenth of the sum borrowed may be repaid each year. Alterna-tively, the borrower may have the power to reduce the loan by open-market operations – buying it on the Stock Exchange as opportunity presents – or it may arrange to repay the whole amount at maturity, and in order to finance this may make such annual payments into a sinking fund as will, with accrued interest, equal the amount due.

7.5 SUBORDINATED LOANS

When 'subordinated' appears in the title of a loan, it means that the lender is prepared to waive some right or rights, which he would normally have, in favour of other claimants. The reason for doing this will vary from case to case but, in essence, will be that the subordinate status fits in with some other goal of the lender.

Some of the biggest subordinated loans in the United Kingdom in recent years were those arranged by the Industrial Re-organization Corporation: £15 million, interest-free for the first two years, to promote the English Electric/Elliott Automation merger, and £25 million on similiar terms to help the Leyland/British Motor Holdings merger in 1967. The I.R.C.'s financial policy called for 'subordination of the I.R.C. loan, so that the recipient's ability to borrow elsewhere is not unduly restricted' [6]. A later example was the 1974 rights issue to shareholders of the Bank of Ireland: £10·25 million-worth of convertible subordinated unsecured loan stock, by which subscribers' claims in the event of the Bank's winding-up would be subordinated to those of all other creditors.

7.6 CONVERTIBLE LOANS

7.61 THE NATURE OF CONVERSION

Such loans may be changed into something else – always into ordinary shares. The right to make this change may rest with the company raising the funds or with the lender; it may be exercisable on only one occasion or on several, and if the latter is the case the amount of equity obtained for a given amount of loan stock may differ on each occasion. The Listing Agreement of the Stock Exchange requires the issue of such convertible securities for cash to be subject, usually, to the prior consent of the members in general meeting – except, that is, for issues to existing shareholders of the company [7].

7.62 EFFECT ON EQUITY

The reason for this is that, although conversion rights may be attractive to lenders – particularly during the early stages of inflation (*see* p. 81) – and although they thus enable borrowers to raise funds more cheaply, the conversion will eventually lead to a deterioration in the position of the original ordinary shareholders, and they must be given a chance to protect themselves against this.

The deterioration may be illustrated by the following simplified example. A company has assets totalling £6 million, financed by 1 million fully paid £1 ordinary shares, £1.5 million of revenue reserves, £1 million of 10% convertible loan stock (convertible on a £ for £ basis), and £2·5 million in trade credit. Profits before interest and tax are £500,000, and corporation tax is at

52%. A comparison of the position of the ordinary shareholders before and after conversion of the loan stock is given in Table 7.1. As a result of the

Table 7.1. Effect on equity of loan conversion

	(a) Before £	(b) After £
Profits before interest and tax	500,000	500,000
Less Loan interest @ 10%	100,000	—
Pre-tax profits	400,000	500,000
Less Tax @ 52%	208,000	260,000
Post-tax profits	192,000	240,000

conversion, the return on the ordinary share capital falls from 19·2% (£192,000 disposable profits on a share capital of £1 million) to 12% (£240,000 disposable profits on a share capital enlarged by the conversion to £2 million). Furthermore, the conversion will cause the asset value per ordinary share to fall. Before conversion, each share is backed by £2·50-worth of assets – total assets minus all prior claims on them, divided by the number of ordinary shares in issue shows:

$$\frac{£6,000,000 - 3,500,000}{1,000,000} = £2.50$$

– but afterwards, each share is backed by only £1·75-worth:

$$\frac{£6,000,000, - 2,500,000}{2,000,000} = £1·75$$

It is of course true that, from the time the loan was first issued up till the date of its conversion, the ordinary shareholders have had the benefit of the lenders' capital working for them – to the extent that it earned more than its servicing cost. But they must weigh against this gain not only the financial disadvantages set out above but also the weakening of their voting power; each of their shares, although having the same number of votes as before, has only half the influence because of the doubling of the number of shares in issue following the conversion.

7.7 LENDING DURING INFLATION

7.71 THE PROBLEM

During inflation, providers of all loans, but especially of long-term ones, suffer in two distinct ways.

1 The value of their money income (i.e. the interest they receive each year) falls in real terms.
2 The value of the capital they have lent also decreases in real terms.

If adequate protection is to be provided for them it must extend to both income and capital. There are three ways in which some degree of protection may be given: conversion rights, variable interest rates, and redemption premiums.

7.72 THE SOLUTIONS

(a) Conversion rights

As set out in the example above, conversion rights may go some way towards meeting both requirements. Lenders, by exercising their rights, substitute for their entitlement to a fixed monetary payment in the form of interest an entitlement to a less-certain equity dividend. Providing the borrowing business operates successfully, however, the money value of its dividends may prove as constant as the interest on the original debt, with the added attraction that the dividends have the possibility of at least moving up as prices rise. This, unless the inflation is thought to be getting out of hand, will be reflected in the value of the shares, so that the capital stake will be, at least to some extent, maintained. Furthermore, as already noted, lenders have a claim expressed in money terms; but the owners of the business have a residual claim on real assets, the money value of which should rise during inflation.

(b) Variable interest rates

These are another inducement which long-term borrowers may offer to meet the needs of lenders during inflation. Such rates are linked with some other money price – perhaps a short-term interest rate – which may be thought likely to move at least to some extent in line with prices generally. This link would aim at providing greater security of real income but, to the extent that it succeeded in doing this, the capital value at which the loan traded would also be enhanced, for a time.

Such loans began to be common in the Eurobond market in 1970, the borrowers being mainly public authorities. Since then they have spread to the domestic market and to commercial bodies. For example, in 1974 the Anglo-Continental Investment & Finance Co. Ltd issued about £5·6 million-worth of unsecured loan stock bearing interest at a rate calculated every six months at $1\frac{1}{2}\%$ above the London rate for sterling six-month interbank deposits [8].

There is, of course, no guarantee – at least in the short run – that interest rates on such deposits will move in line with prices generally, nor that they will even move in the same direction, given the influence on them of political pressures. But at least the lenders normally have no down-side risk (the

Anglo-Continental loan referred to above was unusual in promising sub
scribers no specified minimum rate), and the arrangement may benefit them

(c) Redemption premiums

The third ploy by which a creditor may be brought to lend on a long-term
(or even medium-term) basis during an inflation, aims at providing protec
tion for the real value of the capital stake. It consists of offering redemption
premiums, i.e. of undertaking to give the lender, when the time comes to
repay the loan, a price significantly above its par value. Small redemption
premiums are commonplace; the government, for instance, regularly issue
loans, redeemable at par, at a slight discount, as this enables it to provide
any desired level of yield without resorting to awkward interest rates. What
is involved here, however, is the issue of securities at par which are known
at the time of issue, to be redeemable at a price well above par.

Issues by the French nationalized coal organization, Charbonnage de
France, provide classic examples of this. One in 1967 of $6\frac{1}{4}\%$ debentures
400 francs nominal, provided for redemption of the total loan in three equal
instalments at five-year intervals. The first third was to be redeemed at 41.
francs, the second at 430, and the last at 460. Holders could choose to be
reimbursed in the sixth or eleventh year of the loan's life, but suffered a
penalty (compared with the normal terms) if they did do. Such cases are no
common, but the attraction of the premium is obvious and the idea may
spread – perhaps strengthened by the proposed experiment in inflation
proofing national savings (see p. 37).

7.8 SUMMARY

Both institutional lenders and the investing public may feel happier about
lending if they can claim repayment of their money from assets earmarked
under a fixed or floating charge, but the security they are offered in many
important cases is simply the reputation of the borrower. Inflation reduces
both the income and the capital of lenders in real terms, and they are likely
to look increasingly for compensation for both types of loss. Conversion
rights, which need the prior approval of ordinary shareholders, may be one
way of providing this; redemption premiums and, increasingly, floating
interest rates have also been used.

8 External Sources: Shareholders

8.1 INTRODUCTION

Since the members, i.e. the shareholders, of a company are legally quite separate from it, it may raise funds externally not just by borrowing them, but also by selling more shares. Companies must have ordinary shares, but preference shares are optional and are much less widely used. This chapter looks at some of the great variety of each, and at two peculiarities: par values and registration of securities generally, as found in the United Kingdom and elsewhere. The sums raised by issues of the main types of security are summarized in Table 8.1.

Table 8.1. New issues by companies by type of security

| Year | Debt | | | | Preference | | Ordinary | | Total |
| | Convertible | Other | Total | % of total | | % of total | | % of total | |
	£m	£m	£m		£m		£m		£m
1964	60·2	161·8	222·0	55·3	10·7	2·7	168·9	42·1	401·6
1965	28·1	414·5	442·6	90·1	3·2	0·7	45·5	9·3	491·4
1966	38·4	425·8	464·2	74·5	16·4	2·6	142·5	22·9	623·2
1967	29·7	313·8	343·5	81·5	5·7	1·4	72·6	17·2	421·9
1968	128·3	161·3	289·6	44·1	3·1	0·5	363·7	55·4	656·4
1969	231·7	144·8	376·5	65·9	—	—	195·0	34·1	571·5
1970	101·3	183·0	284·3	80·4	17·2	4·9	51·9	14·7	353·4
1971	96·7	243·7	340·4	51·3	12·8	1·9	310·4	46·8	663·6
1972	96·4	199·2	295·6	30·9	10·9	1·1	649·9	68·0	956·4
1973	21·6	21·3	42·9	20·4	14·0	6·7	153·6	73·0	210·5

Source: Midland Bank, *Review*, February 1974, p. 6.

8.2 TYPES OF SHARE

A share is defined [1] as 'the interest of a shareholder in a company, measured by a sum of money', and it may be thought of as an equal fractional part of the class of capital to which it belongs.

There are two main types of share: ordinary and preference. The latter carry a stated rate of dividend and, *vis-à-vis* ordinary shareholders in the event of a winding-up, preference as to the payment of that dividend and/or to repayment of capital after all the creditors have been satisfied. If there is any surplus on a winding-up, the preference shareholders may share in that too – if the Articles so provide. The ordinary shareholders have the equity in the business. This means that, since as members they have neither guarantee of reward from nor enforceable claim against the company in which they have invested – and therefore stand to lose most if things go wrong – it is only fair that they should have whatever income and capital are left over after all claimants have been satisfied.

8.3 PREFERENCE SHARES

As indicated below, several kinds of preference share may be found. Their features are not mutually exclusive; the issuing firm may endow them with any combination of them that it thinks fit.

8.31 CUMULATIVE

Unless otherwise stated they are all cumulative; that is, any dividend unpaid or partly paid carries forward indefinitely as a prior claim on future distributable earnings. Thus, a 7% preference share in a company which was able to pay only a 4% preference dividend in a particular year, would in the following year entitle its holder to a dividend of 10% (3% arrears plus 7% for the current year). If this in turn were unpaid, the entitlement would rise to 17% the next year, and so on – though this rise in entitlement could well be more than matched by a fall in prospects!

8.32 PARTICIPATING

Preference shares may be made more attractive by being given rights of participation which enable them to benefit twice from the profits available for distribution. They may be paid first when they receive their normal published rate of dividend, profits above this level going to the ordinary shareholders in the usual way. The second part of their reward comes if the profits exceed a figure stated in the Articles; the latter will also say how the excess is to be divided among those entitled to share it. Another form of participation is that used by Associated Hotels Ltd, which in 1959 made a rights offer to its ordinary shareholders to subscribe to $6\frac{1}{2}$% cumulative participating preference shares; in addition to the basic $6\frac{1}{2}$% dividend, these shares are entitled to $\frac{1}{3}$% for every 1% or part thereof dividend paid on the ordinary stock units [2].

8.33 REDEEMABLE

Preference shares of this kind carry an undertaking by the issuing company to buy them back (just like a loan stock) on or after a specified date – usually

not less than twenty years after issue – at par or at a premium. Reed International Ltd, for example, has in issue £1·5 million $4\frac{1}{2}\%$ (gross, i.e. before
deduction of ACT) cumulative preference shares which are redeemable at
the company's option at £1·025 up to 30 September 1974 and at par thereafter [3].

8.34 CONVERTIBLE

Another characteristic which preference shares may have in common with
loans is that they may be convertible into ordinary shares.

8.35 PREFERENCE SHARES *versus* DEBT

Despite all these apparent attractions, preference shares have for long been
the least favoured type of paper issued to raise corporate funds. This is
because a company wishing to raise non-equity capital may sell either preference shares or debt of some kind. The law treats the dividend on the former
as an allocation of income after it has been taxed, and the interest on the
latter as an expense which is allowable as a deduction from income before
the tax on that income is calculated. In effect, therefore, loan interest
reduces the tax bill of a profitable firm, and its effective rate is thus the
net-of-tax rate, i.e. the nominal $\% \times (1 -$ the relevant tax $\%)$. For such a
company, accordingly, the annual cost of servicing, say, £1 million nominal
of 10% preference shares will be £100,000, but with corporation tax at 52%
the cost for the same nominal amount of 10% loan stock will be only £48,000

$$\text{Effective rate} = \text{Nominal rate} \times (1 - \text{Corporation tax} \%)$$
$$= 10\% \times \left(1 - \frac{52}{100}\right) = 10\% \times \left(\frac{48}{100}\right) = 4\cdot8\%$$

This tax disadvantage of preference shares was aggravated by the original
corporation tax arrangements' imposing the full cost of dividends on companies distributing them; although, as explained in Chapter 12, a company
cannot rely entirely on debt issues, Table 8.1 shows the marked increase in
them at that time. However, the tax disadvantage is really due to the basic
difference in law between the two types of capital. As a result, not only do
fund-raising companies avoid issuing preference shares if possible (again,
Table 8.1 tells the story), but they also have good financial reason for with-
drawing any already in issue as the opportunity arises, e.g. as it did for
Woolworth with their £5 million-worth in 1966. Indeed, as Table 8.2 shows,
for the companies in the Department of Industry analysis, the total nominal
value of preference shares outstanding has fallen and that of long-term debt
has risen, both absolutely and relatively, in recent years.

Table 8.2. The changing importance of preference shares and long-term debt*

Year	Preference shares outstanding (nominal) £m 1	Total shareholders' interest £m 2	1 as % of 2 3	Long-term loans £m 4	4 as % of 2 5
1964	1,088	15,304	7·11	2,503	16·36
1971	563	20,524	2·74	5,902	28·75

Source: M3, Company Finance, 5th edn., Tables 3, 5 and 6; values rounded to nearest £m.
*For the companies covered, see Table 3.1.

Fund-raising companies will not be able to have things all their own way however, because of their need to meet the requirements of investors seeking certainty of income and capital repayment. Furthermore, companies receiving preference dividends can pass them straight on to their own shareholders without deducting corporation tax from them, as they have already borne this tax at the hands of the paying company. Income of this kind, called 'franked investment income', is naturally very attractive to its recipients, and the continued use of preference shares may to some extent reflect their success in inducing companies issuing securities to oblige them.

8.4 ORDINARY SHARES

These, despite the apparent simplicity of their status and despite the fact that they can neither be redeemed nor converted, are available in even greater variety than preference shares.

8.41 RESTRICTED-VOTING AND NON-VOTING

As already stated, in principle the owners of ordinary shares – or equities, as they are commonly called – are the residual beneficiaries of the company concerned. As compensation for the possibility that this residual may be very little or nothing – or even negative if liabilities exceed assets and the ordinary shares are not fully paid up when the company is wound up – they have voting power which enables them, in theory, to control the business's activities.

In practice this is where the first major differentiation of ordinary shares appears: they do not all have equal voting rights. (Some of them, indeed, have none.) Thus, for example, each of the Savoy Hotel 'B' shares, largely held by the directors, has twenty times the voting power of each of the much more widely-held 'A' shares [4].

This form of discrimination may, as suggested by the Savoy example,

originate when a private business goes public having been previously dominated by the founder's family; there is a consequent risk of loss of control
by the original directors. In order to preserve their position, while at the
same time benefiting from publicly subscribed funds, the latter issue to
themselves a special class of share with greater voting power than that sold
to the general public. (The case of the Stylo Shoe Co. Ltd provides a good
example of this; *see* p. 151.) Whatever its origin, such discrimination is
increasingly frowned on; in fact, practical suggestions for dealing with it
were officially canvassed in 1973 [5]. Consequently, although the Stock
Exchange's rules [6] so far merely require non-voting and restricted-voting
shares to be so designated, those in issue are gradually being converted into
voting shares. At the end of 1974, however, at least three major firms (Rank,
Lyons, and Great Universal Stores) still had non-voting shares outstanding.

Enfranchisement is, in any case, not without problems, naturally associated with control of the company concerned. This becomes clear when it is
realized that the non-voting shares represent much more capital than the
voting ones: for Rank, the ratio of the nominal value of the non-voting to
the voting ordinary share capital was about 4:1 [7]; for Lyons, about 29:1
[8]; and for G.U.S., about 45:1 [9]! Control would therefore be disturbed if
holders of non-voting shares received the same votes as holders of voting
shares – save in the unlikely event that each class of share was held by the
same people, in the same proportions.

8.42 DEFERRED

Just as the preferred share is entitled to some preferential treatment in connection with dividends and/or capital repayment, so the deferred share
stands back and lets some other class of claimant get in first. But this is the
role normally reserved for ordinary shares – so to what does the deferred
share defer and what, when such shares are found, is the position of the
'ordinary' ordinary shares in the same company?

The answer to the first question is that the deferred shares defer to the
ordinary; the answer to the second is less certain. The common or garden
ordinary shares in a company with deferred shares may be either more or
less attractive to potential buyers of equities because of the existence of the
latter. For example, before it was merged with Reed International Ltd,
Wallpaper Manufacturers Ltd had in issue 5% preference, 10% ordinary
shares, and deferred shares. The ordinary shares were, in effect, preference;
the deferred shares (being the residuary beneficiaries) were effectively the
equity, receiving fluctuating but generally higher rewards, and were accordingly more attractive to income seekers. Jessel Securities Ltd, on the other
hand, in 1969 created deferred ordinary shares which rank *pari passu* in all

respects with the existing ordinary shares of the company except that they carry no right to dividends until 1983, when they will automatically become ordinary shares [10]. Such shares would naturally be less appealing to those seeking current income than would ordinary shares in the company, and would therefore trade at a lower price. They could, nevertheless, because of the prospective capital gain, appeal to investors liable to high rates of tax on income as well as to those interested in increasing their influence in the company in the long term.

Mention of restricted-voting, non-voting, and deferred shares, however, serves only to touch the fringe of the range of shares in issue – the limits to which are set solely by the originality and imagination of their issuers. Although shares are always basically ordinary or preference, this broad grouping permits a wealth of variation.

8.5 PAR VALUES

Comment is called for on two other features of securities as they are commonly found in the United Kingdom. First, they are still issued with nominal, or par, values.

8.51 SIGNIFICANCE OF PAR VALUE

The buyer of such a security will receive a certificate to the effect that he is the holder of so many shares, each of a stated nominal value – which is most unlikely to correspond with the price at which they were originally issued or at which he has bought them. That nominal value appears on the company's balance sheet as an ingredient of the figure for the authorized share capital and also of that for the issued and paid-up capital – to the extent that the authorized capital is so issued and paid up. (The amount of capital shown in a company's Memorandum of Association is its nominal capital – expressed as a monetary amount, in shares of a stated nominal value. When the formalities to bring the company into existence have been completed, that amount becomes its registered capital. This registered capital is the amount which the company is authorized to issue – and is not to be confused with the amount actually raised by an issue. The limit set by this registered figure may be raised whenever the shareholders so resolve. The amount of capital which the company actually issues – i.e. offers in exchange for cash or some other consideration – may be the same as the authorized total; it may never exceed that total though it may be, and indeed often is, less. As issues are now usually made on a fully-paid basis, the paid-up capital equals the issued capital (except to the minor extent that subscription is in instalments or calls and some members have been unable to meet fully the calls made on them). Companies' Articles may provide for the dividend percentage to be calculated on the nominal vaue of the issued share capital, but in the absence of such express provision it is the paid-up value which matters for this purpose [11].)

8.52 IRRELEVANCE OF PAR VALUE

The interesting thing about all this is that it is unnecessary and misleading. A company sells shares to raise capital (if it issues shares in exchange for assets direct, this does not alter the argument). The amount of capital it obtains from the issuing operation is a function of the number of shares sold and their selling price; the nominal value of such shares is irrelevant. It is true that, until 1973, a company could largely avoid the then capital tax by registering a small share capital and raising a much larger sum by selling the shares concerned at a high premium. However, since 1 August 1973, in conformity with E.E.C. Directive 69/335, capital duty has been calculated as a percentage of the assets actually contributed – 1 % at the end of 1974.

An alternative procedure, not permitted in the United Kingdom but used by corporations in the United States and some other countries, is for the company simply to sell so many shares in itself for whatever they fetch, and to show that position in its balance sheet. Then, assuming that it trades successfully, at the end of the year there will be a profit to be distributed among the members. This means that a stated value is to be shared out equally: so much for each share subscribed. Holders of these shares – each of whom has a certificate showing how many he has bought but not saying anything about their value, since that is determined by supply and demand – will then receive a cheque which, ignoring tax, is the product of the amount of profit the company is distributing per share and the number of shares held. There is no mention of a percentage dividend – there is no figure on which such a percentage could be calculated and, anyway, shareholders cannot spend percentages. Only the monetary amount which the company is paying as a dividend per share is mentioned.

8.53 NO-PAR-VALUE SHARES

Shares of this kind are called 'no par value' for the simple reason that they have no stated face value; they are worth only what the market reckons they are worth. This is clearly a more straightforward and realistic way of expressing both a member's stake in his company and the income he receives from that stake, and efforts have been made to permit the use of no-par-value shares in the United Kingdom. In 1954 the Gedge Committee, set up to consider the question of having ordinary shares with no nominal value, reported that such shares should be allowed [12], and eight years later the Jenkins Committee recommended among other things that the principle should be extended to all types of share [13]. Despite these views, the Stock Exchange requirement – ignoring par values – that earnings per share and any dividend paid or proposed be expressed as pence per share [14], and the E.E.C. regulation on capital duties referred to above, no-par-value shares seem no nearer legal recognition. While recognizing the logic of the case for them, the government felt there was no strong practical need to permit their use [15].

8.6 BEARER SECURITIES

The second characteristic of securities issued in the United Kingdom is that they are usually registered securities, as distinct from bearer securities.

8.61 SIGNIFICANCE OF REGISTRATION

Registered securities are so called because they are recorded in the name of a particular holder (joint and nominee holdings are included); these names appear, in alphabetical order in the appropriate register of members or lenders. When shares or loan stocks are sold, the names and holdings shown on the register are amended as required. When the time comes for the company to pay a dividend or distribute interest, the register involved may be temporarily closed, and dividend or interest warrants of the appropriate amounts are prepared for despatch to those whose names are on the register at that time.

8.62 EX DIV. AND CUM DIV.

Hence, anyone buying such securities when a dividend/interest payment is due buys it 'cum div.'; that is, the price includes the value of the dividend or interest payment which will come to him shortly after purchase. If, on the other hand, he buys it after the last date on which the company can register his entitlement to share in the imminent distribution, the price he pays is 'ex div.'; that is, although distribution has not yet been actually made, he will not be able to benefit from it when it is. (Owing to the timing of the Stock Exchange settlement dates – on which securities and cash due in connection with bargains made in the preceding account must normally be exchanged – it is possible for a holder to sell at a cum div. price and then receive the dividend to which he is no longer entitled. In order to minimize claims arising in such circumstances, the Quotations Department 'issues, early each year, a schedule of suitable dates for companies to adopt when arranging dividend programmes for the following year' [16].)

8.63 THE BEARER ALTERNATIVE

Under the above system, registration of holdings is essential if their owners are to receive any income. But it is not the only way in which securities may be held, transferred, and rewarded. The relevant certificate, instead of testifying that a named person is the registered holder of the security concerned, may instead say that the bearer of the certificate is the owner of a stated number of shares in the company named. This company keeps no record of its members, and has no registrar. It has received a capital contribution from the original subscribers and has issued to them numbered certificates for the number or nominal value of the shares they bought (or nominal value of loan stock, as the case may be) – but it does not concern itself with who the present holders of those certificates may be. Title to the securities passes by transfer from hand to hand, with no formality as far as the company is concerned.

Obviously, in such a system there can be no sending of dividend warrants to members; the company has no list of names and addresses to which they could be mailed and no record of bank accounts to which they could be credited. The solution is to print a number of small coupons as an integral part of the security certificate (the Stock Exchange requires them to be on the right-hand side or at the foot of the certificate [17]). Each coupon bears at least the number of the certificate to which it is attached and a serial number. Then, whenever the company wishes to make a payment to holders of this class of security, it simply advertises in the press that a distribution at so much per share or unit of loan stock will be paid to those presenting coupon number so-and-so to the bank(s) named. The holder of the certificate or an agent acting for him then clips off the designated coupon, presents it to the bank, and collects cash in exchange. The paying bank in turn reimburses itself from the company. When the last coupon attached to the certificate is called, the whole certificate is replaced by another one of like value with a fresh batch of coupons attached ready for use in the next, say, 100 distributions. The arrangement sounds very easy and simple for all concerned, but it is not without disadvantages.

8.64 THE SNAGS

Part of the objection to the use of bearer securities is that they make tax evasion easier. The amount which the company pays on each coupon may well be what remains after deduction of the equivalent of some basic rate of income tax, but since there can be no record of who has received the dividend, charging higher rates of tax on those incomes liable to them is practically impossible.

Furthermore, those concerned with the possibilities of violations of foreign-exchange regulations may also have objections to 'coupon clipping', in the absence of arrangements such as the U.K. system of Authorized Depositaries – banks or other agents authorized for the purpose by the foreign-exchange control authorities, with whom foreign-denominated securities must be lodged and who then undertake the collection and crediting of amounts due. The illegal possession of foreign securities, and of the foreign-currency income from them, might be much simpler if there were no means of tracing ownership via dividend warrants.

From the point of view of the company concerned, a practical disadvantage is the possible loss from fraud; this outweighs to a greater or less extent the gain from not having to maintain registers of members and lenders. Certificates and coupons may be forged, and the dividend-paying company does not have the same control over the number of coupons presented to and paid by its agent banks as it does over the value of the dividend warrants which it would otherwise issue itself.

Thus, although U.K. exchange control regulations permit the issue of bearer securities providing they are not in exchange for registered securities existing before August 1963, the facility does not seem to have been greatly used.

8.7 SUMMARY

For incorporated businesses only, shareholders are an external source of funds. Such businesses must have ordinary shares, but for long-standing tax reasons may prefer to issue debt rather than preference shares. Table 8.1 summarizes the amounts raised by issues of the different types, and Table 8.2 shows changes in the relative importance of preference shares and long-term debt. Otherwise indistinguishable ordinary shares may have different voting rights, often designed to maintain a founding family's control of an expanding business. The Stock Exchange disapproves of disenfranchisement and it is less common among listed companies than it was. The characteristics of par values and registration are proving more durable.

9 Specialist Sources of Funds

9.1 INTRODUCTION

A review of the sources from which businesses obtain funds would be incomplete without reference to the gifts and other financial benefits provided by the government, and to the various specialist institutions which exist. This chapter gives brief details of the more important of these.

9.2 GOVERNMENT GRANTS, ETC.

Some of the money given to private firms directly or indirectly by the government is quite visible – for example, the regional development grants under the Industry Act 1972, expected to total about £225 million in 1974/5 [1], and the interest rate subsidy to British shipowners on the credits up to £700 million available under the Shipbuilding Industry Act 1966. Some of the money, on the other hand, is harder to trace and quantify, being tied up with such things as contract prices and procurement arrangements.

Altogether, however, government gifts must amount to a very considerable subsidy to the private sector. A Labour Party publication refers to sixteen separate financial schemes (including those mentioned above) to help privately owned companies and says that, in the four years to March 1974, £3,075 million had been paid under them [2]. Professor Prest suggests that the official figures for government subsidies are inaccurate, and that those to 'Other industry and trade' (i.e. excluding transport and communications, research, and agriculture) in 1972 alone were £1,081 million [3].

Government support for the private sector since then (leaving aside that arranged by the Bank of England to support property and secondary banking firms) has been for less traditional reasons and in a rather different form. In 1974/5, more and more companies have been faced with mounting liquidity problems. These problems stemmed largely from steep increases in costs (with interest rates on borrowed funds remaining at very high levels), combined with curtailment of sales resulting directly or indirectly from the 1973/4 oil price increases (affecting, for example, British Leyland, Aston Martin, and Fodens as sellers of internal combustion engines, and Burmah

Oil as a supplier of oil tanker capacity). For some businesses, these basic difficulties have been aggravated by such factors as the control of profit margins on domestic sales, the general depression of security values, making fund-raising via new issues practically impossible, and the need to pay tax on earlier, inflated, money profits. Under these pressures, firms have been forced to seek government help as an alternative to closing down completely. Such help has usually taken the form of the provision of funds, or guaranteeing of overdraft facilities which would not otherwise have been available, in exchange for some of the equity of the enterprise concerned.

The National Enterprise Board (N.E.B.) – the statutory public corporation provided for under the 1975 Industry Bill – will extend state aid even further. The Board is envisaged as a holding company with a wide and varied role, including looking after shareholdings and other property already publicly owned, promoting industrial democracy in its subsidiaries, and continuing the work of the former Industrial Reorganization Corporation by stimulating structural change in industry. More important in the present context, however, is its job of setting up new industrial enterprises or helping existing ones, and taking profitable parts of manufacturing industry into public ownership. To enable it to do so, the N.E.B. group may obtain, initially, up to £700 million from public dividend capital and borrowings; provision is made to raise this figure to £1,000 million if necessary. (Public dividend capital is that part of a public corporation's finance on which it pays the Treasury a negotiated dividend based on earnings instead of a fixed rate of interest.) The Board will thus have substantial resources at its disposal although, unless the Secretary of State approves, it will not be allowed to spend more than £10 million on the shares of, nor acquire 30% or more of the voting power in, any one company. (This limit on the acquisition of voting power must be read in the light of Rule 34 of the Take-over Code, referred to on p. 145.)

9.3 NATIONAL RESEARCH DEVELOPMENT CORPORATION (1948)

This body exists to finance the development and exploitation of inventions, 1,325 new items having been assessed for support in the year ending 31 March 1974 (including 202 from firms in the United Kingdom and overseas and 509 from private inventors). It has power to borrow up to £50 million from the Secretary of State for Industry but, by March 1974, only about £21½ million had been drawn and, in view of its rising profitability, it did not expect to require further advances during the next few years unless some major demand arose [4].

9.4 FINANCE FOR INDUSTRY GROUP (F.F.I.), (1973)

Finance for Industry, a holding company owned by the Bank of England, the London Clearing banks, and Scottish banks, arose from the merger in 1973 of Finance Corporation for Industry Ltd (F.C.I.) and Industrial and Commercial Finance Corporation Ltd (I.C.F.C.). It had, initially, paid-up capital of £60 million and power to borrow up to four times that figure plus reserves. Official concern over the lack of finance for business investment soon led to expansion of these powers: the borrowing multiple was raised to seven, and the authorized capital was increased to £150 million at the beginning of 1975. If this were all fully paid, and the reserves stayed at roughly £25 million, as shown in the first balance sheet [5], it would in principle be able to raise £1,225 million and lend £1,400. It is hoped that £1,000 million will be absorbed in 1975/6; although the primary intention is to encourage productive investment, lending criteria will be flexible enough to allow the money to be used for such things as funding operations [6]. Successful applicants will be able to borrow for up to ten years at either a fixed or a floating rate of interest.

F.F.I. was formed partly to become the U.K. member of the Association of Long-Term Lending Institutions of the E.E.C. (an Association formed at the request of the European Commission to provide development finance for large-scale projects in the Community) [7], and partly – in connection with that membership – to rationalize the activities of its two subsidiaries, F.C.I. and I.C.F.C. These had both been established in 1945 to provide finance for industrial firms which, although worthy of support, found it impracticable or inconvenient to raise funds directly from banks or the public. I.C.F.C. had been intended to cater for the smaller customers, with financial requirements between £5,000 and £200,000, and F.C.I. for the larger ones needing over £200,000; with the passage of time, this size distinction had become blurred and some fresh assignment of responsibilities was called for.

Other differences between the two organizations have persisted, however. For example, F.C.I. has always dealt through a single office with a few large customers; at the time of the merger it had nine, absorbing some £63 million, in such fields as aluminium smelting and North Sea energy exploration. I.C.F.C., apart from being bigger (its resources, mainly from public debt issues, totalled about £186 million at 31 March, 1974), differs from F.C.I. in serving a large number of clients through a network of branches. Furthermore, it is the channel through which funds (£3½ million at first) flow from the European Investment Bank to projects in Development Areas. Finally, F.C.I. has no subsidiaries, whereas I.C.F.C. has thirty-one – twenty-six of them with accounts consolidated with its own [8]. Three of the most important of them are:

(a) *Industrial Mergers Ltd (1967)*

Established to centralize and develop the advice previously available free from I.C.F.C., it both considers merger proposals put to it and initiates them where it thinks they may be beneficial.

(b) *Technical Development Capital Ltd (1962)*

Under I.C.F.C.'s wing since 1967, this subsidiary concentrates on the commercial development and exploitation of soundly based innovation in the private sector of British industry.

(c) *Ship Mortgage Finance Co. Ltd (1951)*

This company was formed to help British shipowners by providing finance for ships on completion of construction, secured by first mortgages on them. Its activities were curtailed by the official shipbuilding credit schemes (at least one of which it has administered for the government), and at £10·5 million [9] its resources have accordingly stayed fairly small – but it has branched out into ship charter.

9.5 ESTATE DUTIES INVESTMENT TRUST LTD – EDITH (1952)

EDITH helped majority shareholders in properly run family (unquoted) companies find the money to meet death duties while keeping control of their business. It has done this by acquiring a minority interest, mainly in the form of special ordinary shares giving it alone preferential rights as to dividends and capital repayment [10]. It has not sought to influence the running of its client companies, but has been ready to advise any which wished to merge or go public.

The ending of estate duties may temporarily reduce the demand for its services, but the owners of family businesses will still need cash to meet the proposed capital transfer and wealth taxes and, accordingly, in the longer term its role may well expand. Being managed by I.C.F.C., it has ready access to any specialist facilities it may need.

9.6 AGRICULTURAL MORTGAGE CORPORATION LTD (1928)

This body was established by the Bank of England and other banks to make long-term loans against first mortgages of agricultural properties in England and Wales (similar facilities being provided in Scotland by Scottish Agricultural Securities Corporation Ltd). It receives loans, and grants to cover administrative expenses, from the Ministry of Agriculture, Fisheries and Food, but over 90% of its £246 million resources in 1974 came from borrowings from the public and its clearing bank shareholders. It has begun to pay and charge variable rates of interest [11].

9.7 SUMMARY

Either to meet some requirement of national policy or to plug a gap in the range of services provided by conventional financial institutions, various forms of government help and various specialist bodies have developed over the years. Both are already of considerable importance and the former, although not always clearly visible, seem bound to become even more significant when economic conditions worsen generally.

10 Raising Funds From New Subscribers

10.1 INTRODUCTION

When raising funds from friends or relations, a bank, a building society, or another institution, a businessman is not faced with any serious problem of access to or contact with the potential supplier; he just makes up his mind which he wants to approach and gets in touch direct. The type of difficulty which has to be overcome, and the broad issues on which supplier and seeker of funds must agree, have already been indicated. Negotiations on them take place between the parties concerned on a face-to-face basis until a decision is reached.

When, however, the money is to be raised from the public – when, in other words, the organization seeking it is a public company – the question of how actually to obtain it assumes greater importance. On the not unreasonable assumption that the public will not put its money to any great extent into the securities of companies which do not have Stock Exchange listings, the question resolves itself into the related, but not identical, question of how such securities may be sold to investors. On this subject the regulations of the Stock Exchange, set out in the Yellow Book, are critical. (There is now only one Stock Exchange in the British Isles, but it has seven administrative Units: Belfast, Irish, London, Midlands and Western, Northern, Provincial, and Scottish – each with its own list of quoted securities. The London Unit is by far the most important, and its rules dominate the Yellow Book.)

This chapter is concerned with identifying and commenting on the relevant regulations. Some lay down general requirements for new issues, covering all applications for listing, while others (dealt with more fully) relate to particular methods of issue involving new subscribers. Four types of issue which either do not, or may not, add to the funds of the company concerned, are described in the Appendix.

10.2 GENERAL REQUIREMENTS FOR NEW ISSUES

10.21 ADMINISTRATIVE

These cover the submission, to the Quotations Department of the Stock Exchange, of all the documents relating to an application for listing; also they cover the applicant company's entering into a Listing Agreement. Some reference has already been made to this, the details of which run to thirty-three pages of the Yellow Book. Briefly, the Agreement requires the company to follow certain administrative procedures and sets out the standards which the Stock Exchange expects it to maintain as a condition of continued listing; these are largely in connection with the timely disclosure of accurate information to both it and the public.

10.22 MINIMUM SIZE

In addition, the general requirements lay down that, normally, no application for listing will be considered unless the listed securities of the company concerned are expected to have an 'initial aggregate market value of at least £500,000', and any one security for which listing is sought must have an expected 'initial market capitalization' of at least £200,000 [1]. The reason for this minimum size is that, below it, the costs of fund raising by public issues are so high that applicants would be well advised to try to satisfy their requirements by some means other than seeking a listing.

10.23 PUBLIC PARTICIPATION

The Yellow Book further specifies that, normally, 'at least 35% of any class of issued equity capital, or securities convertible into equity capital, is required to be in the hands of the public, that is, persons who are not associated with the directors or major shareholders' [2]. This needs to be taken in conjunction with the previous rule, as it is intended to ensure that those companies large enough to qualify under the minimum size heading do not exclude the public from exercising any influence over their activities. (This subject is referred to again; see 10.6 below.)

10.24 ORDERLY MARKETING

Strictly, the requirement here is one, not of the Stock Exchange, but of the Bank of England. The latter

'. . . exercises [sic] control over the timing of issues, where the amount of money to be raised is £3,000,000 or more, in order to maintain an orderly new issue market. In such cases it is necessary for the sponsoring broker to apply to the Government Broker for a date known as "Impact Day", i.e. the first day on which the size and terms of the issue may be known.' [3].

This procedure is intended to ensure that demand for funds is evenly spread, without periods when everyone is trying to raise money followed by barren times when no one is. Market and general economic conditions in 1973/4 were such that companies, having been allocated an Impact Day, sometimes decided not to go ahead with their issue when the time came. This upset the Bank's timetabling and brought disorder. Accordingly, applicants must state that they genuinely intend to make an issue on the date allotted and are not just trying to keep a place in the queue until conditions improve.

10.3 PROSPECTUS ISSUES

10.31 DEFINITION

This title is rather a misnomer, as it seems to imply that such issues are the only ones for which a prospectus is required. In fact, one is also called for with Offers for Sale, and may be required in other cases too.

A prospectus issue is defined as 'an offer by a company of its own securities to the public for subscription' [4]. (The word 'company' here also covers those statutory bodies, e.g. local government authorities, to which the provisions of the Companies Acts regarding prospectuses apply.) The offer may be at a fixed price or by tender; tender issues are dealt with on p. 103.

10.32 PROCEDURE

The details of the offer are set out in the prospectus – a document required by law to let prospective investors know what they are buying, if they should decide to subscribe. The fourth schedule of the Companies Act 1948 specifies what they must be told: broadly speaking, the names and addresses of the directors, a description of the activities and profit record of the business to date, an indication of financial expectations, and details of material contracts in force. (Strictly speaking, the prospectus is not an offer, but an invitation to treat. The investor's response to this, in the form of his application for shares or stock, constitutes an offer which the fund-raising company may accept or reject.)

The prospectus must be published in two leading London daily papers – unless the application is made for listing only in a Unit list outside London, when the Committee on Quotations may decide that appropriate local papers will do [5]. If attracted by what they have learned about the issue, investors apply for an allotment of shares, or loan stock as the case may be, sending the amount required on application in time to reach the organization concerned when the application lists are formally open; issues are usually payable in full on application but, with loans especially, this is not always so.

The fund-raising body may handle the issue itself if it wishes, but if this is of any size – still more, if it is at all likely to be popular and therefore oversubscribed – the business will be well advised to pay some specialist agency to deal with the job for it, e.g. a merchant bank.

10.33 UNDERWRITING

It is most unlikely that the number of shares or the amount of loan stock applied for will exactly equal what is on offer. If it falls short the issue is said to be undersubscribed, and the unsold portion will have to be taken up by underwriters – assuming, as is probable, that these have been employed. Underwriters are those who are prepared to buy the whole or any part of an issue if the public does not do so. For this they are entitled to a commission which section 55 of the Companies Act 1948 limits to 10% of the price at which the security is issued, or such smaller sum as the fund-raising body's Articles may prescribe. In normal circumstances most public issues are underwritten for $1\frac{1}{4}\%$ of the gross expected proceeds.

10.34 ALLOTMENT

If the issue is oversubscribed, the directors of the company concerned must decide how they will allot it – in other words, what sort of share or loan register they wish to establish. Giving precedence to those who have applied for a small number of shares would mean a larger number of members, with all the extra operating costs involved (e.g. the costs of printing and posting annual reports and dividend warrants, to say nothing of bank charges in connection with the latter). Conversely, giving priority to applicants for large holdings would help keep down the costs of running the register, but that saving may be thought too dearly bought if it entails more critical and professional scrutiny of company policy, or if it means that the company itself may be more easily dominated by a small group of shareholders. (Such considerations of loyalty and control do not arise, of course, if the issue is one of loan stock.) Naturally, if the issue is at a fixed price published in the offer document, all excess subscriptions must be returned to the applicants.

10.35 SCOPE

As explained in 11.2 below, a simple prospectus issue of ordinary shares by a listed company is practically an impossibility. If the company whose shares are being offered for subscription is newly formed and applying for first-time listing at the same time as the issue is being made, it will almost certainly rely on an Offer for Sale. Accordingly, prospectus issues by quoted bodies are almost certainly issues of loan stock. Usually they are also large – not all as big as the £60 million nominal of 8% unsecured loan stock sold by I.C.I. in 1966, but commonly £10 million or more.

10.36 COST

This size of issue makes for substantial economies of scale. Thus the costs of the I.C.I. borrowing just mentioned came to a little over 3% of the net amount raised [6], while those of a £15 million nominal unsecured loan issued by the Industrial and Commercial Finance Corporation Ltd in 1972 – in much more favourable economic circumstances and not underwritten – were only about 0·9% of the net receipts. (The question of costs is referred to again; *see* 10.57 below.)

10.4 OFFERS FOR SALE

10.41 DEFINITION

An Offer for Sale is 'an offer to the public, by an issuing house or broker, of securities already in issue or for which they have agreed to subscribe' [7].

10.42 PROCEDURE

With a prospectus issue, only two parties are involved: the fund-raising body and the potential investors; any intervening organization acts only as an agent of the former. Where an Offer for Sale is concerned, however, the whole issue has already been sold to a third party (overtly, or in effect, at a discount). This third party, e.g. a firm of stockbrokers or a merchant bank, then in turn offers the issue to the public. It is solely responsible for the issue, from organizing the preparation and advertising of the prospectus to eventually producing the register of members or lenders. This intermediary is rewarded either with a fee – in which case it sells the issue for the same price as it bought it – or by selling the issue at a price higher than it paid for it. The Offer for Sale of Rolls Royce Motors Holdings Ltd shares and loan stock in May 1973 illustrates the former arrangement: Rothschild contracted to buy the shares at 90p each and the loan stock at par, and sold them at those prices, respectively [8]. The second is exemplified by the Offer for Sale by Hambros Bank Ltd at the end of 1971 of the ordinary shares of

Newholme Veritas Ltd: Hambros sold the shares at 78p each, having bought them at 76·25p each [9].

10.43 ADVANTAGES

Technically, the gain to the fund-raising company of an Offer for Sale lies in the fact that, once it has arranged such an issue, it need concern itself no further with the matter – not only are the sales proceeds assured (as they are with any underwritten issue), but also the issuing house assumes full responsibility for the prospectus [10].

But another factor, of much greater practical significance, accounts for their use. Since the late 1950s, a feature of business life attracting wide comment has been the number of mergers (an activity considered in Chapter 14). In many such cases, the amalgamation and reorganization of previously separate firms results in the setting up of a new company – an exercise calling for external professional help. Those who provide this help want to see their job through to a proper conclusion just as much as the original principals want to see the new company successfully launched, and the Offer for Sale (bearing in mind the restrictions on other forms of issue) is the simplest and most convenient way of satisfying both desires.

10.44 COST

Working out the cost of this type of issue may be difficult in those cases where the professional advisers and reorganizers charge one fee for all their services combined. Otherwise, scale economies may be expected to be obtained. In the Hambros case, where the net sum produced was about £4·2 million, fund-raising costs were about $4\frac{3}{4}\%$ of this. The Rolls Royce issue collected £38·4 million gross at a cost to the company, the receiver, and the joint liquidators of Rolls Royce Ltd of about 2·3% of this sum; the percentage may, however, have benefited from outlays incurred in connection with the abortive tender just before the Offer for Sale [8].

10.5 TENDER ISSUES

10.51 DEFINITION

A tender issue is one in which securities are sold, not at a price published in advance, but at one based on the offers made by buyers. Both prospectus issues and Offers for Sale may be handled in this way.

Although it is one of the more interesting ways of raising funds, and is

used by the government every week in its borrowings against Treasury
Bills and commonly employed by water companies (the figures in Table
10.1 largely reflect their activities), tender issues have scarcely been the

Table 10.1 Gross domestic issues by U.K. quoted companies

Year	Public issues and Offers for Sale		Tenders		Placings		Issues to shareholders (c)			Total (b)
							Ordinary	Preference and loan		
	£m	%	£m	%	£m	%	£m	£m	%	£m
1964	29	5·3	8	1·5	247	45·5	181	77	47·5	543
1965	55	11·4	3	0·6	322	66·7	61	42	21·3	483
1966	158	22·3	2	0·3	354	50·1	117	76	27·3	707
1967	75	14·5	2	0·4	303	58·5	64	75	26·8	518
1968	31	4·6	10	1·5	178	26·2	352	108	67·7	679
1969	112	17·8	10	1·6	139	22·1	169	197	58·3	628
1970	29	8·0	37	10·2	140	38·8	63	93	43·2	361
1971	102	16·3	34	5·4	253	40·4	170	66	37·7	626
1972	294	26·3	24	2·0	323	28·9	359	117	42·6	1,117
1973	93	32·2	8	2·8	90	31·1	71	27	33·9	289

Source: Bank of England, Quarterly Bulletin – for 1964–6: March 1967, Table 14; for 1967–9:
March 1970, Table 14; and for 1970–3: June 1974, Table 15 (1).

Notes:
(a) Percentages are of the totals and do not always sum to 100 because of rounding.
(b) The totals do not tally exactly with those shown in Table 8.1 for several reasons (e.g.
because those above include some unquoted securities); the differences are explained in the
Bank of England's Quarterly Bulletin, December 1961, pp. 35–7.
(c) The notes to the source tables point out that capitalization issues (i.e. those not raising
fresh funds) are excluded.

staple diet of the capital market. Since the method has considerable theoretical merit, this calls for comment.

10.52 PROCEDURE

The prospectus details are in all respects the same as before, but the securities involved are not offered at a fixed price. Instead, potential buyers are
told the minimum price they must bid if they wish their application to be
taken seriously. (They are also told in what minimum steps they may raise
their bid, over and above the stated minimum.) Underwriting is at the
minimum price, and if the issue is fully subscribed at a price above this
minimum, it will be sold at a price which satisfactorily clears it; this selling
price is called the 'striking price'.

10.53 FIXING THE STRIKING PRICE

The word 'satisfactorily' is critical here. The striking price is not the highest
price at which, on the basis of the bids, the whole issue could be sold, but one
a little lower. The following example illustrates this point.

Suppose a company invites applications, on a tender basis, for 1 million shares; the minimum price specified is 50p and bids above this are to be in steps of 3p. The issue is oversubscribed and, when listed, the bids are found to be as in Table 10.2. At first sight, the striking price would be 68p, since

Table 10.2. Calculation of the striking price

Bid price (p)	No. of shares bid for	Cumulative bids
83	40,000	40,000
74	260,000	300,000
68	700,000	1,000,000
65	1,000,000	2,000,000
59	2,000,000	4,000,000
53	450,000	4,450,000
50	50,000	4,500,000

at this figure the entire offer of 1 million shares is bid for. Prudence suggests, however, that some of these bidders may be weak holders; they may be unable or unwilling to retain, for any length of time, the shares allotted to them. Perhaps they just change their minds; sometimes they have their minds changed for them, by a change in circumstances which makes ready cash more desirable than securities. Most important, however – since the issue is a popular one and oversubscribed – it is reasonable to suppose that there will have been some bids from stags. Stags are those who seek allotments of shares in issues which they believe will be oversubscribed, with the intention of selling them at the earliest opportunity in order to make a quick capital gain. If they made a mistake and subscribed to an issue which did not prove to be popular, they would still sell as soon as possible in order to cut their losses.

Thus, when dealings in the share started there would almost certainly be some selling pressure. The probability is that, with all bids of 68p and above satisfied in the allotment, there would be no buyers to neutralize this pressure, and the market price would drift down. (Some buying might come from those who had bid more than 68p, but it would be unwise to assume that this would be strong enough not only to absorb any selling which took place, but also to edge the market price upwards.)

10.54 EFFECT OF PRICE DRIFT

This downward drift is undesirable for two reasons. First, the reputation of the issuing company suffers, and this may involve a financial penalty later on. Nothing can alter the amount of money which it receives from the tender issue just completed – but it may well wish to make another issue in a few years' time. The terms on which it will be able to do so will be worsened if the present price goes to a discount and stays down for, perhaps, several months. Nobody likes to feel – still less, to have publicly displayed – that he has paid too much for anything; if, in addition, some of the subscribers feel 'locked in' (i.e. prevented from selling the shares they have just bought because of the capital loss they would suffer if they did so), they are not likely to subscribe to more shares in the future.

The second reason is also based on damage to a reputation – this time, to that of the broker or merchant bank sponsoring the issue. If at any time during, say, the first six months of trading, the market price of the new issue goes below that at which it was originally sold, other organizations considering raising funds may doubt the competence of the issue's managers. In selecting the firm to handle their own issue, therefore, they will avoid any which is linked with drooping post-issue market prices.

10.55 ALLOTMENT

The solution to this difficulty is to resist the temptation to be greedy, and to settle for a striking price lower than the one arithmetically achievable. In the example, this would mean selling the issue at, say, 65p instead of 68p a share. Lowering the price in this way would bring in demand for an additional 1 million shares, and since only 1 million are on offer the total number bid for would have to be scaled down to this figure. Offering everyone willing to pay 65p (or more) one share for every two bid would solve this problem – no one would be likely to complain about the lowering of the price, since those who have bid less than 65p cannot expect to receive an allotment while all those who have offered 65p or more would receive half of what they had asked for (in the case of those offering more than 65p, at a price less than that which they were willing to pay). To prevent favouritism, the Stock Exchange has to be satisfied with the price determination and allotment arrangements [11].

Whatever scaling-down occurs does not, of course, completely eliminate weak holders generally and stags in particular. (The latter can still operate in tender issues, but they have to take into account the possibility that, in raising their own bids to secure an allotment, they may narrow the gap between the striking price and the market price and thus reduce their own profit. They may react to this by bidding for multiple allotments at high prices, in the certain knowledge that they will not have to pay such prices, since the issue will be sold at one price.) Scaling-down does mean, however, that when dealings start and some selling occurs, this selling is likely to be more than offset by the large unsatisfied demand which has been deliberately created. Under the pressure of this demand the market price is likely to be buoyant – with corresponding future benefits both to the fund-raising company and to the managers of the issue.

10.56 SCOPE

Tender issues may seem an obvious and simple way of diverting all or most of the popularity premium on an issue from stags to the issuing company, but they cannot be used every time a company wishes to raise funds. The most important reason for this is simply that, as with 'fixed price' prospectus issues, tender issues of ordinary shares may be made on only one occasion – i.e. when the company concerned is first listed. Thereafter, Stock Exchange rules oblige it to make rights issues (*see* 11.2 below). (However, these do not apply to loan issues. Although with these there is very little to fear from stags, it is worth bearing in mind that every one-quarter percentage point improvement in the issue price of £1 million nominal of loan stock, is worth £2,500 – almost enough, at 1974 prices, to pay for the full-page advertisement of the prospectus in the *Financial Times*.) So the question is really why first appeals to the public to buy shares are not more frequently made on a tender basis. For this there may be two reasons.

(a) Effect of price drift

As already noted, some experience of error in fixing the striking price may have resulted in price drift, with consequent disillusionment with the method.

(b) Problem of price setting

Despite first appearance the method does not fully solve the problem of settling the price at which the security is to be issued. If a security marketed at a fixed price is heavily oversubscribed and then trades at a handsome premium over the issue price, its sellers must wonder whether they could not have gained some of that premium for themselves by pitching the issue price more accurately in line with demand. Getting an issue price even roughly right must be counted a considerable achievement – bearing in mind the interval between deciding to go to the market and actually getting there [12], and the uncertainties about what trading conditions will be like when the issue is made. But almost the same problem confronts those who organize a tender issue, because they must fix a minimum price – and the level at which this is set may well affect all the levels at which bids are made.

Thus, in the example of Table 9.2 it is possible that, by fixing a minimum price of 40p, the issue managers might move the whole range of bids down (or, at 60p, they might move the whole range up) without a simultaneous compensating effect on the number of shares applied for at each price. If this were so, fixing a minimum price at too low a level would deny the fund-raising company resources which it might otherwise have attracted, just as certainly as if a fixed-price issue were sold too cheaply.

10.57 COST

From the viewpoint of administrative, professional, and other expenses, a tender issue is not likely to differ greatly from other issues using prospectuses. But the cost of an issue is not just the sum of all the resultant bills the fund-raising company has to settle; the real measure is the difference between the company's actual net receipts from the issue and what the buyers are prepared to give, as shown by the post-issue market price. Newbould indicates that, for an issue of normal size between 1959 and 1963, while administrative costs of offers for sale by tender did not differ markedly from those of fixed-price issues, the 'pricing costs' of the latter (i.e. the extent to which their post-issue price exceeded their issue price) were about five times those of the former [13].

10.58 A FREE MARKET?

Perhaps the most interesting question in connection with tender issues is what would happen if allotment were made to the highest bidders at the prices bid? Since the object of the exercise is to provide funds for the issuing company, and since the market is free and no one is forced to buy, it does not seem unreasonable to let those who want to pay more for their shares, do so. It may be that an issue on these lines would scare away potential bidders; there would possibly be some difficulty in fixing a dealing price (though the striking price arrangements outlined above could still apply), and the more generous bidders might feel upset when they saw that they had paid more than the market price – though the fall in share prices in 1974 must have left practically everyone inured to that sensation. But it would be interesting to see what would happen. If nothing else, it should eliminate stagging.

10.6 PLACINGS

10.61 DEFINITION

The term is used 'to describe the sale of or obtaining subscription for securities by an issuing house or broker through the market and to or by their own clients' [14]. Where this operation is carried out by a private company or an unlisted public one, and is not accompanied by an application to the Stock Exchange for listing of the securities concerned, it is a private placing and, as such, is outside the control of the Exchange.

10.62 PROCEDURE

A business wishing to raise funds in this way contacts an issuing house or broker, tells it how much and what type of paper it is proposing to sell, and asks it to 'place' the securities involved – i.e. find buyers for them. The broker first satisfies itself as to the integrity, past profits, and expected performance of the applicant, the suitability of the securities themselves, and the reasonableness of the price asked. Then it gets in touch with jobbers and those of its clients it thinks might be interested in buying what is on offer, and finds out how much each is prepared to take. When it has found takers for the whole amount involved, it tells the fund-raising company and the placing then goes ahead; share or loan certificates, as the case may be, are made out to the buyers for the amounts they have agreed to take, and their payments, minus the broker's commission, flow back to the company.

10.63 ADVANTAGES

Such an arrangement is attractive to both the recipient and the subscribers of funds. For the latter – especially if they are large-scale investors, constantly on the lookout for good outlets for investment funds – there is the convenience of having suitable opportunities brought to their attention by a reliable contact.

For the former, the method combines speed and cheapness. It is fast because the lapse of time between deciding to raise funds and actually receiving them will not be much longer than the time it takes to satisfy the placing intermediary (and the Stock Exchange, if the securities are of a listed company) on the points mentioned above; the actual placing operation itself may involve little more than half-a-dozen telephone calls to the right people. Its cheapness is due partly to the fact that there is practically nothing in the way of printing, stationery, and postage to pay for, and partly to the saving in underwriting commission – there can be no risk that the issue will not be taken up! Furthermore, Stock Exchange regulations permit reduced advertising [15].

10.64 DISADVANTAGES

From the viewpoint of the Stock Exchange, however, there is a risk associated with placings of ordinary shares: the risk that opportunities to get in on the ground floor of promising investments will be open to its jobber members and to institutional investors, but not to the less well-connected and less well-heeled general public. Thus the profits, when they begin to flow, will largely by-pass the latter. For the Exchange to allow the placings over which it has control to produce this effect, or even seem to do so, would be to invite criticism.

10.65 SCOPE

Table 10.1 shows that the annual total of placings is second in importance only to rights issues as a source of funds from new issues – indeed, in four of the ten years listed, they constituted the most important source. The total, however, covers placings of loans as well as shares, and the arrangement 'is a concession which, in general, is only allowed where there is not likely to be significant public demand for the securities' [14].

To try to ensure that everyone has a fair crack of the whip, the Stock Exchange lays down certain requirements, essentially as to the size of equity placings and the availability of the securities involved. It fixes from time to time an expected market value for equity issues, above which placings will not be allowed; the limit was £$\frac{1}{2}$ million for previously unlisted companies, and £1 million (£3 million for convertible stocks) with an overall limit of 5% of the existing listed equity capital for those already quoted. (Since the expense of underwriting, given the depressed state of securities in 1974, was hindering the raising of fresh capital through the market, the Stock Exchange temporarily relaxed these requirements for listed companies in January 1975 [16].)

Its Committee on Quotations also decides the extent of the market's participation in placings approved for previously unlisted companies, and obliges them to make available specified fractions of their issued capital. Thus, apart from foreign-currency securities, where special arrangements apply, placings by such companies of equity or securities having an equity element (like convertible loans or participating preference shares) must involve at least 35% of the issued amount of the relevant share capital; for those of fixed-income or partly convertible securities, the figures is 30%. Of these percentages, not less than quarter of the equity and a fifth of the fixed-income securities should be offered to the market (i.e. to jobbers) and not kept by institutions. Furthermore, of these market allocations, not more than one-tenth should be retained by the market if there is a demand for the securities; the sponsoring broker is specifically requested to retain none of the placed securities if there is a demand for them [17].

By these rules, the Stock Exchange tries to ensure two things. The first is that a reasonable proportion of the issued share capital of the fund-raising body is made available to investors generally, so that a company cannot abuse the facility by placing small amounts of equity at frequent intervals. If the maximum percentage allowed would entail the raising of a sum smaller than the issuing company had envisaged (or if the minimum percentage specified would bring in more than it had contemplated), it might be forced to adopt another method – by inference, one more open to public participation. Secondly, if the public, after seeing the advertisement or otherwise hearing of the issue, wish to buy some of the securities involved, they will not be frustrated in their efforts to do so by the desire of the market to hold on to a good thing for themselves.

10.7 SUMMARY

After reviewing the main rules designed to promote an efficient and fair securities market, this chapter deals with the methods by which firms may attract capital contributions from new subscribers. Direct personal contact with new potential investors is possible for unincorporated businesses, but not for incorporated businesses – especially the dominant listed company. An outline is given of the more formal approaches they may adopt as a result – prospectus issues, Offers for Sale (at a fixed price or by tender), and placings – and the circumstances in which each is appropriate are described. Table 10.1 summarizes the relevant figures.

APPENDIX: ISSUES NOT RAISING CORPORATE FUNDS

10.A1 INTRODUCTION

New issues, even to new holders of the securities concerned, do not always add to the cash of the company making them. This is so when issues are made in connection with four operations not so far considered (conversions, the exercise of options, the acquisition of assets, and introductions), and sometimes also with one operation which has been considered (placings). These five operations are reviewed below.

10.A2 CONVERSION ISSUES

Such an issue is 'an exchange for or conversion of securities into other classes of securities' [1] – as, for example, when a company 'rolls over' a debt by replacing a maturing loan with another freshly floated one, or discharges its obligation to change a convertible loan stock into ordinary shares. Clearly, it raises no fresh money.

10.A3 OPTION ISSUES

Issues made in 'the exercise of options or warrants to subscribe for securities' [2] are essentially those made in connection with management incentive schemes, under which senior executives are given the chance to buy ordinary shares in their company on preferential terms so that they may make a capital gain from the hoped-for subsequent rise in their market price. Such issues, so far from raising funds for the company concerned, may actually cost it money. The firm must either buy the shares itself – such schemes provide one of the few legal occasions on which a company may do this [3] – or lend its managers the money to do so.

For example, after several experiments J. Lyons & Co. Ltd introduced a stock option scheme in 1973 [4]. Under this, senior managers may be invited to buy the company's 'A' non-voting ordinary stock, to an individual total value of four times their annual remuneration, at the middle market price (broadly, the subscription price) on the day before the option was granted. For these shares they have to pay, immediately, only 1 % of the nominal value acquired; the balance of the subscription price is payable to the company when they exercise their option – normally within the next three to seven years. By that time it is hoped that there will be an attractive capital gain to reward the managers for their efforts on behalf of the business.

10.A4 VENDOR CONSIDERATION ISSUES

These are issues of securities 'in consideration for assets or businesses acquired by the issuing company' [5]. For example, when the owner of a hitherto unincorporated firm turns it into an incorporated one, he will issue shares to himself in exchange for the assets he puts into the company. This issue clearly provides no fresh funds for the business – although the company has assets after it which it did not have before.

Issues of this kind arising in connection with mergers are dealt with in Chapter 14.

10.A5 INTRODUCTIONS

This term 'describes an application [for listing] where no marketing arrangements are required because the securities to be listed are already of such an amount and so widely held that their adequate marketability can be assumed' [6]. Broadly speaking, such applications will be approved either when 'the securities are already listed on another Stock Exchange, where an unlisted company has reached such a size as to fulfil the Council's requirements as to marketability', or 'where a holding company is formed and its securities are issued in exchange for those of one or more existing listed companies' [7]. (It is clear from this that introductions do not always involve new issues.)

An example of an introduction after such a change is provided by Centreway Securities Ltd. At the end of 1972, its directors asked the then Midlands and Western Exchange to suspend the listing of its ordinary shares pending approval by its members of the acquisition of S. J. & E. Fellows (Holdings) Ltd – a company several times larger than Centreway and making quite dissimilar products. Once this was done, Centreway sought approval for an introduction of its enlarged share capital on the London and Midlands and Western Exchanges [8].

The key to the Stock Exchange's attitude to an application for an introduction seems to be the prospect of a stable market price. If the Stock Exchange thinks there is any significant influence which might upset that stability – e.g. the need of executors to sell a large block of the relevant shares to raise money to meet death duties – it is likely to block an introduction.

The advertising needed for introductions is the same as that for placings [9]. In both cases the advertisements carry no application forms and are for information only, since, as mentioned above, no funds go to the company whose securities are involved. Such sales as occur will be made by existing holders for their own benefit. The company gains, of course, from the listing (or restoration or widening of it), and hence from the better market for its securities.

10.A6 PLACINGS

Placings, either private or Stock Exchange, may arise in circumstances which mean that none of the proceeds of the issue go to the company whose securities are placed. Instead, they go to one or more shareholders who are reducing their stake in the company.

For example, in January 1973 G. R. Dawes & Co. Ltd arranged the placing of 1·8 million 10p ordinary shares of Tysons (Contractors) Ltd at 17½p each. The proceeds of the issue all went to the people who had previously owned the shares – directors and their relatives and associates in the private company from which Tysons had developed. No part of the proceeds was received by the company [10].

10.A7 SUMMARY

Option issues and introductions show that new issues do not always raise additional funds for the company concerned, nor even necessarily for its members. Placings also may be arranged to provide cash just for shareholders. Conversion and vendor consideration issues provide the company involved with no extra cash, although the latter will leave it larger than it would otherwise have been.

11 Raising Funds from Existing Members

11.1 INTRODUCTION

The methods dealt with in Chapter 10 rely, in principle, on the establishment of a link between the issuing company and new subscribers to its shares and/or loan stock The methods set out below enable a company to obtain funds from those who are already so linked – principally, its existing shareholders. These methods are rights issues and, to the extent that they are based on current earnings only, capitalization issues.

11.2 RIGHTS ISSUES

11.21 DEFINITION

A rights issue is an offer 'to holders of securities, which enables those holders to subscribe cash for securities in proportion to their existing holdings' [1]. Usually the offer is made on what are meant to be favourable terms. Usually, also, it is made to ordinary shareholders and consists of more equity, but there are exceptions. For example, in 1969 the Bank of Ireland made a rights issue of ordinary shares to the holders of its 7% loan stock; this issue was peculiar also in that the rights could be taken up on any of three occasions, at yearly intervals and rising prices.

11.22 PROCEDURE

The Stock Exchange requires issues for cash of equity capital, or securities having an element of equity, to be offered first 'to the existing shareholders in proportion to their holdings unless the company in general meeting has agreed to other specific proposals' [2]. 'An element of equity' includes convertible loan stocks; thus the issue by the Bank of Ireland of £10·25 million-worth of 10% convertible subordinated unsecured loan stock in 1974 was by way of rights to holders of its capital stock (i.e. ordinary shareholders). The term also covers participating preference shares; for example, the issue of the latter by Associated Hotels Ltd in 1959 was on a rights basis to its ordinary shareholders (*see* p. 84).

The significance of this requirement is that an investor wishing to obtain an initial holding of listed ordinary shares has to buy them second-hand, through the market; he will never get what he wants by subscribing to a public issue, because no such issue will be made.

The Stock Exchange also requires rights allotments normally 'to be conveyed by renounceable letter or other negotiable document' [3]. One of the attractions of rights issues from the viewpoint of marketability is that such allotment letters, if renounceable within six months of the date of issue, are free of the stamp duty of 50p per £50 or part thereof which the Stamp Act 1891 would otherwise require [4].

The allotment letter, just as with other issues, tells the buyer how many shares he has been allotted and invites him to pay for them. If he and all the other members accept this invitation, the company gets the money it is seeking from its existing shareholders exactly in proportion to their existing holdings; they, in the fullness of time, receive new certificates to record this.

11.23 EXAMPLE

An example of a rights issue is provided by the Provident Clothing Co. Ltd which announced, in June 1972, that it was to raise £9·6 million by a one-for-six rights issue, at a price of 300p each [5]. This meant that an existing holder of, say, 300 of the company's ordinary shares would have had the opportunity to buy an additional fifty of them at a total cost of £150; since the market price before the announcement was 348p, this opportunity was clearly on favourable terms. (The offer price is not always quite as favourable as it looks. The announcement of a rights issue is usually accompanied by a fall in the share's market price, other things equal, because jobbers react to a certainty of increased supply and no certainty of increased demand by marking the market price down.)

11.24 CALCULATION OF THE VALUE OF RIGHTS

A shareholder does not have to exercise his right to subscribe; he may instead sell his entitlement, either wholly or in part. What he would receive, if he decided to sell all his allocation, can be calculated from the formula:

$$\text{Value of rights} = \frac{\dfrac{\text{Value of pre-rights}}{\text{qualifying holding}} + \text{Cost of rights}}{\text{Size of post-rights holding}}$$

Thus, in the Provident Clothing issue:

Value of the qualifying holding = 6 × 348p = 2,088p
Cost of the rights allocation   = 1 × 300p = 300p
∴ Value of the post-rights holding   = 2,388p
∴ Value of 1 post-rights share   = 2,388p ÷ 7
                                           =   341p approx.

Hence for 300p the shareholder would have a share which, if he had bought it in the open market, would have cost him 341p (the post-rights price). This difference of 41p would come to him by virtue of his possessing six of the old shares, so the value of the rights may be thought of either as 41p per new share or as just under 7p per old share.

As already noted, the market price of the share immediately after the issue – or, more precisely, immediately after its announcement – is lower than before. Thus, any shareholder who did not react to the offer, either by accepting or renouncing it, would be worse off as a result of the issue, in the absence of the remedial action by the company outlined below; the market value of his holding would have fallen and he would have received no cash from a buyer of his 'rights' to compensate for this.

How long the market price stays below its pre-rights level depends, other things equal, on the use made of the money raised and the dividend performance and policy of the company. It is not unusual for the issue to be accompanied by an optimistic profits forecast, and for the original percentage rate of dividend to be promised for the enlarged capital; if such statements are thought dependable, the market price will quickly return to its original level. On the other hand, some or all of the proceeds may be needed to pay off debt (the rights issue may be linked with the funding operation mentioned in Chapter 5); even if the proceeds are kept in the business and invested straightaway in earning assets, it may well be some time before they are able to make their full contribution to profits. In such circumstances, the market price may remain depressed for some time.

11.25 HANDLING UNACCEPTED RIGHTS

Although the allotment letters state clearly that they are valuable documents and urge the recipients, if they do not know what to do with them, to consult their bank managers or other responsible financial advisers, they do nevertheless get lost, forgotten, or inadvertently destroyed. The issuing company, after allowing at least twenty-one days for the offer to produce its intended effect [6], is normally expected to deal with the resulting unsubscribed shares in one or other of three ways [7]:

1 Sell them for the benefit of the shareholder(s) concerned (the practice favoured by the Stock Exchange).
2 Enable them to be bought by other participants in the rights issue, by providing 'excess' application forms.
3 Where the entitlement is small, sell them for the benefit of the company, which keeps all the sale proceeds.

11.26 ADVANTAGES

As pointed out on p. 114, rights issues are practically obligatory for listed companies making issues of equity or capital with an equity element. They nevertheless offer such companies considerable advantages.

(a) Cheapness

They are cheaper than appeals to the public, partly because no prospectus need be advertised [8], partly because there is no need to organize any allotment procedure, and partly because – assuming the company has the support of its members – no underwriting is required. (This last expense is not always avoided, however. For example, the headline-making one-for-one-fifteen British Petroleum rights issue in 1971, by which it raised just over £123 million, was underwritten – despite the fact that the U.K. government, with a 48·6% stake, had announced its willingness to take up its entitlement [9].)

(b) Time saving

The method may also save time, reducing the interval between the company's decision to raise funds and its actually having them to spend. (It must be remembered, however, that if the sum involved is £3 million or more the company has to join the queue for an Impact Day; see p. 99.) The advantage of this time saving, quite apart from the obvious gain from having additional resources sooner, is that the risk of the market's going sour and of the issue price's being proved wrong is reduced – reduced, not necessarily eliminated. When the B.P. issue referred to above was announced, the shares stood at about 600p, and at the issue price of 514p the company was practically accused of giving money away to the underwriters. In fact, by the time the issue was made the market price has slid to about 520p, and the under-writers must have been biting their nails.

11.27 RESTRICTIONS ON THEIR USE

Despite these advantages, extra funds cannot be raised by rights issues alone. Partly this is because they are bound to disturb the relationship between funds provided by owners and funds provided by lenders, a relationship which sooner or later has to be restored. (This subject is dealt with more fully in Chapter 12.)

The other drawback is that the amount they raise is likely to be small in relation to the share capital already employed. There are three reasons for this, which emerge from a consideration of the effects of a rights issue on the cash position of the potential subscriber, on the composition of his invest-ment portfolio, and on his general confidence in the issuing company – in short, from a consideration of his ability and willingness to buy what is offered. These effects may be illustrated by taking the example used in 11.23 above and first treating it as it was – a one-for-six issue – and then seeing what might have happened had it been a six-for-one issue instead. (It is most unlikely that a normal fund-raising rights offer would be based on such a ratio; its use here is simply exaggeration for the sake of effect.)

Take first the investor's cash position. If he had a pre-rights holding of 300 shares, he would be entitled to subscribe for an additional fifty, which would cost him £150 at the rights price of 300p each. If the issue were six-for-one on the same terms, his entitlement would be 1,800 and the cost to him £5,400. It is not unreasonable to assume that far fewer of the shareholders would be able to lay their hands on £5,400 at all, let alone at fairly short notice, than would be able to find £150. This factor alone would jeopardize the success of a relatively larger issue.

Consideration of the second effect – that of a change in the ratio of the issue on the composition of the shareholder's portfolio – requires an assump-tion as to the portfolio's original composition. Suppose the investor had deliberately chosen to split his purchases (assumed, for the sake of sim-plicity, to have been made at par) equally between five securities, so that no one investment represented more than 20% of the total. His portfolio looked thus:

						B as % of total
			Company			
A	B	C	D	E	Total	
£300	£300	£300	£300	£300	£1,500	20

If Company B were the one to make the rights issue, the position after his acceptance of a one-for-six offer would be:

			Company		Total	B as % of total
A	B	C	D	E		
£300	£450	£300	£300	£300	£1,650	c. 27

Clearly, the importance of Company B would rise, but its share would not be widely out of line with the investor's preference, and he would not feel unduly bothered by the relative fall in the values of the other constituents. If the issue were six-for-one, however, taking it up would produce a portfolio like this:

			Company		Total	B as % of total
A	B	C	D	E		
£300	£5,700	£300	£300	£300	£6,900	c. 83

with Company B representing nearly five times as much as all the others combined. Even if the investors were able to afford the cash outlay involved in such an offer, he might well be unwilling to make it because of the disturbance it would cause to his expressed preference.

Finally there is the question of the investor's confidence in the issuing company. Before the offer was made the investor was, presumably, satisfied with the performance of Company B. If a one-for-six offer were made to him on terms such as those outlined above, he would be likely to interpret it (indeed, it is probable that it would be so explained to him) as a reasonable request for extra funds to carry on, consolidate, and expand a business which had already proved successful. If, however, the offer which came to him were six-for-one, he could be forgiven for wondering what the company planned to do with all the extra money. Such a rapid increase could not be accounted for by steady advance along proved lines (even bearing in mind that it was of ordinary share capital only, not of total resources, and even if the money was to be collected in instalments, as it was in the B.P. case). If the extra resources were to finance a big jump in productive capacity, he might think a slower rate of growth would be wiser; and if they were to be used in a new activity, his doubts as to the scale of the proposed undertaking might understandably be greater still. In any case, the ability of the existing management to handle profitably a greatly enlarged business would be something on which he would like assurance – preferably before his money was at stake.

Such uncertainties may therefore mean that, however able a shareholder may be to subscribe, he will be unwilling to do so. There are, accordingly, good reasons for keeping such issues small in relation to the ordinary share capital already in issue (though, as the B.P. case shows, this does not mean that the amount raised will be absolutely small). As can be seen from Table 10.1, the total sums raised in this way are quite large and, apart from three years in the mid 1960s, have regularly represented one- to two-thirds of the gross proceeds of issues by U.K. quoted companies.

11.3 OPEN OFFERS

Another 'specific proposal' (*see* 11.22 above) to which the company in general meeting may agree is an open offer, i.e. one which enables holders of securities 'to subscribe cash for securities otherwise than in proportion to their existing holdings' [10]. Within the total set by the issue, there is thus no limit to the number of shares each member may apply for. Since the smaller investor may be squeezed out by the big in the ensuing free-for-all, such issues meet with little official approval.

11.4 PINK FORM ISSUES

Rights issues must not be confused with 'pink form' issues, by which a specified number of shares are simply earmarked for the employees of a company raising funds by a public issue. The employees may apply for the shares on special pink application forms, and the shares are sold to them at the same price as to everyone else. The arrangement is just to ensure that some shares are available to staff and that their applications are not over-looked.

11.5 CAPITALIZATION ISSUES

11.51 DEFINITION

Such issues, sometimes called scrip or (rather misleadingly) bonus issues, are defined as issues 'to holders of securities, by which further securities are credited as fully paid up out of the company's reserves in proportion to existing holdings, not involving any monetary payments' [11]. As the Appendix shows, there are several possible ways in which this 'crediting' may be done, but only one of them – the capitalization of current earnings – can be said to provide fresh funds for the issuing company. Paradoxically, it does so precisely because no monetary payment is involved.

11.52 PROCEDURE

The explanation for this is that, with such an issue, the company is author-ized by its shareholders to plough back some of the currently available earnings – or, in extreme cases, all of them. Instead of dividends, the share-holders receive fully paid shares to the same value. Their stake in the company will thus grow year by year; any individual shareholder who needs cash has to get it by selling part of his holding.

11.53 EXAMPLE

An example of a modified form of this procedure is provided by Gestetner Holdings Ltd, which in 1972 offered holders of its ordinary shares the chance to convert some or all of them into 'capital' shares. Such 'capital' shares entitle their holders to only a tiny cash dividend (not exceeding 0·1p per share annually; on the nominal value of 25p, this equals 0·4% maximum); the main part of their reward is in the form of additional fully-paid capital shares. The number of these is determined in accordance with a formula laid down in the Articles and based on the dividends declared on the dividend shares and the market value of the existing capital shares. Holders of approximately 30% of the ordinary shares took the opportunity to con-vert, but some subsequently reconverted back to the regular dividend-bearing shares [12]. The exercise can be repeated indefinitely, as long as the earnings are there to be capitalized and the shareholders are happy with paper instead of cash. Providing the retained earnings are used as effectively as the funds originally held, earnings per share do not suffer.

11.54 ADVANTAGES

For the members, the appeal is presumably that, on a net-of-tax basis, the value of the capital gains expected outweighs that of the current income foregone.

For the company, three benefits may be identified:

1 It enjoys the uninterrupted use of the earnings it retains. The capital shares accepted instead of dividends may be turned at will by their holders into ordinary shares entitled to receive future dividends – but never back into a dividend already declared.

2 It saves the cost of attracting back to itself the money distributed as dividends, should it need this for its development programme.

3 It eases its liquidity problem because one cash outflow which has either shrunk or stopped completely is that for dividend payments. Gestetner

reckoned that by mid 1974 its scheme had saved it about £1·2 million gross, which would otherwise have been paid out [13].

11.55 DISADVANTAGES

Issues of this kind are open to the same objections regarding breaking up the capital market as apply to retentions generally (*see* Chapter 3). Furthermore, because of the scope they seem to offer to evade whatever norm rate of increase in income is currently approved, they may again attract particular official attention whenever a statutory prices and incomes policy is being enforced, as they have done in the past. The Prices and Incomes Act 1968, section 6(2) (*a*), for example, seemed to ban them altogether while it lasted.

11.6 SUMMARY

Any public company may, in principle, raise more funds by selling securities additional to those already in issue. However, the Stock Exchange requires listed companies selling equity or equity-type securities for cash to give their existing members, as of right, the first chance to subscribe. The advantages and limitations of such rights issues are noted, as are the possibilities of financing a business partly by capitalizing what would otherwise be dividends. The gross amounts raised by U.K. quoted companies via rights issues have been earlier shown in Table 10.1.

APPENDIX: OTHER CAPITALIZATION ISSUES

11.A1 INTRODUCTION

Capitalization issues are not generally paid for from current earnings, and the other ways of financing them do not provide the business involved with any funds. This Appendix reviews these different ways, and also the reasons for making such issues.

11.A2 FINANCIAL BASIS

A business may build up the reserves referred to in 11.51 above from four sources: premiums received from share issues, partial retention of previous years' earnings, profits from the sale of fixed assets, and revaluation surpluses.

11.A3 CAPITALIZATION OF SHARE PREMIUMS,

Ordinary shares are now never sold at par, and the sum received over and above their nominal value may not be credited to the Share Capital A/c since the total on the latter may not exceed the product of the nominal value of the share in question and the number of such shares sold. Instead, the company records this sum in a Share Premium A/c – though it uses the premium proceeds just like any other permanently subscribed funds.

However, the way in which the actual balance on this Share Premium A/c may be used is restricted by law [1] and, for reasons set out below, the company may eventually find it convenient or necessary to incorporate this balance in the Share Capital A/c – where, after all, it may be said to belong. In this case, the sum required is transferred by journal entry from the Share Premium A/c to the appropriate Share Capital A/c (there may be more than one), and the members concerned are sent certificates for fully paid shares in the same ratio to their existing holdings as the capitalized premiums were to the original share capital. The introduction of no-par-value shares would, of course, enable a start to be made on the elimination of such manoeuvres.

11.A4 CAPITALIZATION OF PREVIOUS YEARS' RETENTIONS

Profitable firms do not usually distribute all their current earnings. The amounts retained in any one year may, of course, be paid out in later years; indeed, as noted in 3.41 above, it is part of their function to provide the accounting means – as distinct from the monetary means – by which dividends may be kept stable. (Remember (i) that to pay a dividend a company needs both a profit legally available for distribution and a bank balance large enough to meet the dividend cheques, and (ii) that retentions, like other reserves, are *not* normally held in the form of cash.)

However, although the retentions (recorded in a Revenue Reserve A/c) *could* be liquefied and distributed to members, after a time no large part of them *would* be so treated, since the assets acquired with them would have become an essential and permanent part of the business. The balance sheet can then be made to reflect more accurately the true position by merging some or all of the Revenue Reserve A/c with the Share Capital A/c. When this book-keeping transfer of value is made, fully paid shares are issued to members in the proportion appropriate to their existing holdings.

Effect on potential creditors

Although a capitalization exercise of this kind does not directly result in any extra funds for the company concerned, it may provide access to them by meeting the requirements of potential lenders

Suppose, for example, that a profitable business, with resources concentrated in current assets, decided to seek more long-term funds by borrowing £1 million. In an exaggerated and simplified form, assuming the loan proceeds were used to increase all existing assets by the same percentage, the balance sheets before and after the proposed fund-raising might look like those in Table 11.1(*a*).

Table 11.A1. Capitalization of retained earnings

(*a*) *Balance sheets (i) before and (ii) after proposed borrowing of £1 million*

	£m			£m	
	(i)	(ii)		(i)	(ii)
Ordinary share capital	1	1	Plant and machinery	1·0	1·2
Revenue reserve	2	2	Stock	1·75	2·1
Secured loan*	—	1	Debtors	1·75	2·1
Trade creditors	2	2	Cash	0·5	0·6
	5	6		5·0	6·0

*In view of the nature of the assets, the security would be a floating or general charge (*see* p. 76).

The borrower's record indicates little risk that the loan might not be serviced properly and, if anything did go wrong, the position of secured creditors would be very strong since over 80% of the assets could be lost before their claim was at risk. Nevertheless, such creditors might be unwilling to lend the desired amount, because of the size and importance of the revenue reserve. It would be quite legal for the directors to distribute it as dividends, and quite easy for them to obtain the cash to do so simply by letting stocks run down and curtailing supplies to customers as they settled their accounts. Part (*b*) of the Table indicates how the position might appear after such an operation.

(*b*) *Balance sheet (ii) after distribution of reserves*

Ordinary share capital	1	Plant and machinery	1·2
Revenue reserve	—	Stock	0·7
Secured loan	1	Debtors	0·9
Trade creditors*	1	Cash	0·2
	3		3·0

*With smaller sales, smaller purchases would be required.

This contraction of the business (which, incidentally, the lenders would have helped to finance) would mean an absolute decline in its earning capacity – and hence of its ability to service its debt – and also a halving of the creditors' cover. Furthermore, the largest single item in that cover would be the least liquid and, from the security point of view, least satisfactory asset, namely plant and machinery. Accordingly, before putting up any money the prospective lenders may insist that a large part of the revenue reserve be capitalized in the way already described. With previously mobile resources thus tied down, they might then feel happier about parting with their money.

11.A5 CAPITALIZATION OF PROFITS FROM SALE OF FIXED ASSETS

A profit may be made from the sale of an asset which was part of a business's permanent productive capacity, not of its current assets. Such a profit may be treated like a trading profit, but initially it may appear in the accounts as a capital reserve. Later, the directors may decide to deal with this reserve in the same way, for the same reasons, and with the same results, as indicated in 11.A4 above.

11.A6 CAPITALIZATION OF REVALUATION GAINS

Revaluation may affect such assets as patents and copyrights, but it is in freehold real estate that by far the commonest and most spectacular increases in monetary value in recent years in the United Kingdom have occurred. For example, in 1972 Sears Holdings Ltd showed a net surplus of £95 million arising from revaluation of group properties [2].

Since this extra book value represents part of the true equity interest in the company, sooner or later it will be transferred to the appropriate Share Capital A/c; most of the Sears Holdings Ltd revaluation surplus was dealt with in this way by a one-for-one issue to ordinary shareholders in 1973 [3].

11.A7 REASONS FOR CAPITALIZATION ISSUES

These issues are commonly said to be carried out in order to bring the capital formally employed in a business more closely into line with that actually employed in it – but that leaves in the air the question of why bother to do so? The two explanations already given – to retain current earnings, and to satisfy potential lenders – apply to only a minority of cases, so other considerations must be taken into account

(a) Share marketability

One explanation may be to improve the marketability of the shares affected by lowering their market price. If a share is 'dear' – i.e. if its price is high, relative to its face value – some people may not be interested in buying it simply because the holding they would get seems to them unattractively small compared with the outlay they would have to make. (A dear share is not the same as a 'heavy' share – i.e. one with a high market price and a high nominal value too.)

One way of tackling this disadvantage is to split the share into a larger number of units, each with a lower nominal value, e.g. a £1 share being divided into five shares each with a nominal value of 20p. Splitting, although the simplest way of curing 'heaviness', really has very little effect on 'dearness'; the gap between the nominal and market values after the split, although absolutely smaller, is relatively unchanged. However, it does bring the market price down and thus lowers the psychological barrier in the path of prospective investors. The reality of this barrier was acknowledged by the Chairman of The Savoy Hotel Ltd, for instance, when he said, 'In view of the very big price in the market of Savoy Ordinary shares, both A and B, it is considered that it would be advantageous to shareholders if these were split into five, making the shares more attractive to the smaller investor, of whom the Company has always had a large number' [4]. (Before the split, the 50p A shares stood at about £4 and the 25p B at about £13.)

The other way of dealing with 'dearness' is to make a capitalization issue. With a rise in the number of shares in issue and no change in assets or earnings, the market price of the share falls, and trading in it may be stimulated as a result. Thus, if the market price of a share on an assets basis were £5, dealings in it might be at $\pm 10p$ (dealers buying at £4·90 and selling at £5·10). After a three-for-one capitalization issue had lowered the price to £1·25, the dealing margin might be $\pm 2p$. The issuing for cash of £5-worth of shares would then have cost the company only 8p instead of the previous 10p – or a given amount of capital could be raised by issuing fewer shares. This is highly simplified, and the price range would not be the same for a large issue as for transactions in a small number of shares – but there would be some tangible benefit to the company from lowering the market price by a capitalization issue.

(b) Dividend rate

Another possible explanation for capitalization issues is that they lower the percentage rate of dividend. In the case above, if the shares were originally receiving a dividend of, say, 80%, after the three-for-one issue the same amount of profit distributed among four times the number of shares would give a dividend rate of only 20%. The shareholders would, of course, be almost unaffected by this change; a dividend of 80% on one share gives the same income as a dividend of 20% on four shares of the same nominal value. (The total value of their holdings, however, would be fractionally higher after the issue if the 'marketability' argument above is valid – one share previously worth £4·90 net having been replaced by four, each worth £1·23 net.)

The company, however, may consider high percentage rates of dividend undesirable, for several reasons:

1 They may arouse the interest of other firms, and stimulate competition more rapidly than would otherwise have been the case.
2 They may attract attention because of the possibility of monopoly that they imply.

3 They may provide representatives of their employees with a useful bargaining weapon in negotiations over pay and working conditions.

Lowering the percentage rate of distribution by means of a capitalization issue may serve to head off these dangers.

(c) Company–Shareholder relations

It is clear from what was quoted earlier from The Savoy Hotel report that such issues may also serve to strengthen the bond between a company and its shareholders. They provide favourable publicity for the former, and because the term 'bonus' is still often used for them, although they may give little in the way of direct benefit to shareholders, the recipients may feel more inclined to support their directors in whatever they happen to be doing (especially the more loyal and compliant individual members).

(d) Shareholder compensation

Finally, capitalization issues may be made to provide compensation to shareholders for some loss suffered by them. Thus, when Sears Holdings Ltd enfranchized its non-voting A ordinary shares in 1972, it weakened the control over the company previously exercised by the holders of the voting shares. The attractiveness of the latter were thus reduced, and their market value, relative to that of the previously non-voting shares, fell. Accordingly, at the same time as the A shares gained the vote, holders of the original voting shares received a one-for-ten capitalization issue as an offset to the detriment suffered [5].

11.A8 SUMMARY

Capitalization issues may be financed from sums raised via share premiums and the sale of fixed assets, but the largest of them have been based on past earnings and, even more, on property revaluations. They do not directly raise funds but may provide a financial benefit to the issuer indirectly, by facilitating its borrowing or by improving the marketability of its shares. The issuing company may also gain by attracting less unwanted attention through them than through high percentage rates of dividend, as well as by promoting shareholders' loyalty.

12 Gearing

12.1 INTRODUCTION

From what has been said in the preceding chapters, it is clear that all forms of business, irrespective of the purpose for which they wish to use the funds raised, rely on two main sources: members and lenders. However, which of these sources they are able to use at any particular time – as well as the terms on which they are able to use them – are not matters entirely of their choice. Both depend on the providers' assessment of the risk involved in the appeal addressed to them.

12.2 RISK AND THE PROVISION OF FUNDS

The connection between risk and the type and terms of funds provided can be seen if the procedure of a business in need of finance is looked at. Such a business reviews the means by which its need may be satisfied; in other words, it lists and examines all the possible sources from which the funds required may be raised. The potential fund-raiser will not be completely indifferent as between these possible sources; indeed, it will grade them in order of attractiveness, taking into account the amount each may be good for, what it is likely to charge, what security or share in the business it is likely to require – all the terms and conditions, in fact, which each source may seek to impose.

The important point is why those terms should differ. The applicant for funds and the proposal put forward will be the same in each case – yet the response, if any, will not. The reason for this is that each potential supplier of funds will view the proposition put to him in a slightly different light. For one it may be a routine transaction, indistinguishable in type and size from many others already handled; for another, however, it may be abnormal in one or more ways and present unfamiliar problems. Each source, therefore, will quote terms which reflect its estimate of, and its reaction to, the risk which it thinks the proposal entails. The risk which the proposal actually embodies is, of course, constant; only the subjective assessment of it varies. Some financers are not attracted by the 'swings and roundabouts' of ownership; they seek security of income and capital – at least in money terms – and will contribute to a business only as lenders. Others will insist on rights of membership and come in as shareholders. This risk-based difference in the terms on which resources are supplied to an enterprise gives rise to the phenomenon of gearing or leverage.

12.3 MEANING

The word 'gearing' has to carry a heavy load of meaning. Basically, gearing is a mechanical term. Most people are familiar with the working of a watch or bicycle where, in essence, two or more toothed wheels of different sizes are linked, with one driving and the other(s) being driven. If the drive wheel has forty teeth and the driven wheel has eight, one complete revolution of the former will cause the latter to rotate five times, or one complete revolution of the latter will cause the larger wheel to make one-fifth of a turn. (The purist who wishes them to rotate in the same direction – as the analogy requires that they should – will at this stage add either a third eight-toothed wheel or a continuous length of suitable chain.) Accordingly, if anything turns the drive wheel (e.g. arm action or pedalling, as appropriate!) the driven one will also turn – but five times as fast.

In the financial sense, the drive wheel is the level of earnings – treated here, for the sake of simplicity, as those before interest and tax – and the driven wheel is the reward going to the ordinary shareholders. If some power (e.g. economic growth or a change in tastes) is applied to the drive so that earnings rise, the equity reward should also rise. What gearing is concerned with is whether the increase is proportionately more than, the same as, or less than the increase in earnings. It will differ if there are unavoidable fixed charges on the earnings which have to be settled before the ordinary shareholders get anything.

12.4 EFFECT

Table 12.1 shows what difference gearing makes to the reward going to ordinary shareholders following a rise in earnings (as defined above). Figures are given for three hypothetical companies, each capitalized in a different way, and the rise is from £100,000 to £180,000, i.e. 80%.

From this table it can be seen that, at the original level of earnings, the shareholders of each company received a 10% reward – either (i) in the form of a dividend, if all the earnings were distributed, or (ii) as capital appreciation of their shares due to larger asset backing for them, if they were not, or (iii) as any combination of distribution and retention absorbing £100,000.

Table 12.1. Effect of capital structure on equity reward

Capital:	Company A £	Company B £	Company C £
10% debentures	—	200,000	800,000
Fully paid ordinary shares	1,000,000	800,000	200,000
Total	1,000,000	1,000,000	1,000,000
Allocation of earnings:			
(a) of £100,000:			
Debt interest	—	20,000	80,000
Ordinary dividend	100,000	80,000	20,000
Ordinary dividend %	10	10	10
(b) of £180,000:			
Debt interest	—	20,000	80,000
Ordinary dividend	180,000	160,000	100,000
Ordinary dividend %	10	20	50

Suppose earnings then rise to £180,000. The result is that in Company A the ordinary shareholders' reward also rises by 80%; all the profits are attributable to them, and if they are all distributed the dividend also rises from 10% to 18% – i.e. by 80%. In Company B, their reward doubles (in money terms it rises from £80,000 to £160,000, and as a dividend from 10% to 20%); while in Company C it quintuples (from £20,000 to £100,000 in money terms, and from a dividend of 10% to one of 50%). The same unequal rate of change can be seen if the level of earnings is cut.

12.5 FACTORS INFLUENCING GEARING

12.51 AMOUNT OF PRIOR-CHARGE CAPITAL

Where a change in earnings produces the same proportionate change in equity reward, the company is said to be ungeared – as in Company A above. If it produces a more than proportionate change in equity reward, the company is geared – like Companies B and C. The greater the induced change, the higher the gearing; C is thus more highly geared than B. From this it seems that the simplest way of expressing gearing – but one which will have to be modified later – is to say that it is the ratio of prior-charge capital to the ordinary share capital, both being expressed in terms of their paid-up value. Prior-charge capital is, of course, that part of a business's capital which has to be rewarded before the ordinary shareholders receive anything. In A, this ratio is infinitesimal; in B it is 1:4; and in C, 4:1.

It is worth noting that, in the interests of consistency, the ratio must be expressed as prior-charge capital to equity, not the other way round. For example, putting the equity first would lead to an original gearing ratio in B of 4:1. If B then issued £200,000-worth of debt, its gearing ratio would obviously rise, but with the equity first the new ratio would be 2:1, which is clearly lower than 4:1.

12.52 COST OF SERVICING PRIOR-CHARGE CAPITAL

However, it is not just the relative amounts of prior-charge and equity capital which matter in assessing the extent of gearing; it is the cost of servicing that prior-charge capital in relation to earnings.

For example, Company C is shown as having a high gearing ratio (4:1), so that any given change in earnings would have a disproportionately large effect on equity rewards. However, if the rate of interest on the debt were reduced to, say, 5%, there would be no difference in the 4:1 capital ratio, but the prior charges would be halved and the gearing ratio thus effectively lowered. Instead of quintupling after an 80% rise in earnings, the equity dividend would be multiplied by 2⅓ – rising from a rate of 30% to one of 70%.

Thus a more satisfactory measurement of gearing would seem to be 'the ratio of prior charges – i.e. the cost of servicing prior-charge capital – to earnings before interest and tax'. The higher these prior charges, the greater will be the impact of any given change in profits on the reward going to ordinary shareholders, and although these profits will constantly change, this ratio will always be higher in a high-geared company than in a low-geared one.

12.53 INCREASES IN EQUITY STAKE

Both the concept of equity reward and the nature of the prior charges which bring gearing into effect need further attention. The reward of the equity holders was expressed earlier as a percentage of the nominal value of the ordinary share capital in issue. However, as noted in the Appendix to Chapter 11, this value is unlikely to reflect accurately the contributions which members have made to the firm's capital, or the value of the stake they have in it. Both the premium which they paid when they bought their shares, and the earnings which have been retained on their behalf since, must be taken into account. Both these adjustments will, other things being equal, lower the gearing ratio.

Thus, assuming the same level of earnings for Companies A, B, and C, consider the effect in each of a Share Premium A/c of £80,000 and retained earnings of £120,000. Company A is unaffected, as it was ungeared before. In B, however, the equity contribution rises to £1 million and the capital gearing ratio falls from 1:4 to 1:5; while in C the equity contribution rises to £400,000 and the capital gearing ratio falls from 4:1 to 2:1.

Now clearly, although a reward of, say, £10 may be regarded as one of 10% to the holder of £100 nominal or ordinary shares, it cannot be so regarded if it comes to that holder by virtue not just of the shares he holds but also of the premium he has paid the company to get them and of his share of the past profits which the company has retained. (Nor can it be for anyone buying the shares second-hand in the open market at a price above par.) In A this reward (the basis of the yields explained in the Appendix to Chapter 14) would initially be $8\frac{1}{3}\%$; in B it would be 8%; and in C, 5%. After the £80,000 rise in earnings, it would be 15%, 16%, and 25% respectively.

12.54 OTHER INFLUENCES ON GEARING

So far, perhaps, so good. The return or yield which an ordinary shareholder is looking for, and which it is a major purpose of gearing to increase, must obviously be calculated on what he has really put into – or paid to get into – the business concerned. Equally obviously, it will be affected by the amount of debt interest and/or preference dividends which must be met.

This, unfortunately, is not the end of the story. If interest on long-term debt constitutes a prior charge on earnings, why not also that on medium- and short-term borrowings such as bank advances? Similarly, if the commitment to pay interest on debt or dividends on preference shares is taken into account when calculating the effect of fluctuations in earnings on ordinary share dividends, why not take into account all the other payments made under commitment or obligation – legal or other – such as rent, rates, insurance premiums, and depreciation? Why not, in other words, develop the gearing ratio until it incorporates all prior claims on earnings, not just those of a formal and legalistic kind?

The argument against doing so is not that such payments do not represent the costs of obtaining resources, which may then earn (for the benefit of the equity) more than those costs – many of them do just that. It is simply that information on most of these payments is not regularly and openly available – the relevant data appear only in the business's internal but unpublished Profit & Loss A/c. Accordingly, the calculation of such an 'effective' gearing ratio can be done by those outside a business only on a piecemeal basis, if at all.

Nevertheless, the artificiality of the formal gearing ratio, and the desirability of finding some better means of expressing the relationship between variations in earnings and in equity reward, have led at least one commentator to go the whole hog and stretch gearing to cover the differential rate of increase of total costs and total revenues. Writing in *The Guardian* of 1 November 1968 on the results of the Shell Transport and Trading Co. Ltd, which showed revenues up by 10·2% and costs up by 9·4%, he said, 'Then the high gearing effect of the company's enormous costs and expenses came into its own.' That 0·8% difference between the rates of increase of total costs and total revenues meant an extra $96 million, which boosted net earnings by 18·2%.

The snag with this approach is that, if the idea of gearing is partly to give ordinary shareholders some clue as to how they would be affected by future profit fluctuations, information after the event is not much help; since total costs include variable costs, which to a large extent are not known in advance, they will not be able to get this clue. Accordingly, although the basic concept of gearing is both simple and sensible (i.e. sensible from the viewpoints of both the ordinary shareholder and the provider of prior-charge capital), defining it in some reasonably precise and practically helpful way is not as easy as it sounds.

12.6 REASONS FOR GEARING

These fortunately present less of a problem. Three may be identified: to attract lenders, to benefit shareholders, and to please managers.

12.61 LENDERS' PREFERENCE

It was pointed out on p. 128 that prior-charge capital, on which the formal definition of capital gearing was based, would emerge from meeting the requirements of those who would provide funds for an enterprise only on some secured or preferential basis. One explanation for gearing is, therefore, the desire to accommodate this kind of investor and to gain access to the finance which such investors control.

12.62 EQUITY BENEFIT

It must not be supposed from this, however, that the issuing of such prior-charge capital – on either the first or subsequent occasions – is against the wishes of the equity holders. After all, if their business needs funds to continue or expand, they presumably regard the price they have to pay for those funds as lower than the price they would have to pay for not having them, in the form of lost opportunities for profit or even the possible collapse of the firm. Nobody forces them to raise the extra money.

Furthermore, a business which is able to obtain all the funds it requires in the form of equity may still find it worthwhile deliberately to raise some on a prior-charge basis – as long as that finance can be used to earn more than it costs. If money can be borrowed at, say, 15% per year, and used to earn on average 20% per year, the amount represented by that five-percentage-point difference will be, in principle, extra pre-tax profits for the ordinary shareholders. If the borrowed money earns only 15% per year, these share-holders will be no better and no worse off; if it earns less than 15% per year, they will suffer because the deficiency will have to be made good from profits which would otherwise go to them. In other words, a second major reason for gearing as a deliberate device is to raise the reward going to ordinary shareholders.

This attraction of borrowing is all the greater during inflation, which enables a profitable company to make substantial real gains at the expense of lenders. If prices are rising by 15% a year, debt carrying interest at 15% has a real annual interest cost of zero. Since the interest is a tax-deductible expense, the net-of-tax cost of the borrowed funds is lower still; with corporation tax at 52%, the money cost of servicing the debt is 7·2% a year (see 8.35) and, after allowing for inflation, the real net annual interest cost is minus 7·8%. However if profits are not made, the full 15% money gross rate has to be paid – and doing so will present the borrower with just as big a problem as if prices had been stable.

12.63 MANAGERS' PREFERENCE

The third factor which may account for gearing (in the formal sense) is the scope it offers for meeting the requirements, not of the providers of different types of capital, but of those who will be responsible for its use: the borrow-ing firm's managers. Gearing may be attractive to the latter as a means of making their lives easier, because, if the funds used to buy the assets under their control have been raised partly on a prior-charge basis, they may need to be less efficient in operating them than if these funds have not.

Suppose, for example, that a company had a paid-up capital of £1 million (£100,000 of it in the form of a 10% debenture, the rest in ordinary shares, giving a formal gearing ratio of 1:9), and a target rate of earnings for the equity of 15%. Ignoring tax, the total earnings required each year would be:

		£
To service the debt (10% of £100,000)	=	10,000
To satisfy the equity (15% of £900,000)	=	135,000
Total required	=	145,000

or an overall rate of return of $14\frac{1}{2}$%.

Suppose further that, having traded satisfactorily and met this target, the company decided that it should expand and that, in the process of obtaining the extra funds to finance this, it should raise its gearing to 3:7. Selling (for the sake of simplicity, at par and on the same terms as before) an additional £500,000 each of debt and equity would raise the total capital to £2 million and give the desired gearing ratio. With an unchanged target of equity reward, the total earnings required would then be:

		£
To service the debt (10% of £600,000)	=	60,000
To satisfy the equity (15% of £1,400,000)	=	210,000
Total required	=	270,000

or $13\frac{1}{2}$% return overall.

If such an increase in gearing occurred, the management of the business would have three choices. They could continue to operate the assets under their control as effectively as before, so that the $14\frac{1}{2}$% overall return achieved would produce £290,000 on the enlarged capital of £2 million. They would need only £270,000 of this to satisfy everybody, so they could use the extra £20,000 to pay higher dividends to the ordinary shareholders. Alternatively, still achieving $14\frac{1}{2}$% overall, they could retain the £20,000 and thus help the company to grow faster still. (Of course any combination of these two possibilities, absorbing the £20,000 available, would also be open to them.) But the third line of action they could take would be simply to relax into an easier life – the assets they managed could be operated so as to produce £20,000 a year less than before, yet still to earn enough to keep lenders and members content.

Raising gearing, then, may be a prescription for inefficiency. Perhaps, in the interests of stimulating economic growth, corporate issues of long-term debt should be banned – at least for companies making profits. Those earning too little to pay debt interest might be stimulated to greater efforts in order to do so – but until their success was demonstrated they would scarcely make attractive borrowers.

12.7 SUMMARY

Apart from gifts – mainly from the government (*see* Chapter 9) – all the resources used by a business must come from its members or its creditors. These contributions will be on different terms, partly because of different attitudes to risk. Meeting these terms means establishing some form of prior-charge capital, as a result of which the business concerned becomes geared. Gearing effects, however, arise otherwise than through the terms on which funds are raised. Furthermore, no matter how beneficial it may be to the contributors of capital, gearing may not always be so to the economy as a whole.

SECTION D

ALTERNATIVES TO CASH PURCHASE OF NEW ASSETS

13 Leasing/Hire Purchase

13.1 INTRODUCTION

In the two previous sections, attention has been given to various ways in which funds may be raised. But businesses do not need funds – whether borrowed or owned – as such; they want them for the productive assets they will buy. Buying assets for cash, however, is not the only (legal) way of getting them, nor necessarily the most suitable way. Assets may also be leased – with or without a formal agreement about eventual purchase – or bought on credit terms; any form of business may do this, perhaps drawing on one or other of the sources reviewed earlier (for at least the initial hire payments).

The word 'leasing' covers also hiring and renting; there seems to be no consistent distinction in the use of these terms. However, there is an operational difference between leasing which is intended to be for just one short period or possibly two or three such periods at irregular intervals, and leasing which is intended to offer the client continuous use of the asset involved. It is to the procedure, advantages, and disadvantages of the latter that this chapter applies.

13.2 LEASING

13.21 DEFINITION

Leasing is an arrangement by which the owner of an asset grants exclusive possession and use of it to someone else, in exchange for an agreed monetary payment at stated intervals. This owner may be a specialist subsidiary of the firm actually making the asset; the latter sells the product outright to the former (which pays with funds raised from minority shareholders, the deposits it attracts, and the loans it arranges); then, in turn, it leases the asset to the user.

13.22 TERMS

These naturally vary with the type of asset and the institution involved. Basically, the period is likely to be that during which the asset may be expected to pay for itself – perhaps half its working life, with annual renewal options thereafter. For the biggest items, e.g. whole sections of processing plant, this could be up to fifteen years, but most contracts would be for smaller and shorter-lived items and would run for three to five years.

Incidentally, the large outlays involved for the owners of some of these assets may bring about changes in their organization. Thus Kleinwort Benson, when they extended their leasing activities beyond ships, computers, and machine tools to cover large commercial jet aircraft, recognized that the expense of buying such aircraft for subsequent leasing was so great that no one bank would do it on their own; they therefore established Airline International Management Ltd to do so – the first-ever legal partnership between banks [1].

As to the amounts available, Kleinwort Benson had, as part of the normal criteria, a minimum lease value of £100,000 or the foreign-currency equivalent, but firms handling less expensive items would obviously set much lower limits. The Bolton Committee said that, apart from manufacturer's leasing, £1,000 was often quoted as the normal minimum size of transaction. Under manufacturer's leasing:

'. . . products are offered automatically for leasing by customers under a guarantee provided by himself. In such cases the manufacturer's guarantee may obviate the need for investigation of the lessee and the manufacturer will assume responsibility for final disposal of the goods; amounts of £200 or even less may be available in these circumstances.' [2]

The range of values suggests that no asset for which leasing is appropriate will be out of reach of a suitable client.

13.23 ADVANTAGES

1 *Release of capital.* As already indicated, compared with outright purchase there is the fundamental gain of securing the use of assets without having to find and commit the resources needed to buy them. The capital which, if so raised, would have been tied up in a bought asset, is free for use elsewhere.

2 *No down payment* is required with leasing as it is with hire purchase. However, leasing contracts may call for the 'rent' to be paid in advance; this advantage is significant, therefore, only if the period paid for in advance is short.

3 *Technical improvement* is perhaps a more important gain – though one less easily quantified. Using leased rather than owned assets may stimulate

the businessman concerned to replace them more frequently, as technical advances are made, and thus to keep up-to-date. Investing financial capital in assets is risky enough anyway; investing emotional capital in them can be fatal.

4 *Creditworthiness.* It is also argued that, since no liability shows on the user's balance sheet as it would if he were buying the leased asset with borrowed money, his other credit lines are unimpaired; that is, if he should subsequently wish to borrow, a potential lender would not be put off by seeing that an existing creditor already had a claim on the assets which might constitute his security. The weakness of this argument is, of course, that there is no asset on the balance sheet either. However, other things being equal, profit expressed as a proportion of assets owned is higher in a business leasing some assets than in one buying them; to the extent that potential creditors would look to profitability as a guide to their lending, the former would be more attractive to them.

5 *Wider markets* become a benefit to the manufacturers of the assets which are leased. Since the annual leasing charge must be less than the asset's purchase price, and since, other things being equal, more of anything is demanded at a lower than at a higher price, producers are able to tap markets otherwise inaccessible to them. (Their higher sales may lead to scale economies which are, in turn, reflected in lower prices.)

13.24 DISADVANTAGES

1 *Cost.* The periodic payments are fixed at a level which, if the competition is not too savage, enables the owner to make money. Since he has to protect himself against damage caused by the least careful user, a more careful user may be penalized. Where this applies – e.g. as it may with construction equipment – the latter may be able to strike a better bargain after he has established his reputation.

2 *The effective gearing of the lessee is raised* by the payments due under the leasing agreement since they must be made irrespective of his profits. While these are buoyant no problem arises, but, if they fall, such prior claims may cut deeply into the operator's reward.

3 *Tax effects.* Although the charges are a tax-deductible expense analogous to the depreciation they replace, the lessee cannot benefit directly from any of the government's investment-stimulating arrangements; these help only the buyers of assets. It is, of course, always worth checking that the charges made under the lease are reduced to take account of such investment incentives; Kleinwort Benson pointed out that theirs were.

4 *The owner may impose conditions* on the use of the asset which the user may find onerous, e.g. a specification as to the number and/or the qualifications of the people authorized to operate it.

13.25 WHEN TO BUY

These advantages and disadvantages will be present even if the money needed to buy a particular asset is available. In principle, leasing is worth investigating when the operation of any specialized and relatively costly assets is under consideration – especially those assets requiring expert maintenance and servicing, or subject to rapid depreciation. The relative attractiveness of leasing assets or buying them outright – assuming either is possible – depends on several factors which, without overriding the specialization argument advanced earlier, set it in a wider context. Three such factors follow.

1 Probably the most important is the period for which the asset concerned would be leased. If this were long, the charges would fairly quickly exceed the purchase price. More precisely, the present value of the future payments at the lessee's rate of interest would exceed the current cost. The meaning of this is considered in Chapter 17.
2 The appeal of a leasing contract which had provision for the asset to be looked after by the owner, would be reduced or cancelled completely if the potential lessee had his own facilities for servicing and repairing it.
3 If a businessman were not bothered by the prospect of a fall in the value of the asset he was contemplating buying, leasing would be less attractive to him.

13.26 SCOPE AND EXTENT

The practice seems to have begun in the United States in about 1950 and spread from there to Canada, Europe, and the United Kingdom, becoming important in Britain in about the mid 1960s [3]. Simultaneously, the range of assets available on lease spread well beyond the conventional land and buildings, vehicles, and ships; building equipment, office furniture, and computers are now leased.

Expenditure on the hire of plant and machinery by the companies covered by the Department of Industry analysis referred to earlier, was approximately £144 million in 1968 (when the figure for this outlay was first shown separately) and rose to about £330 million by 1971 [4]. Although this is the fastest rate of increase under any heading, it is still negligible in relation to total assets, as shown in Table 5.1.

13.3 HIRE PURCHASE

13.31 DEFINITION

Hire purchase must be distinguished from leasing and from credit sale agreements. The main difference between it and leasing noted by the Bolton Committee is: with a leasing contract, although the asset concerned is usually re-leased or sold to the customer for a nominal sum at the end of the lease period, there is no formal agreement to do so; with an H.P. contract, there is.

There is a basic difference between H.P. and credit sale agreements. Under the former, ownership of the goods involved does not pass to the hirer until final payment is made; the owner, in the event of default, may repossess the goods (although, once one-third of the H.P. price has been paid, this right may be exercised only on the authority of a court order [5]). Under a credit sale agreement, however, ownership of the goods concerned passes as soon as the first payment is made; the creditor has no right to repossess them, and in the event of default he must sue for the outstanding balance.

13.32 ADVANTAGES

Like leasing, hire purchase enables a business to have the use of an asset without immediately paying the whole cost of it. It scores over leasing in that, since the client is buying the asset concerned, he is entitled directly to any grants or allowances against tax which go with it.

In addition, H.P. firms rely entirely on the creditworthiness of their customers and do not require any collateral security from them. ('Collateral' is used here in its conventional rather than its banking sense. For the latter, collateral security is that put up by a third party to secure a customer's account – as distinct from direct security, which is lodged by a customer to secure his own account [6]). This reliance on clients is a considerable advantage compared with, say, a bank or leasing organization, which almost certainly would require such security – either collateral or direct! – from the customer, who almost equally certainly would not be able to provide it.

Finally, it is claimed that, as the hirer must meet his payment obligations irrespective of his earnings, and as he finishes up owning an asset which he would not otherwise have had, hire purchase acts as a form of compulsory saving. Since, in this context, the economic significance of saving is the investment which it makes possible, this argument is misleading. In real terms, the investment occurs as soon as the producer of the asset makes it, not when the client decides to buy it – on hire purchase or otherwise.

13.33 DISADVANTAGES

If, as already indicated, it is use rather than ownership of assets which matters, hire purchase is in principle less appealing than leasing. Given that the whole purchase price has to be paid in a period usually shorter than the lease contract, outlays under H.P. contracts are likely to be larger than under comparable leasing ones.

Whether the cost of borrowing is greater under hire purchase than leasing is uncertain; neither type of contract seems renowned for openness in expressing a true rate of interest. Such true rates on H.P. contracts for consumers' goods may, if calculated on the opening balance of the sum borrowed, work out at about twice the rate apparently charged. It would be nice to think that such things did not happen in industrial H.P. contracts. A rule of thumb for finding the true rate of interest is given [7] as:

$$\text{True rate} = \frac{\text{Nominal rate} \times 2 \text{ (No. of instalments}}{\text{No. of instalments} + 1}$$

Nominal rate = Rate applying to original debt

As with leasing, the payments are due irrespective of the level of profits, and the seller may impose conditions as to the way in which the asset may be used or as to the terms of repayment, which make the use of the facility dearer or less convenient than at first appears.

Indeed, a potential user may find that the asset is out of reach entirely – at least temporarily. The Bolton Committee, after pointing out that 'Normally the only background information needed is the last three years' accounts, although personal guarantees are frequently required', noted that 'New firms, which by definition have no record of achievement, find it difficult to obtain facilities, as do those without up-to-date accounts' [8].

In addition, all clients must bear in mind that the government regulates H.P. facilities as part of its general machinery for trying to manage the economy. A customer may find that the terms he has relied on getting have been made unobtainable by an unforeseen change in the law.

Finally, in certain circumstances, if the purchaser fails to meet the terms of his contract, he may find that the seller can exercise his rights of repossession.

13.34 SCOPE AND EXTENT

This financing technique is by no means confined to the acquisition of consumers' durables; using it to help firms buy machinery, equipment, and vehicles is standard practice for companies like United Dominions Trust Ltd and Bowmakers Ltd. The Bolton Report quotes [9] a Finance Houses Association estimate that 12% of the January 1971 total of instalment debt of £1,377 million (covering both hire purchase and leasing) was for industrial plant and agricultural equipment, and that a further 11% was for commercial vehicles. 'This facility is in principle available even to the smallest firms, but the amount the finance houses are willing to advance varies with the size of the borrower. Most will not lend more than about half the owner's stake in the business, and impose a minimum loan size of £200.' However, little is published on amounts, availability, and terms (although three years seems to be usual); each applicant has to negotiate individually with his local office manager.

Complaints about high, concealed rates of interest and the burden of ill-considered commitments have made H.P. transactions the subject of growing concern. The Hire Purchase Act 1964 aims at protecting customers in H.P. and credit sale agreements where the sum involved does not exceed £2,000. (The proposals contained in the 1973 White Paper [10] would, if enacted, have raised this limit to £5,000 and also laid down formulae for calculating credit charges – together with many other changes to improve consumer protection in this field.) With such a monetary limit, the protection provided may well be important to sole traders and partners, but, in any case, the law does not apply to any agreement where the hirer or the buyer is an incorporated body. These two restrictions mean that much commercial and industrial hire purchase is outside the scope of this specific legislation.

13.4 SUMMARY

There seems little doubt that the facilities for the leasing of assets, or purchase of them on instalments, are widely available and increasingly used. This expansion must not be allowed to distract attention from their cost and, for the companies covered by the Department of Trade analysis, their relative insignificance. Although they, especially leasing, offer scope for the extension of specialization, circumstances may exist in which it is better to buy the asset(s) concerned outright.

14 Take-over/Merger

14.1 INTRODUCTION

All the methods so far considered by which a business may acquire fresh funds or assets and, with them, expand its operations, have assumed that no change in the number of enterprises occurs. Some firms are, of course, affected by the activities of the expanding business – either as suppliers or customers – but their number does not alter.

In real life, this is not so. Much expansion certainly depends on the institutions and techniques mentioned earlier, but, especially since the late 1950s, great reliance has also been placed on an apparently simpler approach to growth – not piecemeal additions to one's stock of assets, but acquisition of an entire existing collection of assets as a going concern. (Such growth is, of course, not economic growth in the macro-economic sense. Total national output and productive capacity are unchanged as a result of the exercise, other things equal; all that happens is that they become associated with a smaller number of business units. National output will grow only if the 'greater efficiency' aim of many take-overs is realized by producing a larger output with the same factor inputs, not by producing the same output with fewer factor inputs. Productive capacity may well shrink if plant is shut down for good following rationalization – and doing just that may be the main reason for the merger in the first place.)

Any form of business which has the will and the resources is free to adopt this approach. However, given the additional means available to incorporated businesses – especially public listed ones – of paying for assets with their own stocks and shares and given also the much greater economic significance of such companies and the much fuller public record of their activities, this chapter is concerned primarily with their take-over/merger operations. The distinction between these two terms, incidentally, is by no means clear-cut – though a take-over may be more likely to be resisted, and a merger to be generally approved, by the board of directors at the receiving end.

14.2 PROCEDURE

The actual process of acquiring assets already owned and used by another business may occur in two different ways. Given that both acquirer and acquired are companies limited by shares, the former must either buy the latter's assets direct or buy its shares and gain ownership and control through them.

14.21 PURCHASING OF ASSETS DIRECT

If the expanding company buys another firm's assets, it may give in exchange for them either cash, some of its own securities, or a combination of the two (the influences affecting its choice are considered later). From the seller's viewpoint, whatever form the payment takes the directors will have to decide, once they have accepted the offer, what the future of their company should be. They may decide to distribute any cash received – including the proceeds of the sale of any securities forming part of the purchase price – and to wind the company up. (This assumes that the securities received are marketable; if they are not, the directors' first job will presumably be to think up a satisfactory explanation of why they accepted the securities in the first place.)

Or the directors may decide to stay in business in some way. In this case, having made up their minds what this business is to be, they use the funds derived from the sale of their original assets to start up again. In doing so they must abide by any restrictions imposed on them by the buyer as a condition of his purchase. For example, when Tesco bought the Adsega supermarket group in 1965, it required the owners to stay out of the grocery business for five years [2].

The third possibility is for the selling company to continue to operate as a sort of investment company – not doing anything, but just receiving dividend income from the shares etc. it was given in exchange for its operating assets. This, however, would be pointless, because the company might just as well not exist. Its owners would save themselves the costs of running it by splitting the share portfolio – its only earning asset – among themselves *pro rata* to their holdings in it (after, of course, they first satisfied any prior claimants to capital).

14.22 PURCHASING SHARES

If the expanding company buys another company's shares, again it may offer cash, its own shares/loan stock, or both. The Take-over Code requires the offeror to be able to prove that he has the necessary cash for a cash offer or the cash element of an offer [2]. Under the Code's definition, 'References to purchases for cash and cash prices paid for shares shall be deemed to include contracts or arrangements for the acquisition of shares where the consideration consists of a debt instrument maturing for payment in less than three years' [3]. Furthermore, if, during the offer period and the preceding twelve months, a bidder and anyone acting in concert with him buy over 15% of the relevant shares for cash, the offer for the rest of those shares must be in cash or have a cash alternative, unless the Take-over Panel specifically approves something different [4].

Whichever consideration is given, the directors of the selling organization have no worries about what to do next with their company – they no longer control it. (As indicated on p. 14, to get this control the buyer does not, in law, have to acquire all the equity; apart from special resolutions, his position is unassailable if he has 50% + 1 share of the relevant class, and operational control is usually gained with considerably less than this. The Take-over Code, however, has a certain requirement for anyone who, singly or in concert with others, either (i) acquires shares carrying 30% or more of the voting power (not having held that much voting strength already), or (ii) holding in June 1974 shares with not less than 30% nor more than 50% of the voting power, acquires in any twelve-month period shares increasing that voting power by more than 1%; anyone so doing must extend an offer on a specified basis within a reasonable time to the remainder of the equity share capital – voting or non-voting [5]). The bought company may, indeed, have ceased to exist. Its shareholders and long-term lenders will have exchanged the share and loan certificates they previously held for cash or similar securities of the buying firm. The latter may treat the securities so obtained as assets and show them as such on its balance sheet. If so, the identity of the bought company is unaffected by the change in ownership. But the buyer may decide to cancel the bought securities and merge the bought company completely with itself. In that case, the company taken over is finished as a separate entity, and its assets and liabilities are all, by the exchange of securities, transferred to the buyer. (The factors influencing the buyer's decision are referred to in 2.63 above.)

14.3 VALUATION OF SHARES

Whether the formal process of merging goes smoothly or not – indeed, whether the assets sought are in fact bought and, if so, at what price – depends to a large extent on the valuation which the buying company puts on the assets, and on the way in which it proposes to pay this valuation, once it is agreed, Assuming, as is usually the case, that it is the securities of the offered company which are being bought, not its assets direct, two aspects of the operation must be considered: (i) how may those securities (essentially the voting shares) be valued, and (ii) how may they be paid for.

14.31 ASSETS-PER-SHARE BASIS OF VALUATION

(a) Procedure

The initial calculation involved in the first step should present no problems. The potential buyer, working from the potential seller's most recent balance sheet, and adjusting this to take account of any later information which may be available, arrives at an asset value per share. To do this, he simply sums the asset values shown (deducting any fictitious ones which may be present), subtracts the value of all claims – including those of any preference share-holders – and then divides the resulting figure by the number of ordinary shares in issue. The answer is the value of the assets attributable to each ordinary share.

Thus, taking Reed International Ltd as an example, the parent company's balance sheet for the year ending 31 March 1974 [6] revealed total assets of almost £401 million, with nothing identifiably fictitious about them. Claims on these assets in the form of current liabilities amounted to £34 million; roughly £123 million was owing to long-term lenders, and just over £4 million to holders of preference shares of various kinds. The £240 million remaining after deduction of these amounts would have been attributable to the holders of the ordinary shares. Since there were 90 million of these in issue at the time, the assets per share on this balance sheet valuation would have been approximately £2·67.

(b) Divergence from market price

This does not mean that anyone seeking to buy control of Reed International would have been able to do so by paying this average price per ordinary share, nor that the market price of those shares would have been £2·67, either at the balance sheet date or after. (In fact, 31 March 1974 was a Sunday; the market price on the following Monday was about £2·01. Such discounts on asset values are not uncommon in times of economic un-certainty.)

There are several factors to be borne in mind when assessing, by the type of calculation made above, the accuracy of the valuation of a share as shown by the assets apparently underlying it. For instance, whenever a value is ascribed to an asset, the questions at once arise of how and when (and, perhaps, by whom) the valuation was made. As already noted on p. 125, the value of land may change quite markedly – sometimes quite quickly. Hence, if land appears in the balance sheet (as either freehold or long-leasehold property) and if it has not been recently professionally valued, the balance sheet figure for it may be much too low, and the ordinary share value calculated on an assets basis also much too low. In the case of the Reed International parent, 'properties and plant' were only £1·3 million, i.e. about 0·3% of total assets. However, nearly 84% of total assets consisted of investments in subsidiaries, and the written-down group figure for land and buildings at cost or valuation was about £89 million – with valuations totalling £22·5 million made in 1964 or earlier [7].

The other side of this coin is that most assets do not appreciate with the passage of time – they depreciate. This again raises the question of whether their balance sheet valuation is a true one; but this time, of course, the possibility is of over- rather than under-valuation. Without knowing the method and the consistency with which plant, machinery, and other fixed assets have been written down, and what provision had been made, for example, for bad debts, it is impossible to say whether the values shown are true reflections of the earning power of the resources concerned. This situation will eventually improve through the efforts of the professional bodies concerned to establish a body of standard practice leading to consistent treatment (e.g. through the Exposure Drafts of the Institute of Chartered Accountants).

But undoubtedly the biggest reason why the asset value of a share differs from its market price is that the former embodies the past, while the latter embodies the future. Accordingly, even if all the assets (and, of course, all the liabilities) are accurately valued at the time the balance sheet is prepared, they will still represent only what the business has achieved up to that date. When a share is traded in an open market, however, potential buyers are likely to be much less interested in past achievements than in prospective performance, and their decision to buy or not buy will be based, to a large extent, on what they expect the company to do in the months or years to come. This being so, all manner of uncertainties may alter the prospects of a company for good or bad, so that, although nothing can change the value of its assets on some date in the past, the earnings which those assets may be able to generate in the future may become quite different. As a result, it makes sense to buy shares in an undertaking with good prospects at prices above the historically-calculated asset value – and, similarly, to buy those of companies with poor or weakened prospects at prices below those so based (if they are to be bought at all).

One final point must be remembered. The value of the share calculated from the assets shown in the balance sheet may be below its market price because the whole is greater than the sum of the parts. The business is not just so many million pounds-worth of land and buildings, plus so many more million pounds-worth of plant and machinery, stock, debtors, etc. If, starting from scratch, all these individual parts were assembled on their existing locations, they would not produce anything at all – even if connected to the appropriate sources of power and energy. Since the society in which the firm operates is not a slave society, labour may not appear on the balance sheet as a bought asset – but without a workforce no output can emerge.

The asset pool at a firm's disposal is thus not just a collection, however big, of material resources, however sophisticated. All these things must be in a dynamic union. not stopped and idle, but working together as a going concern. If the whole productive operation came to a halt – as it might, perhaps, through a strike – the assets themselves would not suddenly change their values. Debtors would still owe the same amounts; stocks would still exist to the same extent, as would land, buildings, plant, patents, investments, and everything else – but it would be reasonable for the market price of the share to drop, simply because the assets, being stopped, might be unable to earn as much as usual in a given period. (Incidentally it should be noted that output so lost might, if produced, have been unsaleable; alternatively, it might have been made good by higher production later [8].) Similarly, when production restarted the market price might well move up once more – not because the value of the assets had changed on an historical cost basis, but because their earning power had risen or been restored. In other words, market price reflects the fact that the business concerned – any business – is not just a collection of material assets but a functioning and, hopefully, profit-making entity.

(c) Significance of asset value per share

If the comments made earlier about the accuracy of the balance sheet entries and the possibility that the shares might be trading at a discount on asset values are remembered, (a) above provides a means of establishing a *minimum* price for the shares of a company which another proposes to buy. It does not necessarily determine the *actual* price which will be paid, still less the maximum that a bidder may be induced to offer. This, like the market price, depends on his expectations.

14.32 BIDDER'S EXPECTATIONS BASIS

In making an offer for a company, the bidder must have in mind some gain which he hopes to obtain, or some damage or injury which he seeks to avoid. What he is prepared to pay to realize these hopes, added to the genuine asset value, determine how much he will offer, acting rationally.

(a) Asset stripping

In some cases, less common now than they used to be, the advantage looked for can be quantified quite easily. There may be some undervalued asset, particularly land, which the bidder has identified and appraised. Such appraisal was the basis of the practice of asset stripping, where a business was bought not primarily to maintain its operations but in order that some or all of its assets might be sold – at a figure well above the balance sheet valuation and, of course, well above what the assets cost the buyer. An offeror now, however, is expected to declare the long-term commercial justification for the proposed offer, his intentions regarding the continuance of the offeree's business and the employment of its workforce, and any major changes envisaged, including redeployment of fixed assets [9].

(b) Competitor control

Another advantage contemplated may be that of being able to control a particular competitor; a bidder might know quite clearly in advance what an amalgamation would save him in marketing expenses, for example, and the costs of rivalry generally.

(c) Return on assets

In a broader way, he may reasonably hope to make the bid-for assets work as profitably for him as those assets he already uses; his upper limit then is set by capitalizing the gain expected from them. This gain may present itself in two distinct ways, as can be seen from the following example.

Table 14.1. Basis of offer by X for Y

Company X	£	Company Y	£
Total assets	5,000,000	Total assets	1,000,000
Represented by:			
2 million £1 ordinary shares	2,000,000	500,000 £1 ordinary shares	500,000
Reserves	3,000,000	Reserves	250,000
Long-term debt	—	10% debentures	250,000
Profits, after interest and tax:			
1973	1,000,000		120,000
1972	800,000		125,000
1971	640,000		115,000
Market price of equity	£4		£1·44
Last dividend (1973)	30%		18%

Company X is considering making an offer for Company Y, which is in the same line of business but obviously doing less well (see Table 14.1). How much would it be justified in bidding? Comparison of the two companies shows the following:

	X	Y
(a) Assets per share	£2·50	£1·50
*(b) Dividend yield	7½%	12½%
*(c) Dividend cover	1⅔	1⅓
*(d) Earnings yield	12½%	16⅔%
*(e) Price: earnings multiple	8	6
(f) Return on capital employed	20%	12%
(share capital + reserves + long-term debt)		

*These terms are explained in the Appendix.

An offer based on the asset value of Y's shares would provide a minimum bid, but at only 6p above the existing market price it would be unlikely to receive an enthusiastic welcome. After all, if X started buying Y's shares in the market at any speed, it would probably push the price up to the 'asset' value anyway and, given that it would have to bid for all the shares as soon as it had 30%, it would almost certainly have to pay more than just the asset value in order to get the benefit of complete control.

The directors of X would presumably hope to get from Y the same results, in the long run, as they now achieve in their own company. One form of the hoped-for gain would be the same return on capital employed. If this were realized, Y's stagnant profit record would be radically changed; a 20% return on capital would bring its profits up to £200,000 a year (net of interest and tax). Since X's equity is currently selling at eight times earnings, Y's would be worth eight times these hoped-for earnings, i.e. £1·6 million – which for half a million shares would be £3·20 each.

However, such a long-run expectation would not be a realistic foundation for a once-and-for-all payment now – and payment in instalments as the expected gains actually materialized, however attractive to buyers, would be unlikely to commend itself to sellers. Accordingly, a reasonable offer would be based on the second aspect of the expected gain, i.e. the rate of growth of profits. It would take into account the probability of some delays, occurring before the improvement planned for Y showed fully in its profits. Inspection of the recent performance of X reveals that its disposable income has been rising by 25% a year, while Y's has changed very little over the period given. If Y's profits could be made to grow at the same annual rate as X's, they would reach £150,000 a year after the merger; that level of earnings, capitalized at X's price:earnings multiple of 8, would give a total consideration of £1·2 million, or £2·40 per Y ordinary share. Such a price would have the advantages of not being based on extravagant demands on X's management in handling both their existing resources and those acquired from Y, while at the same time offering Y's shareholders a sizable premium over the current market price.

14.33 UNQUANTIFIED OR NON-COMMERCIAL BASIS

In cases such as the hypothetical one above, where there is a clearly defined and straightforward commercial assessment underlying the bid, the maximum price which it makes sense to offer – and, more important, the actual price which would leave both parties satisfied – can be established without inordinate difficulty. However, the situation is quite different if the benefits to be gained (or the losses to be avoided) are either (i) not precisely formulated, or (ii) if they are so formulated, not properly priced. When expansion is justified because it will 'round out the product line' or 'provide complementarity of production and marketing', the monetary value of the expected advantage may be as hard to work out before the merger as it is hard to realize after it.

The decision then on where to fix the maximum price may depend on such factors as (i) the optimism or otherwise of the bidding directors and/or their advisers, (ii) the extent to which they may worry about losing face if, having encountered opposition or rivalry to their bid, they decide not to pursue it, and (iii) the existence and nature of any personality clashes between directors in the bidding business itself, or between them and those of the bid-for company or any competing bidder. These factors may be imponderable, and the upper limit to a bid may thus become unpredictable. All that can be said is that in many cases the bid price has been too high. Commenting on Ajit Singh's *Take-overs* (London: Cambridge University Press, 1971), Professor W. B. Reddaway said [10]:

> 'Dr. Singh's research into what happens *after* a take-over provides no support whatever for the idea that profitability is, on average, increased by applying better methods to the assets which have been taken into new management ... in each of the five industries he finds that over half the acquiring companies show a worse movement than the rest of the industry.'

14.34 NON-COMMERCIAL REJECTION OF A BID

By the same token, offering a higher price than a competitor is no guarantee of success; the more generous bidder may be thwarted by the fact that his face does not fit. A classic illustration of this was provided in 1964 by the contest [11] between Sir Charles Clore's British Shoe Corporation and Stylo Ltd for ownership of the shoe firm W. Barratt Ltd (values decimalized). B.S.C. bid £1·10 for each voting, and £1·07½ for each non-voting, ordinary Barratt share. Stylo offered one of its low-voting ordinary shares plus 37½p in cash for each voting, and one low-voting ordinary share plus 30p in cash for each non-voting, ordinary Barratt share. Since Stylo low-voting shares then stood at 60p, its offer was worth 97½p and 90p respectively – well below the rival bid.

Of Barratt's shares, 28% were held by its directors and a further 17½% by the company's pension fund. The directors were opposed to the B.S.C. bid anyway, and the trustees of the pension fund accepted the Stylo offer, allegedly because there would have been no benefit to Barratt's employees from the higher bid since their pensions were predetermined, and because they thought jobs would be safer under Stylo management. The B.S.C. said it was ready to give the same guarantees regarding pensions and jobs as Stylo (though presumably this did not extend to the Barratt directors!), but it was not asked to do so by Barratt. The Stylo bid prevailed – just – with 53% of the voting and 25% of the non-voting Barratt shares accepting.

(Incidentally, the success of the Stylo offer at once created two problems. One was for the former Barratt shareholders who found themselves holding Stylo paper which they did not wish to keep. Since Stylo was a small director-controlled company, its shares could not resist heavy selling, so such ex-Barratt members found themselves locked in. The other problem was a potentially awkward one for the Stylo directors. The company was controlled via 'management' shares, i.e. ordinary shares with eight votes each as compared with the low-voting ordinary share's one. The issue of low-voting ordinary shares in exchange for Barratt's shares jeopardized this control, so the Stylo directors proposed, successfully, that it be restored by raising the management share's voting power to sixteen – with no compensation to the ordinary shareholders for this. In essence the latter, having been deprived of a monetary gain in the form of a higher bid but having, as a result, gained control over those who had so deprived them, freely gave up that control. Reporting this sorry tale must have brought *The Economist* close to spontaneous incandescence.)

14.4 PAYMENT FOR SHARES

Once the bidding company has decided to try to secure the extra assets it seeks by making an offer for an existing business, and has, presumably, established a maximum price for itself, it must also consider the separate but related issue of the form its offer is to take.

14.41 DEALING WITH NON-EQUITY SECURITIES

To some extent, what the bidder does will be conditioned by the securities which the 'victim' already has in issue. For instance, preference shareholders and long-term lenders would be unlikely to want to change their status to that of ordinary shareholders in the bidding company. Accordingly, if they were not bought out for cash, an appropriate part of the offer might have to be in the form of suitable prior-charge capital. However, classes of non-equity capital need not be the subject of an offer [12], and the main problem is bound to be what, and how much, to offer the ordinary shareholders; after all, they control the sought-after assets. The 'what' must be either cash or ordinary shares (or something with an equity element) in the bidding company. Incidentally, to the extent that cash is used, the bidding company will not be enlarged by the acquisition, since it will merely have exchanged cash for other assets.

14.42 CASH OFFERS

Several points have to be borne in mind where cash offers are concerned. The first one which naturally arises is whether the cash required is available or can be easily produced. This is not simply a matter of meeting the requirements of the Take-over Code, important though these are. The bidder presumably has activities other than the take-over to finance. The cash available must therefore be enough for the latter and also for all the other known commitments, or outlays likely to arise, in the period which must elapse before the anticipated benefits materialize. It would, for instance, be foolish to settle the bill for the equity of the acquired company in cash and then to find that the money needed to pay the usual dividend a couple of months later was not there, or that capital outlays already authorized could not be met on time because of lack of cash. (Avoiding this sort of embarrassment is one reason for maintaining up-to-date and accurate cash flow forecasts; *see* p. 171.)

And, of course, if the purchase of a company's shares is just the first stage of a reorganization of the joint, bigger enterprise, it would be prudent to keep a sizable amount of cash in hand to pay for whatever developments the merger might make possible. It is not very helpful to buy assets and then find, for example, that they cannot be employed properly because the working capital needed to utilize them has been used in acquiring them.

But if there is enough of it, paying cash for paper has advantages – to both buyer and seller. For the former, there is the simple fact that the transaction is completed at once, with no further payments to be made. If, instead, shares are exchanged, they will have to be serviced all the time they are in issue; a series of relatively small but as yet unknown claims on the resources of the new organization will replace one relatively large but definite claim on the buyer's resources now. If the buyer thinks the future is bright enough, he may prefer to block those claims now.

Furthermore, a cash offer, once accepted, leaves control of the bidder undisturbed; whereas a paper bid necessarily dilutes the influence of the bidder's original members – save in the improbable event that the sellers can be persuaded to take shares with restricted or no voting rights.

From the sellers' point of view, cash has the attractions of certain, predictable value and of being immediately ready for reinvestment if this is desired. It is true that, on the form of the early 1970s, cash is unlikely to produce any gains in real terms; it may not generate anything very exciting in the way of income (taking cash to include balances on interest-bearing deposit accounts), and to convert it into anything more lucrative must involve expense of some kind. These disadvantages, however, may be small compared with those of being given a security which has to be sold before redeployment of funds can take place, which trades at prices which cannot be known in advance, and which accordingly may quite easily have to be sold at a loss.

14.43 SHARE EXCHANGES

Despite these points, it is not difficult to see that an exchange of securities has considerable appeal to both parties.

From the offeror's viewpoint, not least is the knowledge that, unlike cash, he may legally print securities himself. Paying with paper protects his liquidity at the time of the take-over and eases the financial strains associated with it.

Table 14.2. Acquisition of subsidiaries by quoted companies in manufacturing, distribution, etc.* (£m)

Year 1	By issue of shares and loans 2	By cash 3	Total expenditure (a) (2 + 3) 4	Total uses of funds 5	2 as % of 4 (b) 6	4 as % of 5 (b) 7
1964	232	274	505	4,592	46	11
1965	275	219	493	4,929	56	10
1966	274	123	397	4,578	69	9
1967	554	185	739	5,302	75	14
1968	1,412	281	1,694	6,895	83	25
1969	649	186	835	6,821	78	12
Revision of Cover						
1970	629	183	812	6,903	77	12
1971	544	330	875	5,931	62	15

Source: M3, Company Finance, 5th edn., Tables 1 and 5; values rounded to nearest £m.

*For the companies covered, see Table 3.1.
Notes:
(a) Does not always equal 2 + 3 because of rounding.
(b) % taken to nearest whole number.

Sellers who accept securities avoid the interruption of their income and the bother and expense of reinvestment which arise from a cash settlement. Even more important for larger investors is the fact that an exchange of securities, unlike acceptance of a cash offer, does not constitute a realization for capital-gains tax purposes; hence their tax libility under this heading does not crystallize.

Whichever of these considerations has been dominant in the past, it is clear from Table 14.2 that a far higher proportion of assets has been acquired with paper than with cash, between 1965 and 1971 at any rate.

14.44 USE OF CONVERTIBLES

The main variation in the actual form of the offer is likely to derive from (i) the buyer's consideration of the dilution of earnings which will initially arise from taking over badly-run assets, and (ii) the seller's consideration of the uncertainties of the whole scheme. The use of a convertible loan stock for at least part of the payment may serve to overcome both these reservations. The low cost of servicing such a security makes it attractive to the buyer, especially in the early post-merger years during which the assets acquired are being brought up to the desired level of profitability. At the same time it offers the acceptors some certainty of income during the period when the merger is getting over its teething troubles, and the prospect of full participation in profits later when, hopefully, everything is going well.

14.5 THE TAKE-OVER CODE

Some of the Code's requirements have already been noted – especially Rules which ensure fair treatment of all those affected by an offer; other relevant ones are set out below.

Broadly speaking, partial bids are regarded with disfavour – i.e. bids for less than 100% of the voting capital not already owned. They may be made only with the prior approval of the Panel, and the same offer must be made to all shareholders of any particular class (Rule 27). If an offeror does not make a formal offer within a reasonable time of announcing its intention of doing so, it must be prepared to justify its inaction to the Panel. An announced offer cannot be withdrawn without the Panel's consent, which is given only in exceptional cases (Rule 9). Offers must initially be open for at least twenty-one days after they are posted and, if revised, for at least fourteen days from the posting of the revision. Unless contested or declared unconditional, they must close at the close of business on the sixtieth day after they were posted. An offer which has not become or been declared unconditional within these sixty days may not be replaced by another offer without the Panel's permission (Rule 22).

The word 'unconditional' has a special significance in connection with offers. All offers are made on the assumption that certain conditions, which must be stated in the formal announcement, will be fulfilled. These conditions normally include:

1 Approval by the bidding company's shareholders of the creation of any extra nominal capital called for.
2 Listing by the Stock Exchange of the securities which it is proposed to issue.
3 Acceptance in an approved fashion by any non-voting shares being bid for at the same time.
4 Avoidance of reference of the whole deal to the Monopolies and Mergers Commission (Rule 8 requires specific mention of this particular condition, if it applies).

Individual bidders may add such other conditions as they think fit in order to protect themselves from unforeseen events. To ensure that, if successful, they finish up with the assets they expect, they may bid on condition that the offeree company does not declare and distribute any abnormal dividends during the course of the offer, or may specify that the assets of the offeree should not be 'materially damaged by fire, flood, Act of God or the public enemy, regardless of insurance cover' [13], as G. D. Searle Inc. did in bidding for Gold Cross Hospital Supplies Ltd in May 1974.

The critical thing is that, until an offer is declared unconditional, any acceptor of it is entitled to withdraw his acceptance after twenty-one days from the first closing date of the original offer (Rule 22). Accordingly, as soon as an offer is made unconditional, all acceptances are irrevocable. Therefore, to protect the shareholders of the offeree company from the possibility that the offeror may get enough acceptances to influence, but not to control that company, the Code in general requires offers to be made on the condition that they 'will not become or be declared unconditional unless the offeror has acquired . . . by the close of the offer shares carrying over 50% of the voting rights attributable to the equity share capital' (Rule 21). In addition,

'Except with the consent of the Panel, where an offer has been made but has not become unconditional, the offeror and persons acting in concert with the offeror may not, within 12 months from the date on which such offer lapsed, acquire any further shares of the offeree company if the offeror or persons acting in concert with the offeror would thereby become obliged under Rule 34 to make an offer.' (Rule 35)

(Rule 34 was referred to at 14.22 above.)

14.6 EXTENT OF TAKE-OVERS

Information on the acquisition of companies covered by the Department of Industry analysis is given in Table 14.2. This table shows the persistence and generally rising importance of this form of activity; even the check to the economy from the 1966 'squeeze and freeze' only brought it down to 9% of their total uses of funds, and over the years shown it has averaged $13\frac{1}{2}\%$ of that total.

14.7 SUMMARY

Business growth, as distinct from economic growth, may occur through a firm's buying the assets or shares of one or more existing enterprises, and it is clear from Table 14·2 that the larger companies have found this approach attractive. Consideration of true asset values and the performance expected from them sets the commercial limits within which the purchase price will be agreed, but other influences may produce a price outside these limits. Payment may be in either cash or securities. Whatever attraction cash may have for the seller, the buyer must keep his operational requirements for it clearly in view, and he is likely to find securities a more suitable form of consideration. Whichever he chooses, he must keep the Take-over Code in mind.

APPENDIX: YIELDS AND YIELD GAPS

14.A1 DEFINITION

The essence of a yield is that it is return in relation to outlay. With securities, it may be shown in three different ways: dividend yield, earnings yield, and redemption yield.

14.A2 DIVIDEND (CURRENT, RUNNING, OR FLAT) YIELD (DY)

If securities have par values, dividend or interest payments on them are expressed as a percentage of the nominal value of the relevant capital. Their rates of return can be found from the formula:

$$\text{DY (of X)} = \frac{\text{Nominal value of X}}{\text{Current market price of X}} \times \text{Last annual payment } \%$$

Thus, a £1 nominal share which last paid a dividend of 20% and now costs £4 would have a DY of 5%; a £100-nominal loan stock, carrying interest at 10% a year and standing now at £80, would have a running yield of 12½%.

If par values are not used,

$$DY = \frac{\text{Last annual money payment}}{\text{Current market price}} \times 100$$

Values must always be expressed in a common monetary form.

14.A3 EARNINGS YIELD (EY)

This yield takes into account a share's total earnings, whether retained or distributed. It applies only to equity, not to securities having no retentions. Par values are irrelevant.

$$EY = \frac{\text{Last reported post-tax earnings per share}}{\text{Current market price of the share}} \times 100$$

If the year's distributable earnings for the share in 14.A2 above were 40p (20p being used for the dividend and 20p retained), the EY would be 10%, since $(40 \div 400) \times 100 = 10$.

The fact that the EY is twice the DY here means that the dividend is twice covered – cover being the number of times a dividend could have been paid at the stated rate if all the available earnings had been distributed. Thus EY = DY × Cover.

Price: earnings ratio or multiple (p:e)

This is simply the reciprocal of the EY. Given a market price of £4 and last reported post-tax earnings of 40p per share, the p:e ratio is 10:1 (the reciprocal of 10%) – commonly expressed simply as a p:e multiple of 10.

A few companies, because of heavy overseas taxation or large depreciation allowances, have little or no U.K. tax liability against which to offset the ACT due on any dividend they pay in the United Kingdom. (ACT may be set off only against corporation tax. It is to recoup such ACT that overseas trading corporations have bought, or have tried to buy, businesses with satisfactory U.K. earnings, e.g. Bowater's attempted take-over of Hanson Trust Ltd in 1973.) Treating such unrelieved ACT in the approved way, as part of the company's tax charge, means that 'net' or actual disposable income falls because of a tax payment arising from a dividend distribution; in other words, disposable earnings depend on dividends, rather than the other way round. However, for the vast majority of companies, 'net' earnings and earnings based on a 'nil' distribution are the same. Since the former more accurately depict a company's actual disposable income, they are the earnings used in calculating p:e multiples.

14.A4 REDEMPTION YIELD (RY)

This is the return an investor obtains by holding redeemable securities – i.e. most loans and some preference shares – which he has bought at a price different from that at which they will be redeemed. It equals the annual value of the capital gain represented by this difference, plus the DY. It is measured by the rate of interest which, used to discount the amount due on redemption and the future income payments, makes the security's present value equal to its cost. (The discounting of future sums is dealt with in Chapter 17.)

The outlays on which yields are calculated should include stamp duties, commissions, and other acquisition costs, as well as the price of the securities. Net-of-tax yields differ according to investors' individual tax positions; RY in particular may attract income tax on the current element as well as capital gains tax on the redemption element.

14.A5 THE YIELD GAP AND THE REVERSE YIELD GAP

Although it might be thought that investors would quickly react to close any gap which emerged between current yields on comparable securities (i.e. those having no redemption element and being equally secure), both a yield gap and a reverse yield gap have appeared and persisted at different times.

(a) The yield gap

Comparison between the histories of U.K. government debt ('gilt-edged') in the form of $3\frac{1}{2}\%$ War Loan and of top-grade industrial ordinary shares ('blue chips', named after the highest denomination of token used in poker) shows that for many years the former yielded less than the latter. This yield gap was attributable to two main factors.

1 Periodic depressions of employment and output could be relied on to reduce firms' ability to maintain dividends, or even pay them at all; by contrast, the risk of the U.K. government's defaulting on its debt interest was regarded as nil. Those expectations pushed the market price of gilts up and reduced the prices of blue chips, thus producing higher yields for the latter than for the former.

2 Prices were known to move down as well as up; there was not, before World War II, an expectation of continuing inflation. Falling prices not

only made profitable trading more difficult for firms, but made income from gilt-edged doubly attractive, because (i) it was certain and (ii) its real value was rising. This too was reflected in the respective market prices, and tended to widen the yield gap.

(b) Emergence of the reverse yield gap

During and after the war, however, the gap first closed and then reopened the other way in 1959, for several reasons;

1 because policies to maintain full employment largely removed the threat to profits and dividends arising from inadequate aggregate demand. Apart from in freak periods such as the winter of 1962/3 and the three-day week in early 1974, the peak rate of unemployment after the war was about 4% in 1971/2. This rightly gave cause for concern, but compared with the prewar maximum of 22% [1] it was scarcely noticeable.
2 because rising prices improved companies' prospects of making at least larger money profits, and simultaneously lowered the appeal of the fixed interest paid on debt – however riskless.
3 because of the preoccupation with economic growth. This, if it occurs, must mean more output which will go only to those with readily adjustable incomes, since experience shows no recent case of sustained growth in this type of economy with completely stable prices. Ordinary shareholders would be able to benefit from it, but not lenders.

Largely for these reasons the appeal of fixed interest securities declined relative to that of equities. The traditional position was upset and between 1959 and 1973 there emerged a reverse yield gap, i.e. equity yields below debt yields.

(c) The yield gap re-emerges

The slide in share prices in 1973/4, coupled with unprecedentedly high interest rates, restored the yield gap in its original form; in December 1974, the earnings yield on industrials (not all of them blue chips) was over seventeen percentage points above the flat yield on $2\frac{1}{2}$% Consols [2].

SECTION E

USES OF FUNDS

15 The Liquidity Goal and Overtrading

15.1 INTRODUCTION

Raising funds is one thing; deciding how to use them in the best way is another. No business can expect to get very far on the basis of first obtaining money and then deciding what it will be used for – although during the speculative mania associated with the South Sea Bubble, there was a 'gentleman who in one morning collected a thousand subscriptions for a company "for carrying on an undertaking of great advantage, but nobody to know what it is", and decamped with the cash the same afternoon' [1].

The decision depends on a balancing of the basic requirement of survival with the other, not necessarily compatible, objectives of the business – mainly the desired combination of liquidity, profitability and growth. Growth and profitability, based on take-over or investment in specific assets, are considered in Chapters 14 and 16 respectively. This chapter looks at the liquidity goal of a business and the dangers of overtrading which may beset it if it misjudges its working capital requirements.

15.2 WORKING CAPITAL

15.21 DEFINITION AND CALCULATION

Working capital is defined as the liquid resources available to meet day-to-day operating expenses, of which the most important item is almost certainly the payroll.

It is calculated by subtracting the total of current liabilities from the total of current assets; it thus shows on the balance sheet as net current assets.

15.22 SIGNIFICANCE

Output emerges from a combination of assets. Plant, machinery, and fixed assets generally cannot produce unless they have co-operating with them at least some of the inputs of labour, energy, and raw materials which their technical specification prescribes. Thus, any decision on the use of fixed assets is likely to have inseparable repercussions on the amounts of these other inputs required, as well as on the investment in the circulating assets (stock and trade debtors). In other words, efficient production depends not only on the availability of the right quantity and type of the appropriate physical assets, but also on the availability of the right amount of working capital.

15.23 REQUIREMENT

How much working capital a business should have depends on the type of organization involved; a holding company would probably need less than an operating one, for example. The industry it is in also makes a difference; manufacturing, with its relatively long production cycles and consequent large tie-up of value in work in progress, is likely to require much more than retailing, with its fast stock-turnover and predominantly cash sales. If the activities it engages in are seasonal, a firm needs more working capital at one time of the year than another, and there may well be other variables peculiar to it which affect its requirements.

The evidence of the Department of Industry analysis suggests that firms were operating with relatively less working capital in 1971 than in 1964. The average ratio of current assets to current liabilities for quoted companies fell during this period from about 2:1 to about 1·6:1; for unquoted companies it was roughly stable at about 1·3:1.

15.3 OVERTRADING

15.31 DEFINITION AND ORIGINS

Overtrading means trying to run a business with too little working capital in relation to turnover (total sales). It is essentially a hazard for the expanding and successful – indeed, profitable – business, not for the failure, although this only makes it more insidious and harder to deal with. Typically, an overtrading firm faces buoyant demand at existing price levels. It has the physical capacity to meet this demand, so for a time higher sales can be and are made. But the finance essential to support this expansion is not there.

What the managers of an overtrading business do not grasp (or what they lose sight of) is the fact that each stage of a productive process must be financed by somebody – from the provision of basic inputs such as fuel and raw materials to the eventual sale of a finished product. That somebody may be suppliers, processors, or any of the specialized institutions already mentioned, but every movement of real things must be matched by an equal and opposite movement of money values. Any attempt, therefore, to increase the flow of real things must be backed by a corresponding, and simultaneous, ncrease in the ability to finance this greater material flow. An overtrading irm cannot provide this extra finance, but still seeks to maintain the bigger volume of production which the buoyancy of its market seems to justify. This leads to certain predictable characteristics of such a firm, illustrated in a simplified and exaggerated manner in Table 15.1.

Table 15.1. Balance sheets of an overtrading firm (a) before overtrading begins, (b) after one year's overtrading, and (c) after two years' overtrading

Assets:	£(a)	£(b)	£(c)
Fixed			
Land and buildings	10,000	10,000	10,000
Plant and machinery	5,000	5,000	5,000
Vehicles	2,000	2,000	2,000
Total fixed assets (i)	17,000	17,000	17,000
Current			
Stock	10,000	15,000	21,000
Trade debtors	20,000	30,000	41,000
Cash	1,000	—	—
Total current assets (ii)	31,000	45,000	62,000
Total assets (i + ii)	48,000	62,000	79,000
Financed by:			
Capital	30,000	30,000	30,000
Revenue reserves	5,000	5,840	8,600
Profit & Loss A/c (current year	840	2,760	6,480
Current liabilities:			
Trade creditors	5,000	7,500	13,500
Dividend (gross)	3,000	3,000	—
Tax due @ 52%	4,160	6,240	7,020
Overdraft or other borrowing	—	6,660	13,400
Total current liabilities (iii)	12,160	23,400	33,920
Total liabilities	48,000	62,000	79,000
Turnover (iv)	100,000	150,000	225,000
Working capital (v) = (ii−iii)	18,840	21,600	28,080
(v) as % of (iv)	18·84	14·4	12·48

Balance sheet (a) shows a promising business. It is profitable; the year's pre-tax profit is £8,000, of which £840 is retained, and previous years' retentions total £5,000. It has plenty of working capital; current assets total £31,000 and current liabilities only £12,160, so there is £18,840 to meet operating expenses. Its other ratios, as shown in Table 15.2 are generally good. Suppose the directors, impressed by this performance and aware that there were plenty of profitable orders going which they had the physical capacity to handle, decided to accept more work. Sales would rise (and so would profits initially) – but with them stock, debtors, and creditors would inevitably rise too.

15.32 DEVELOPMENT OF OVERTRADING

Suppose, for the sake of illustration, there were a 50% increase in sales the following year, and that stock, debtors, and creditors rose similarly. (There is no guarantee that they would keep pace exactly with sales; indeed, as is pointed out in 15.33 below, they probably would not, but for the sake of simplicity it is assumed that they do.) The situation would then be as shown in balance sheet (*b*). There, although the operating ratios are still satisfactory and the net margin is maintained at 8% (net margin equals profit before tax as a percentage of turnover), the sudden appearance of a sizable overdraft suggests that something has gone wrong.

Just what, and how, can be seen by asking what balance sheet (*a*) means. The owners of the business have started it off with £30,000 capital, to which have been added another £5,000 in retained profits over the years, plus £840 from the most recent year's trading. This total of £35,840 has been used to acquire £17,000-worth of fixed assets, leaving £18,840 (the working capital figure) to finance actual production and trading operations – buying, processing, and 'carrying' inputs until the output embodying them has been finally paid for.

When expansion starts, trade suppliers oblige by making larger amounts of raw materials etc. available, so the value of their outstanding claims rises to £7,500. With higher production, stocks of all kinds rise to £15,000; with higher sales, trade debtors go up to £30,000. The small cash balance previously held is absorbed in the expansion. So far, so good: the current liabilities, at £16,740, still seem well covered by the current assets of £45,000; the net margin is still 8%; and the business has clearly grown, assets now totalling £62,000 instead of last year's £48,000. The question is, just how is this extra £14,000-worth of (current) assets being financed? Who is putting up the money for them to be provided for the business? They certainly have not been given to it, free.

Remember what the figures mean. The proprietors put £30,000 into the business to start with and have since left in it another £8,600 (revenue reserves plus current year's profit), making £38,600 all told. Fixed assets have absorbed £17,000 of this, leaving £21,600 in working capital to cover the firm's running costs. This £21,600, plus anything obtainable from any other source, is what is available to carry, in a financial sense, any stocks of materials held and any output sold but not yet paid for, and also to provide whatever cash balance is thought desirable. So it is increased by the sums borrowed from suppliers (£7,500), from the owners (£3,000, i.e. the as yet unpaid dividend), and the tax collector (£6,240). This gives a grand total of £38,340 – to cover both the cost of all the stocks held (£15,000) and the value of trade debtors (£30,000). Whether the desired cash balance is zero or not, there is in fact none. Altogether, these requirements come to £45,000 – which is £6,660 more than the resources available. In other words, this increase in output, although physically within the original powers of the business, financially was not. Achieving it calls for an extra £6,660 – to be raised either by overdraft, by an increased proprietors' stake, or by whatever other suitable means presents itself.

The firm may be able to obtain these additional funds without serious dificulty – although its chances of doing so, and the terms it might be offered, would be improved if it were able to ask well in advance of the need actually to spend the funds. (This ability is strengthened by the cash flow forecasting dealt with in Chapter 16.) But that does not mean that it would always be able to do so – still less that the owners would always be able to rely on other organizations to finance their expansion, without themselves making any further permanent contribution to their business's resources. The paradox for the owners is that the expansion they embark on seems to offer them the prospect of being able to take more out of the business, whereas in reality, unless external funds can be tapped, its continued existence depends on their putting more into it.

Suppose the directors were able to arrange overdraft facilities and, hoping that further expansion would solve their problems, in the ensuing twelve months again raised sales by 50%, with appropriate increases in stocks, trade debtors, and creditors. The position at the end of the second year is shown in balance sheet (c). The overdraft has doubled to £13,400; the bank manager may not be too happy at seeing his share of the resources of this particular customer risen from about 11% to about 17%.

Furthermore, it has been assumed that the business's output and sales could expand without any increase at all in plant or other fixed assets. Spare capacity, however, is finite; sooner or later extra output would require more fixed assets, even if it were only another vehicle to carry the bigger loads involved. But any allocation of funds to pay for such items would at once aggravate the existing shortage of finance to carry the current assets, and the pressure to get more money to pay for the desired rate of growth would thus become even greater. If the money could not be produced, the business would be heading for rapid collapse.

15.33 EVIDENCE OF OVERTRADING

Signs of this trouble will appear partly in the firm's balance sheet and partly in a deterioration in the operating ratios summarized in Table 15.2.

Table 15.2. Operating ratios of the business in Table 15.1 as overtrading develops (%)

	Year 1	Year 2	Year 3
Current assets: current liabilities	255	192	183
Stock: sales	10	10	9·3
Trade debtors: sales	20	20	18·2
Trade creditors: sales	5	5	6
Trade debtors: trade creditors	400	400	304
Net margin (profits before tax: sales)	8	8	6
Net-of-tax profit: capital + retained earnings	10·7	15	14·4
Working capital: sales	18·84	14·4	12·48

There will be a chronic shortage of cash, since for every penny that can be laid hands on there are several pressing and essential claims. If the bank manager is willing, an overdraft will appear and persist; if he is not, some other form of indebtedness will emerge. (Whichever it is, its cost must lower profits.)

Because of the cash shortage, the business will delay settling with its suppliers as long as possible; trade creditors as a percentage of sales will tend to rise. Conversely, in an effort to speed up the inflow of cash, an over-trading firm will push stocks out to customers as quickly as possible, in order to move output one stage nearer the point at which it will produce a return flow of desperately needed funds; under this influence, stocks as a percentage of sales will tend to fall. The influence may be offset to a greater or lesser extent by the inability of the business to complete orders; the extended credit which suppliers have to give may make them, in turn, either slow to deliver goods or unwilling to do so at all. Accordingly, items required to finish work in progress may be delayed, causing capital to be tied up in partly completed goods much longer than would normally be the case.

Furthermore, since in normal circumstances a business reckons to sell things for more than it paid for them, trade debtors will considerably exceed trade creditors. The size of this excess will depend on such things as the amount of value added and the degree of competition in the industry concerned; in many branches of manufacturing the difference between the two values may be ten times what it is in, say, food retailing. In this example, the important signal is that debtors are shrinking in relation to not only sales, but also creditors.

Those having business dealings with the overtrading concern will have other clues to its predicament. Suppliers will become aware of the cash discounts forgone and of the delaying tactics used to keep them quiet, e.g. the issuing of post-dated cheques and payments made on account at the last moment. Customers will become aware of the urgency of the pressure on them to pay, and of the discounts offered for early settlement. The bank manager will see the post-dated cheques, and the overdraft running perman-ently at its limit and exceeding that limit on paydays. All these may there-fore infer, even if they do not actually know, that something is badly wrong; they will realize that the liquidity problem must eventually erode profits. In this example, although return on capital employed goes up sharply in year 2, and in the following year is still well above that obtained in year 1, profits are falling under the impact of the cost of borrowing and price cutting; the net margin in year 3 is down from 8% to 6%.

15.4 SUMMARY

Businesses raise funds in order to reach goals such as survival, profitability, and growth. These goals are not always mutually consistent, and growing businesses, in particular, must ensure that their financial resources expand in line with their physical output. The overtrading which otherwise results shows in worsening operating ratios and the general business behaviour of the firm concerned. Failure to cure the overtrading with additional funds and a slower, more soundly-based expansion leads to collapse. Attention must therefore be constantly given to maintaining the right level of working capital.

16 The Profitability Goal and Investment Decisions:
(i) Preparation of Cash Flow Forecasts

16.1 INTRODUCTION

Assuming that a proper balance between fixed and current assets can be established and maintained and that overtrading does not occur, there remains the major question of how to choose the 'right' or most profitable assets in which to deploy the funds available. The funds could be used either for portfolio investment, i.e. the buying of share/loan certificates and other paper titles to income and capital, or for real investment, which means the physical creation of fresh productive capacity. Everything which follows applies equally to both types, whether the investor is an individual or a company and whether he is contemplating buying an existing enterprise, stocks, or shares for a portfolio, or plant and equipment for some productive operation.

Ultimately, however, there can be no income from paper securities unless real investment has occurred. (Bear in mind that the subject here is business, not public, finance. Although in a real sense there can be no income unless physically productive investment has taken place, money income – of real significance to its recipients! – can be and is distributed to holders of government debt; this debt has been largely issued in wartime, and the distribution occurs despite the fact that the resources transferred by the original capital transaction have long since been burned, sunk, blown up, or otherwise destroyed.) Attention will therefore be concentrated on the problem of real investment, i.e. on:

1 How to identify the potentially most profitable outlays on such things as plant, machinery, and equipment.
2 How to identify less profitable proposals and downright losers, in order to avoid them.

As already noted, looking at investment in fixed assets has the advantage that it always entails the consideration of associated investment in current assets. Concentrating on the latter would not necessarily lead to the consideration of fixed assets at all; some types of businesses, e.g. publishers and those providing professional services, may operate successfully with very little in the way of fixed assets of any kind.

This chapter reviews the reasons for investment, and the first step in making correct investment decisions: the preparation of proper cash flow forecasts. (The second step. i.e. the evaluation of these forecasts, is dealt with in Chapter 17.)

16.2 DEFINITION OF INVESTMENT

Investment means the commitment of resources now, or in the immediate future, in the expectation of rewards spread over the more distant future. In the case of major capital works, e.g. building a large power station, the immediate future may mean the next five or six years.

16.3 REASONS FOR INVESTMENT

The first consideration of an entrepreneur may simply be survival. In this context, if the business ceases to exist nothing else matters. Linked with this, or as a separate concern, he may wish to preserve his share of a particular market; this seems to be at least a partial explanation why chemical companies invest in synthetic fibre plant at times when they know all their competitors are doing the same. He may seek to retain leadership in a particular field, or to keep up with the real or imagined demands of 'progress'; much of the initial outlay on computer installations may have been for this reason.

The rewards expected from investment are clearly not necessarily profits, nor is profit maximization the only reason for investment. Profit maximization is, in any case, an ambiguous concept covering both (i) the largest absolute profits (whether made as quickly as possible, or more slowly and discreetly in order not to attract attention) and (ii) the largest profits relative to outlays. However, profit maximization – usually in the second sense – is generally assumed to be the goal of the investor because it is no less plausible than the other objectives and has the advantage of being more quantifiable than some.

16.4 TYPES OF INVESTMENT

Investment can be classified into three types, according to its immediate purpose.

1 The installation of fresh plant to turn out new products not yet on the market – not, at least, as far as the particular producer is concerned. This

comes first in the chronological sequence of a business's development and also in terms of the risk involved.

2 The expansion of existing productive capacity, either to meet growing demand in markets already served, or to cater for markets so far untapped.

3 The maintenance of existing production facilities by replacing parts of them which are worn out or have become obsolete. This is the least risky investment.

Two comments may be made at this stage.

1 Replacement, in times of technical change, is not likely to be exact substitution; the new asset is an improvement on the old by virtue of the design changes and new knowledge embodied in it. Strangely enough therefore, some expansion of capacity will result from simply maintaining it intact!

2 The installation of new capacity, whether as a net addition to the capital stock or not, does not necessarily mean the generation of any income at all – it may remain idle.

16.5 SIGNIFICANCE OF CASH FLOWS

For whatever reason an investment proposal is contemplated, a decision on it will require the calculation of certain financial characteristics called its 'cash flow'. (Unfortunately, this term has more than one meaning, like some others in this field; it is not used here in the sense given on p. 42.)

The necessity for this calculation is based on the critical importance to a business of the movements of cash into and out of it. It is true that for all businesses cash (i.e. cash in hand plus bank balances) is either a non-earning or a low-earning asset which is usually kept to a minimum – *pace* Slater Walker in 1974. The size of this minimum, relative to other assets, naturally varies with the type of activity carried on; most banks, for example, probably want a larger one than most manufacturing companies.

But just because the *stocks* of cash are relatively unimportant at any one time, it does not follow that the *flows* of cash are equally unimportant. They are, in fact, absolutely vital. A business may not necessarily start with a formal input of cash – its proprietor(s) may bring the required assets into it direct – but all its operations will depend on movements of cash into and out of it. It may seem obvious, but it must never be forgotten that, although a firm's balance sheet normally reveals a situation predominantly in a non-cash form, every item in that balance sheet has resulted from the cash flows (actual transfers of bank balances) into and out of that firm, with the minor qualification in the previous sentence. Also, the size of every item has been determined by those cash flows. The owners' equity and the long-term liabilities, if any, represent a flow of cash which has come into the business over the years, while the current liabilities comprise claims the discharge of which will cause movements of cash out of the business in the near future. Similarly, the fixed assets have been acquired as a result of cash outlays, while the current assets will shortly result in cash inflows.

The success or failure of any business depends on the balance between these cash inflows and outflows. If the latter are consistently less than the former, the business will survive and perhaps flourish; if the reverse is true, it will shrink and eventually fold up.

As with the business as a whole, so with the individual assets which make it up; the contribution of each asset to the health of the whole organization depends on the balance of the cash flows associated with it. Hence, in considering the attractiveness or otherwise of an investment proposal (either by itself or as part of a collection called a project), attention must be focused on the cash flows, i.e. the movements of cash in and out, which may reasonably be expected to arise in connection with it.

16.6 CASH FLOW FORECASTS FOR LIQUIDITY CONTROL

Before concentrating on their use in investment appraisal, and bearing in mind the dangers of overtrading reviewed in Chapter 15, it is as well to note that the preparation of such forecasts is scarcely a new development, based on concern with ways of assessing investment opportunities. It is, in fact, a job which must be regularly done in any rightly conducted enterprise, partly in order to guard against overtrading and partly (and more commonly) to ensure that the business maintains the desired level of liquidity – no more and no less. The following example illustrates this 'liquidity control' aspect of cash flow forecasts.

16.61 PREPARATION OF A CASH FLOW FORECAST

Suppose a company finance officer has before him the information set out below, from which to determine the availability of, and the need for, cash in his firm for the next six months (August to January):

Bank balance and cash in hand: £5,000.
Expected sales: 10,000 units at £10 per unit (one-quarter on a cash basis, the rest on two months' credit). Monthly sales have been at this volume and price since the beginning of the year, and an approved 5% price increase taking effect on 1 October is not expected to affect volume.

Raw materials' cost: £40,000 a month. Suppliers allow one month's credit and, since their prices have recently risen, no further increase is likely in the next six months.

Tax: Taxable income was £150,000 last year. Corporation tax at 52% is payable on 1 January.

Wages: £6,000 a week, with an approved 10% rise to take effect from 1 January. There are five paydays in August and November, four in each of the other months. A bonus of two weeks' pay is to be given in December (by which time any remaining price and income controls will have been removed).

Other cash outlays: Other operating expenses will be £18,000 a month throughout the period. A progress payment to contractors engaged in extending the plant will absorb £50,000 in October.

Table 16.1 gives the cash flow forecast that the finance officer will produce using the above data.

Table 16.1. Cash flow forecast: August to January (£)

Item	Aug.	Sept.	Oct.	Nov.	Dec.	Jan.
Opening balance	5,000	17,000	35,000	4,250	17,500	28,500
Receipts:						
Cash sales	25,000	25,000	26,250	26,250	26,250	26,250
Credit sales	75,000	75,000	75,000	75,000	78,750	78,750
Total in (a)	105,000	117,000	136,250	105,500	122,500	133,500
Payments:						
Purchases	40,000	40,000	40,000	40,000	40,000	40,000
Wages	30,000	24,000	24,000	30,000	24,000	26,400
Bonus	—	—	—	—	12,000	—
Tax	—	—	—	—	—	78,000
Expenses	18,000	18,000	18,000	18,000	18,000	18,000
Progress payments	—	—	50,000	—	—	—
Total out (b)	88,000	82,000	132,000	88,000	94,000	162,400
Balance forward (a−b); negative in brackets	17,000	35,000	4,250	17,500	28,500	(28,900)

16.62 USE OF THE CASH FLOW FORECAST

From the forecast he can see that the business will be comfortably liquid for four out of the six months, and it will then be his responsibility to extract the maximum advantage from such temporary surpluses consistent with their size and the required degree of liquidity. (They may, for example, be placed on deposit with a bank, invested in Treasury Bills (if they reach the minimum bid size of £50,000), or lent through a loan broker as mentioned on p. 58.) He can also see that the safety margin will be rather slim in October, and that there is a predicted shortfall of the cash required in January. On the strength of this warning he should take whatever precautionary action is appropriate – arranging overdraft facilities (if they do not already exist) or some similar access to funds, on a stand-by basis for October and for use in January.

Then month by month, he updates the forecast by omitting the first month and adding another one, six months ahead, and making whatever changes that more recent information justifies. In this way he keeps the cash position of the business under constant review. Thus he avoids such embarrassment as not being able to pay employees at the end of the week because nobody has thought about making sure the cash required is at hand. It would be little consolation to the unpaid workforce that their money and jobs were quite safe and the business quite solvent; a minimum of liquidity is also essential. This cannot be relied upon to be present, all the time, just by chance; it must be arranged. That is what cash flow forecasts of this type are for, and when used in this way they have nothing to do with investment appraisal.

(What they do fit into is funds flow plans, which are drawn up for some longer period, generally a year. These plans show the expected balance sheet changes in not just bank accounts but also earning assets generally; they show too the sources, other than cash holdings, which will finance the acquisition of those extra assets as the business develops.)

16.7 CASH FLOW FORECASTS FOR INVESTMENT APPRAISAL

16.71 INTRODUCTION

For a business to make the best use of the resources available for investment, it must take two related steps.

1 *It must prepare a cash flow forecast* for each proposed investment; this will be similar in principle to the one above, but will obviously differ in the detail recorded. It will set out as accurately as possible the anticipated amounts and timing of (i) the capital and running costs involved (including any changes in working capital, and any effects in the cash flow of other parts of the firm), and (ii) the benefits expected to emerge – in the form of either lower costs (hence reduced cash outlays) or higher sales (hence increased cash inflows) or both.
2 *It must appraise or evaluate this forecast* in order to see how attractive the proposal is. If there are two or more competing claims on the available resources, each cash flow forecast must be appraised, by the same technique, before a rational choice between them can be made.

This second step is dealt with in the next chapter, but it is important to grasp that each of the two is essential. Neither alone is sufficient. Thus, no matter how accurately and painstakingly a cash flow forecast is prepared, it will remain just a bewildering mass of figures – misleading and perhaps even useless – if it is not properly assessed and if the signals it gives are not properly understood. Similarly, the most sophisticated and reliable assessment technique will not lead to correct resource allocation and investment decisions if it is applied to inaccurate material. The computer maxim 'Garbage in, garbage out' holds in this field too.

The first of these two steps is illustrated below with two competing proposals; the rest of the chapter describes the terms and calculations involved.

16.72 THE PROPOSALS

Proposal A is to replace a machine which has been completely written off for tax purposes with a new one costing £8,000. This investment will result in the saving of one man's wages, National Insurance, and other employer's contributions totalling £2,500 in the first year. The new machine will have an effective life of five years, during which it will produce the same quantity and quality of output as the one it replaces.

Proposal B is to buy a new machine, costing £6,400. It will have an estimated life of four years, will not save labour, but will increase output. The expected benefits in the form of higher net sales revenues are £1,000, £2,500, £8,000, and £4,000 in years 1 to 4 respectively.

The business must take into account certain additional information, and make certain assumptions, as follows.

1 Its wage and other related costs in Proposal A will rise by 10% a year. This increase is quite specific; the problem of inflation, i.e. of generally rising prices, is considered on p. 178.
2 Each machine will be depreciated for tax purposes at 25% a year on the reducing balance of its cost.
3 Corporation tax at 52% is payable one year in arrears.
4 Enough profits from other activities are available to enable the firm to make full use of its depreciation allowances at the earliest opportunity. (If this were not so, the calculations would be significantly different).
5 A and B will require £500 and £2,000 respectively in extra working capital, recoverable in full at the end of the machines' working lives.
6 Scrap values (A: £200. B: nil) will be similarly recoverable.
7 Outlays and proceeds, unless immediate, occur at the end of the year in question.

With this data, the relevant cash flow forecasts can be drawn up (*see* Table 16.2).

Table 16.2. Cash flow forecasts for Proposals A and B (£)

Year	Outlay	Net proceeds	Tax effects Due on higher earnings	Tax effects Saved by depreciation allowances	Net cash flow
	(a)	(b)	(c)	(d)	(e) = (a + b + c + d)
Proposal A					
0	(8,500)	—	—	—	(8,500)
1	—	2,500	—	—	2,500
2	—	2,750	(1,300)	1,040	2,490
3	—	3,025	(1,430)	780	2,375
4	—	3,328	(1,573)	585	2,340
5	—	3,661	(1,731)	439	2,369
6	700	—	(1,903)	1,316	113
Proposal B					
0	(8,400)	—	—	—	(8,400)
1	—	1,000	—	—	1,000
2	—	2,500	(520)	832	2,812
3	—	8,000	(1,300)	624	7,324
4	—	4,000	(4,160)	468	308
5	2,000	—	(2,080)	1,404	1,324

16.73 THE TIMING OF THE FLOWS

As will become clear later, this is most important. Year 0 represents now. Given assumption (7), proceeds in year 1 arrive at the end of that year (i.e. one year from now); similarly, outgoings in year 5 occur at the end of that year (i.e. five years from now).

This does not provide a completely accurate record of the movements of cash into and out of the business. For example, if Proposal A were adopted, the cash savings would start to accrue at once at the rate of roughly £50 a week – not in a lump sum at the end of the year. Since this is likely to be true of all the other cash flows too, however, it does not affect their relative impact on the business concerned, and the possible loss of accuracy due to working in yearly intervals is more than offset by the saving in time and effort it permits. If, however, there is some predictable and large 'lumpiness' in the cash flows associated with an investment proposal – e.g. big cash movements at one- or six-monthly intervals – the time divisions in the forecast should be altered to accommodate them.

16.74 OUTLAYS

Entries in this column basically refer to the net movements of cash out of the investing business due to the acquisition of the assets under consideration. They must be recorded in some way which distinguishes them clearly from inflows; each firm has its own convention for this, and here they are shown in brackets.

In Proposal A, the new machine will cost £8,000 and £500 is needed for extra working capital; the sum of these constitutes the outlay involved. If any scrap value were obtained for the old machine, that would serve to reduce the cash outlay and the £8,000 would be lowered accordingly, assuming, of course, that the scrap proceeds were available immediately - if not, they would have to be shown as proceeds in the appropriate year.

A's scrap value is shown as being recovered in year 6 – an entry without brackets signifies an inflow, even if it occurs in an 'outlay' column. The working capital is also recorded as being recovered in year 6. Again, such an entry may not reflect completely accurately the cash movement involved; while it is unlikely that a whole year would pass before the working capital was released, it is unrealistic to suppose that all the funds tied up in this way would be freed the minute the machine's life ended. Hence, recording the recovery in year 5 would not accord with common sense. (When cash grants to stimulate investment were provided by the government, they also served to cut net cash outlays. Since they were not received as soon as the qualifying outlay was made, they were best treated as 'proceeds' in year 1. Extra columns for these and other items may be inserted into the forecast form as required. The critical things to get right are the amounts and the timing; the heading they come under is a matter of convenience.)

Bear in mind that these two proposals are highly simplified for the sake of exposition. Many real investment projects involve payments to contractors as construction and installation work progresses, so that outlays cannot appear in the relevant cash forecasts as one lump sum in the present, but must be shown as a series of instalments spread over perhaps several years. However, this does not alter the meaning of the term 'outlays' as those outflows of cash which a business incurs if it undertakes an investment, which would not otherwise have occurred. This meaning may properly be expanded to include quantifiable opportunity costs, e.g. rent of floor space which has to be forgone if a proposed investment occupies that space. But it specifically excludes any share of existing overheads from the whole appraisal procedure; it takes into account only those overheads which will be affected if the proposal is undertaken – and then only to the extent of the extra cash movements involved.

16.75 PROCEEDS

Less needs to be said about this term. Proceeds measure the net cash benefit which a business will receive, year by year, if a proposed investment is undertaken. In Proposal A, this benefit comes from reduced cash outflows, because one fewer employee is needed; in B, it comes from higher cash inflows arising from higher sales proceeds (net of all the associated running costs).

Proceeds are not the same as profits. The difference between them is due partly to the different impact of overheads, mentioned above, and partly to the effect of depreciation. The latter, as was pointed out in Chapter 4, rarely involves a cash flow directly – but it can make a critical impression on the cash flow of a proposal because of the way it affects tax payments.

16.76 CALCULATIONS

The calculations of the figures shown in the cash flow forecast for Proposal A are set out below; those for B in general follow the same pattern, and where this is so they are not repeated.

(a) Proceeds

Assumption (1) requires A's first year's savings of £2,500 to be raised by 10% annually. B calls for no adjustment and is a straightforward list of the net sales revenues over the four years.

(b) Tax due on higher earnings

If, as a result of accepting A, the business's operating costs are cut by £2,500 in the first year, its profits in that year will be £2,500 higher – other things being equal. If its profits are higher it will naturally have to pay more tax; how much more will depend on the rate at which profits are taxed. Assumption (3) gives this rate as 52%, so the extra tax payable will be 52% of £2,500, i.e. £1,300. Assumption (3) also says that payment of tax is one year in arrears, i.e. one year after the taxable profit has been made. This outflow of cash to the Revenue authorities will therefore occur in year 2. The other tax payments are calculated in the same way, as 52% of the preceding year's proceeds.

(c) Tax saved on depreciation allowances

As explained in Chapter 4, the size and timing of the payments to settle a tax liability on profits are influenced by the depreciation allowed by the Revenue authorities. For new machinery, they now permit either 100% of the cost to be charged against profits in the asset's first year, or 25% of the reducing balance of the cost to be charged each year [1]. The latter has been chosen here, to enable the calculations to be shown.

If A is accepted, in year 1 the firm will be able to claim £2,000 as depreciation allowable for tax purposes (25% of the cost of the new machine;

working capital does not qualify for any allowance). As a result, profits liable for tax that year will be lower by £2,000, other things being equal, and if profits are lower the tax on them will also be lower. At a 52% tax rate, the tax saved will be £1,040. Since savings, like payments, take effect one year after the profits to which they relate have been made, this sum appears in year 2.

In the second year of the asset's life, the business will be entitled to charge 25% of the asset's remaining value against its taxable income. This value is £6,000 (£8,000 —£2,000, as shown above); 25% of £6,000 is £1,500, and this amount of depreciation will save the business £780 (52% of £1,500) in year 3. Note that, to arrive at the balance outstanding on the asset account at the start of a year, the previous balance must be reduced by the last depreciation charge – *NOT* the last tax saving.

This calculation is repeated up to and including the penultimate year of the asset's life. Then, since the depreciation allowances are intended in principle to enable the full cost of the asset to be set against taxable income over the course of its life, any balance remaining on the account is charged to the final year's profits. For A, this balance will be £2,531, and the tax bill will thus be reduced by 52% of this, i.e. by £1,316. (In practice, current U.K. arrangements provide for the pooling of all qualifying expenditure, and for the calculation of allowable depreciation on this pool figure rather than on the value of individual items [1]).

(d) Net cash flow

This, as the column heading shows, is a horizontal sum of the entries appearing in each year. For reasons which will become clear later, the columns are not added vertically, although it may be noted that column *(d)* must total 52% of the cost of the asset which qualifies for depreciation allowances.

16.8 INFLATION

If the purchasing power of money is expected to remain reasonably constant, the net cash flow is ready for appraisal. However, in a time of inflation the value of future payments and receipts is falling in real terms. Therefore, before any appraisal can be made, the cash flow forecast must be adjusted so that the individual pounds in it have a standard purchasing power. If this is not done, investment proposals will be made to look attractive just because inflation is raising their monetary benefits; in real terms, they may not look good at all. This adjustment is made by discounting the net cash flow – as shown in Chapter 17 – at the expected rate of inflation.

The vital point to grasp about this adjustment (which may be up instead of down, as the general price level has been known to fall and to stay down for long periods) is that it is required only if the value of money is expected to change. Not only will the adjustment be unnecessary if prices are thought likely to be generally stable, but if change is expected only in some particular prices or costs it can be accommodated in the cash flow forecast, as shown in column (b) of Proposal A.

16.9 SUMMARY

Although investment – portfolio or real, individual or corporate – may be undertaken for various reasons, profit maximization is assumed to be the dominant one. The profitability of a business in general, and/or of any investment proposal in particular, depends ultimately on the size and timing of the cash inflows and outflows generated by it. Therefore, in order to identify the most attractive of the competing opportunities open to him, the investor must first prepare for each a forecast of these expected cash flows. (Such cash flow forecasts are not used only for investment appraisal; their preparation and inspection should be a routine procedure in all businesses, to ensure that prospective cash deficits and surpluses are foreseen and properly dealt with.) The forecast must show, as accurately as possible, both the amount and the timing of the expected cash outlays and proceeds – as affected by current taxation and as adjusted, when necessary, for changes in the purchasing power of money.

17 The Profitability Goal and Investment Decisions: (2) Appraising the Forecasts

17.1 INTRODUCTION

Since all investors have some resource constraint which makes it impossible for them to accept every opportunity open to them, a satisfactory appraisal technique must be able not only to separate good proposals from bad ones but also arrange the former in some acceptable order of merit, e.g. that of producing the highest return in the resources employed. Using the net cash flows calculated for Proposals A and B in Chapter 16, this chapter considers evaluation by the pay-back period method and by discounting techniques, emphasizing the advantages of the latter.

17.2 THE PAY-BACK PERIOD

17.21 DEFINITION

The pay-back period is defined as the time which must elapse before the outlay on a project is completely recovered from the rest of the net cash flow expected from it. The shorter this time, the more attractive the proposal.

17.22 CALCULATION

The period is calculated by summing these expected cash flows, from the start of the proposal's life, until they equal the outlay.

Applying this method to Proposal A shows that it has a pay-back period of about 3·5 years:

Year	Net cash flow £	Cumulative net cash flow £
1	2,500	2,500
2	2,490	4,990
3	2,375	7,365

At the end of year 3, £1,135 is yet required to reach the total outlay of £8,500, this requirement being roughly a half of year 4's net cash flow of £2,340. Although cash flows are conventionally recorded as occurring at discrete yearly intervals, the pay-back period calculation assumes that they occur evenly throughout the year to which they refer. A similar calculation shows that Proposal B has a pay-back period of approximately 2·6 years. With this criterion, therefore, B is better than A.

17.23 ADVANTAGES

1 The method is simplicity itself – nothing more than elementary arithmetic is required.
2 By emphasizing the importance of the early recovery of outlays, it seems to take account of the basically risky nature of investment and of the fact that the further away in time proceeds are, the greater the probability that they will not come up to expectations – or appear at all!

Indeed, a concentration on proposals with short pay-back periods makes good sense in those industries where technical change is rapid and where assets with apparently long earnings lives, based on physical durability, are in constant danger of being overtaken by obsolescence. Furthermore, any firm – whether in a rapidly changing field or not – which has a chronic cash problem will not want to commit itself to investment outlays which do not generate a speedy flow of cash back into the business; that is, any firm which finds that expansion on sound lines is being constantly held back by the sort of liquidity strains which may lead to overtrading if not properly handled, will not want to make such commitments.

17.24 DISADVANTAGES

Not all firms fit into one or other of these categories, however, and the pay-back period approach has grave drawbacks even for those that do.

1 It ignores differences in the timing of inflows *within* the pay-back period. For example, although Proposal A is inferior to Proposal B in that it has a longer pay-back period, it recovers nearly 60 % of its outlay in the first two years of its life while B recovers only about 45 % in the same period – and it is always better to recover a given amount of money earlier rather than later.
2 It ignores what happens in a proposal *after* the pay-back period is over. It happens that B has a slight edge over A on this score, recovering about

52% to A's 44% of outlay during that time – but its pay-back period can give no indication of this, and the positions might easily have been reversed.

17.25 USEFULNESS

Actual and potential discrepancies of the kinds mentioned above should not appear in a satisfactory appraisal system. Probably the best way of using the pay-back approach is as a screen to eliminate any project not worth further attention, and to provide a short list of potentially worthwhile proposals which will justify more careful assessment.

17.3 DISCOUNTED CASH FLOW TECHNIQUES

17.31 INTRODUCTION

From what has been said so far, it is clear that an acceptable method of appraising competing investment proposals must be capable of two things:

1 Giving proper weight to the incidence over time of the cash inflows and outflows associated with them.
2 Being able to do so to the whole of those flows, during the entire expected lives of the proposals.

It is because of their ability to meet these two fundamental demands that techniques involving the discounting of cash flows have become widely accepted. Such techniques are based on the need to give less weight (because they carry less value) to given outlays and proceeds which will arise in the future, than to ones of the same nominal amount arising in the present.

17.32 THE NEED FOR DISCOUNTING FUTURE MONEY VALUES

Before examining the application of the techniques, it is as well to understand the truth of the proposition a sum of money now, is worth more than the same nominal amount available in, say, a year's time. There are three reasons for this.

(a) Default of payment

A given sum of money now is more attractive to the recipient than a promise of the same sum later because the promise may not be kept. Any of a vast range of possibilities may prevent the payment's being made, e.g. the dishonesty or death of the promiser. All the uncertainty may be removed by having the money now.

(b) Subjective time preference

Anyone offered a choice between a sum of money, a new suit, or a car *now* and the same sum of money or material gain *in a year's time* will be sensible to take the offer now. This is so, not because the benefit may not materialize – the supply side of the situation can be guaranteed in a variety of ways – but because next year the potential beneficiary may be too busy, tired, or ill, perhaps even dead, and the chooser will then have lost, to no purpose, that which he sought merely to postpone. There is no question here of being rewarded for abstinence if the chooser denies himself what is on offer now; the exchange is of a car now for the same car next year – not a superior model to compensate him for the year he will have gone without. In such circumstances there is no point in not enjoying whatever is available now; present satisfactions count for more than future ones. Expressing this in its simplest monetary terms, £1 now is worth more than £1 in the future.

(c) Investment gains

The £1 now can be invested, so that with accrued interest it will be worth more than £1 after a year. How much more will depend on the rate of interest and the frequency with which it is applied, but as long as that rate is positive (in nominal, not necessarily real, terms) the £1 now will grow to more than £1 in the future. This reason, incidentally, does not depend on the existence of inflation – nor, if it exists, on its degree. Interest is paid on loans when prices are completely stable, and even when they are falling. Naturally, when prices are rising, not only does the present £1 become more attractive and the future £1 less so because of the larger amount of goods and services which the former will command, but also the interest which the present £1 will earn becomes more significant, rather than less, if prices rise in the meantime.

17.33 THE BASIC DISCOUNTING FORMULA

Clearly, if £1 now is worth more than £1 in the future, £1 in the future must be worth less than £1 now. How much less depends, as before, on the rate of interest at which it is discounted and on the frequency of discounting.

Assume, for the sake of convenience, that this discounting occurs once a year. Then, if £1 could be invested at 10% to become £1·1 in a year's time, £1 in a year's time discounted at 10% would be worth £1 divided by 1·1, or £0·909 now. (The proof of this is that £0·909 invested now at 10% would amount to £1 after a year: £0·909 + £0·0909 = £1, for all practical purposes.) As a general proposition, the present value of a future sum may be found from:

$$P = S \div (1 + i)^n$$

where P is the present value to be found

S is the future sum of money

i is the rate of interest (expressed as a fraction of 100) at which S is to be discounted

n is the number of years S is in the future

Suppose, for example, that someone due to inherit £10,000 in four years' time has a pressing need for the money now. If 10% were the going rate of interest, the present sum for which this expectation would exchange would be found by substituting these figures in the formula:

$$P = £10,000 \div \left(1 + \frac{10}{100}\right)^4$$

$$= £10,000 \div \left(\frac{110}{100}\right)^4$$

$$= £10,000 \div \left(\frac{14,641}{10,000}\right)$$

$$= £6,830$$

(This is shown worked out the long way. The answer could be obtained much more easily by looking in the appropriate discount table, finding the present value of £1 four years away at 10%, and multiplying that figure (£0·683) by 10,000. However, these tables are built on the above formula; knowledge of it will always enable answers to be worked out if discount tables are not available.) From the £6,830 should be deducted the fees of the lawyer who draws up the assignment, and the cost of the insurance cover on the beneficiary's life; this cover would have to be arranged to safeguard whoever advanced the money against the possibility that the beneficiary might not live to collect the inheritance. The rest is the beneficiary's, and he should not settle for less. Remember that, at the stated rate of interest and for the stated period, £6,830 now is the same as £10,000 then (add interest at 10% a year compound to £6,830 for four years and see), so that in no real sense is the beneficiary getting less than he is entitled to.

17.4 DISCOUNTED CASH FLOW (D.C.F.) YIELD

This basic valuation formula is the essence of the discounted cash flow (d.c.f.) appraisal methods. Applying it to the cash flows expected from investments enables calculations to be made of their yields (also called their 'internal rates of return') and/or their net present values. (The yields discussed in the Appendix to Chapter 14 may be thought of as showing external rates of return, just as the p:e ratio shows a pay-back period.)

17.41 CALCULATION

Working out the d.c.f. yield of an investment entails finding, by trial and error, the rate of interest which, when used to discount the relevant cash flows, will make the present value of the outlays exactly equal to that of the inflows. This sounds not only forbidding but also interminable; fortunately, it turns out to be a good deal less daunting and slow than it appears.

The operation can be broken down into a series of steps.

1 Select an interest rate. Literally any rate will do, but if discount tables are available it will obviously pay to select one which they cover; if they are not, choose one which keeps the arithmetic as simple as possible.
2 Use this rate to find the present value of the net cash flow for each year.
3 Add up these present values to find the net present value of the proposal.

The resulting figure will be either (i) negative, signifying that the present value of the expected outlays exceeds that of the expected proceeds((ii) positive, showing that the present value of the expected proceeds exceeds that of the expected outlays, or (iii) zero, indicating that the present values of the expected outlays and proceeds are equal. If this last result is obtained, the rate of interest used for discounting *is* the d.c.f. yield of the investment, since it meets the requirement given earlier.

However, the chance of finding this yield rate at the first attempt is pretty remote, and it is as well to assume that more trials will have to be made. If the net present value (n.p.v.) resulting from the first trial is positive, the present value of the proceeds must be reduced further; the second trial must, accordingly, be made with a higher rate of interest. Conversely, if the n.p.v. emerging from the first trial is negative, the rate used was too high and another trial must be made with a lower one. How much higher or lower will depend on the balance (positive or negative) of n.p.v. to be eliminated; the bigger it is, the bigger must be the adjustment to the interest rate first used.

In principle, as indicated earlier, this procedure is repeated until the n.p.v. is zero. In practice, this may not be so. One reason for this is simply that, if working with ordinary discount tables, the investor will not be able to discriminate by more than $\frac{1}{4}\%$ or perhaps $\frac{1}{8}\%$ between one trial rate and another, and this may be too crude to allow the present values of net proceeds and outlays to be brought to exact equality. If a computer is used for the calculations, it can easily deal with this problem and produce a yield rate of interest which will exactly balance the present values concerned – going to as many decimal places as are necessary to do so. This, however, serves to emphasize the second and major reason why the exact yield rate may not be found; this is that such a degree of precision is both spurious and useless. It is spurious because, even though a rate of interest to several decimal places might show the precise cost of obtaining investment funds (the annual servicing charge expressed as a percentage of the net amount actually received might easily produce an answer in such a form), the uncertainties inherent in the cash flow forecast itself invalidate the apparent accuracy obtained. It is useless because no one would justify selecting between competing proposals on the basis of a difference in the yield rate of interest to the right of the decimal point. Even the units are suspect! The third reason why repeated trials to find the yield rate of interest are not made is that interpolation will provide a short-cut. Thus, if PV_1 and PV_h stand for the present values of the net proceeds discounted at the chosen low and high rates of interest respectively, then

$$\frac{PV_1 - \text{Outlay}}{PV_1 - PV_h} = \times \text{ Difference in the rates used}$$

will give a figure which, added to the low rate, will give the yield.

17.42 APPLICATION TO PROPOSALS A AND B

This procedure will now be applied to Proposal A, the first rate of interest used to discount the cash flows being 10%. Table 17.1 shows (from column (e) of Table 16.2) how many pounds are expected to move in and out of the investing business as a result of A, and at what yearly intervals they will move. Column (f) shows, to three decimal places, the present value of £1 in different future years. Multiplying each annual amount by the appropriate present value of £1 gives a present value for each future sum.

Table 17.1. Present values of net cash flow at 10% (Proposal A) (£)

Year	Net cash flow (e)	Present value of £1 expected (f)	Present value of (e) (g) = (e × f)
0	(8,500)	1·0	(8,500)
1	2,500	0·909	2,273
2	2,490	0·826	2,057
3	2,375	0·751	1,784
4	2,340	0·683	1,598
5	2,369	0·621	1,471
6	113	0·565	64
		Net present value =	747

Column (g) may then be totalled. On p. 178 it was mentioned that the amounts shown in the cash flow forecasts could be added horizontally but not vertically. The reason for this should now be clear: the amounts in the columns other than (g) are not in a common form. Before the basic arithmetical operations of addition or subtraction may be carried out in money terms, the amounts to be dealt with must first be expressed in some common form and notation. Notation is taken for granted; few people are likely to be confronted with a calculation involving amounts expressed in, say, Chinese, Roman, and Arabic numerals. Form may present more of a problem in two different ways – one obvious, the other less so. The obvious aspect appears when the amounts to be dealt with are expressed in different currencies; clearly, no meaningful addition of, say, dollars, yen, and francs can be made, and their aggregate value can be determined only after they have been converted into some common currency. The less obvious aspect is the one which matters here; it is that the sums involved may contain different amounts of time. It has already been emphasized that £1 in the future is not the same as £1 now, and that £1 in three years' time is not the same as £1 in four or any other number of years' time. Therefore, although a cash flow forecast uses a common notation (in this case, Arabic), and shows amounts expressed apparently in a common form (in this case, sterling), the figures in it may not be added or subtracted vertically (i.e. across time) until the time element in them has been standardized. This is achieved by converting all the net cash flows into their present value form – as shown in column (g). Then – and only then – may they be regarded as genuinely homogeneous and hence amenable to addition and subtraction.

Inflows for A total £9,247, outflows £8,500; the balance of these present values is (positive) £747. Thus, the d.c.f. yield is not 10%, and it can be inferred from the sign and the size of the balance that 10% is well below the yield rate. (A similar calculation for B shows that, at 10%, there is a positive n.p.v. of £1,364, so the adjustment required there is larger still.) A second trial, using 16%, gives the results in Table 17.2.

Table 17.2. Present values of net cash flow at 16% (Proposal A) (£)

Year	Net cash flow (e)	Present value of £1 expected (f)	Present value of (e) (g) = (e × f)
0	(8,500)	1·0	(8,500)
1	2,500	0·862	2,155
2	2,490	0·743	1,850
3	2,375	0·641	1,522
4	2,340	0·552	1,292
5	2,369	0·476	1,128
6	113	0·410	46
		Net present value =	(507)

Since the sign of the balance has changed, the yield rate of interest must lie between 10% and 16%. Interpolation shows it to be approximately 13·6%:

$$\frac{9{,}247 - 8{,}500}{9{,}247 - 7{,}993} \times 6\% = \frac{747}{1{,}254} \times 6\% = 3{\cdot}6\% \text{ approx.}$$

(This 3·6% is added to the low rate of 10%.) Applying the same procedure to B shows that its d.c.f. yield is roughly 16·2%. The general rule is that the higher the yield, the more attractive the investment. Hence, if the investor had to choose between A and B, the preferable proposal would be B.

17.43 SIGNIFICANCE OF THE D.C.F. YIELD

For proposals with a normal cash flow pattern of outlays followed by proceeds, the significance of the d.c.f. yield is that it is the highest rate of interest an investor can afford to pay – and not be worse off – in order to obtain funds to carry out the proposed investment, assuming that it is financed with borrowed money which is repaid, with accrued interest, from the proceeds of the investment as they come in.

Thus, Proposal A has a yield of about 13.6%. If the investor borrows at this rate the £8,500 needed to finance it, undertaking to repay the loan with interest from annually generated proceeds, the position will be as given in Table 17.3.

Table 17.3. Significance of the d.c.f. yield rate of interest

	£	£
Amount borrowed at 13·6% to finance Proposal A		8,500
At end of year 1, add interest @ 13·6%	1,156	
deduct proceeds	2,500	1,344
Amount owing at end of year 1		7,156
At end of year 2, add interest	973	
deduct proceeds	2,490	1,517
Amount owing at end of year 2		5,639
At end of year 3, add interest	767	
deduct proceeds	2,375	1,608
Amount owing at end of year 3		4,031
At end of year 4, add interest	548	
deduct proceeds	2,340	1,792
Amount owing at end of year 4		2,239
At end of year 5, add interest	305	
deduct proceeds	2,369	2,064
Amount owing at end of year 5		175
At end of year 6, add interest	24	
deduct proceeds	113	89
Balance (attributable to yield rate's being slightly below 13·6%, and to using only three decimal places in present values).		86

If the investor had undertaken to pay more than this 'yield' rate of interest, the borrowing charges would have been higher and the proceeds would not have covered the full amount of the debt. Equally, if he had been able to obtain the funds needed at a lower rate, there would have been a surplus left over for him. The higher the d.c.f. yield, the more likely it is that the investor will be able to find the funds he requires at a price below the yield rate; the bigger the difference between the two rates, the bigger is his potential gain. Another way of looking at it is that, given the cash flow forecast and the repayment arrangements, if the investor has to compete for funds, the yield sets a ceiling on the rate of interest he can afford to pay to get them.

It may be objected that the arrangements for repaying borrowed funds are unlikely to be on this sort of 'overdraft' basis, with the outstanding balance reduced as receipts come in; they are more likely to call for periodic fixed instalments of interest and capital, or for the regular payment of interest during the life of the loan and a lump-sum capital repayment at the end of it. This is not necessarily so; borrowers usually have some bargaining power, and lenders are not always averse to having repayments tailored to suit the borrowers' requirements. In any case, as Table 3·1 shows, a considerable amount of investment is financed from internal resources, which may conform closely to this pattern. However, if some more rigid repayment schedule had to be adopted, the calculations might need adjustment to take account, for example, of what the proceeds might earn if they could not be handed over completely to the lender at yearly intervals.

17.5 D.C.F. NET PRESENT VALUE

As mentioned in 17.4 above, d.c.f. appraisal may be based on either a proposal's yield or its n.p.v.

17.51 CALCULATION

The establishment of the n.p.v. of an investment differs in two respects from the establishment of the yield.

1 Instead of finding, by trial and error, the appropriate rate of interest, the appraiser uses a known rate – the business's cost of capital – and carries out one discounting operation with it.
2 Having done this, the appraiser simply subtracts the present value of the outlays from that of the proceeds to find the n.p.v. of the proposal under consideration.

17.52 APPLICATION

This has already been done for Proposals A and B; at a discount rate of 10%, the former had a n.p.v. of £747 and the latter one of £1,324 (both positive). It will be clear from what has been said that (i) if a proposal's n.p.v. is positive, it will do more than cover its costs, including interest at the stated rate, (ii) if zero, it will only just cover these costs, and (iii) if negative, it will fail to do so.

The rule, therefore, is that the higher the n.p.v., the more attractive is the proposal. However, a particular investment may show a large n.p.v. simply because it is on a large scale. In order to guard against selecting investments solely on the basis of the absolute size of their n.p.v.s, the n.p.v.s are often expressed as a percentage of the outlays involved and ranked accordingly. Nevertheless, if the proposals under consideration are mutually exclusive, the absolute size of the n.p.v.s involved may be the dominant influence in the choice. Put simply, an n.p.v. of £10 on an outlay of £1,000 (1%) is better than an n.p.v. of £9 on an outlay of £100 (9%) if only one of the two can be undertaken.

17.53 SIGNIFICANCE OF NET PRESENT VALUES

The n.p.v. figure represents the largest amount the investor can afford to borrow (to do with, now, exactly as he chooses, and not be worse off) over and above the sum required to finance the investment – assuming, as before, that the investment is paid for with borrowed funds and that the total loan (i.e. n.p.v. plus project cost) is repaid, with accrued interest, from the proceeds of the investment as they come in. Thus, in the case of Proposal A the n.p.v. (at 10%) is £747 and the cost of the proposal £8,500. The investor could therefore afford to raise the combined sum (£9,247) at that rate; spend the £747 *now* on wine, women, and song (singly, or in any preferred combination); invest the £8,500 in the proposed way (assuming he were still capable of doing so); and repay the whole amount plus interest from the proceeds as they were generated. A calculation similar to that in Table 17.3 will show that this is so.

Any positive n.p.v. is the present value of a proposal's expected net earnings. The investor contemplating A could, if he so desired, borrow just the £8,500 needed to pay for it, and then wait until the end of its earning life to collect as his reward the balance left after the loan plus accrued interest had been repaid. This balance would be £1,323 but, as was pointed out earlier, the investor would not be any better off through waiting – at a discount rate of 10% a year, £1,323 in six years' time is equal in value to £747 now.

17.54 THE COST OF CAPITAL

The n.p.v. approach assumes that the appraising business knows the rate of interest to be used in discounting the cash flows of any proposal – i.e. that it knows its cost of capital. This knowledge may be based on reliable information as to (i) how much it would have to pay to get the funds required to carry out the proposal it is contemplating, or (ii) if it already has the necessary resources, what they could earn in their next best employment. (The return it could reckon on as a lender would be less than what it would have to pay as a borrower. The latter has to meet the expenses of raising funds. Since these expenses are rewards for the services of intermediaries, they do not appear as income in the hands of lenders.)

This cost of capital is an average of the costs of the different types of capital that the company has in issue, weighted by their market values. Thus, if there are ordinary shares worth £1 million on which it reckons to earn 15% net of tax, and £500,000-worth of loan stock on which it pays $4\frac{1}{2}\%$ after tax, the weighted average cost of its capital is:

$$\frac{(2 \times 15) + (1 \times 4\frac{1}{2})}{3} = 11\frac{1}{2}\%$$

It is true that only one type of security may be issued for the purpose of financing any one particular investment, so that the rate paid at any one time may be above or below this weighted average. Over time, however, gearing considerations will lead the business to try to keep roughly constant the appropriate ratio between equity and prior-charge capital; if the balance between these two was about right to start with, it would be better to test all proposals with the $11\frac{1}{2}\%$ average rate than to submit some to 15% and others to $4\frac{1}{2}\%$ – depending on which type of capital was being raised to finance them..

17.6 D.C.F. AND PAY-BACK METHODS COMPARED

17.61 ADVANTAGES OF D.C.F. METHODS

The great advantage of the d.c.f. techniques – whether they produce the yield or the simpler, more relevant, and more widely used n.p.v. – is that they are able to deal properly with the critical problem of the timing of the cash flows of investment projects. By giving less weight (i.e. less value in present-day terms) to outlays and proceeds, the further away they are in time, and by taking into account all such outlays and proceeds over the whole anticipated life of proposals (not just those occurring in some arbitrarily-fixed shorter period), d.c.f. techniques overcome the two major defects of the pay-back approach. They have therefore been increasingly used for investment appraisal in both the public and the private sectors; government also, in its efforts to stimulate greater efficiency and faster growth, has urged all those responsible for investment decisions to use them [1].

17.62 DISADVANTAGES OF D.C.F. METHODS

Against them, it may be argued that they involve much more work than finding pay-back periods. There seems more than enough to do even if discount tables are at hand; if they are not, the sheer volume of arith-metic involved in applying the valuation formula is rather intimidating. D.c.f. methods may also be thought more difficult to grasp – probably largely because of the unfamiliarity of the discounting exercise.

Regarding the first point, tables of discount factors are usually readily available, as are computation aids of various kinds; thus, in any real-life situation the strain of actually finding the d.c.f. yield or n.p.v. of one or more proposals is greatly eased. As for the second point, discounting as a technique will at least have been heard of before (e.g. in connection with bills of exchange and invoices), and a little experience of what it involves soon removes its terrors.

17.7 DEALING WITH UNCERTAINTY

17.71 INTRODUCTION

Before the subject of investment appraisal is left, one other point should be noted. In view of the uncertainties inherent in investment, it will be prudent for a firm contemplating it to safeguard itself as much as possible against the unknown. It may do so at either or both of the two stages indicated earlier, i.e. either when preparing the cash flow forecasts and or when appraising them.

17.72 AT THE FORECAST STAGE

Uncertainty at the first stage may be reduced by preparing more than one forecast for each proposed investment, each forecast being based on different assumptions regarding future costs and benefits:

1 One based on certain reasonable assumptions about, say, the rate of growth of population or gross national product, the impact of advertising

on sales, and the behaviour of other important influences such as future levels of tax.

2 One prepared on a pessimistic basis, assuming that some things do not work out as well as they might.

3 One based on an optimistic view of the proposal's performance.

(In preparing such forecasts, the investing organization will be helped if it has already been able to compile a 'sensitivity index', showing the probable effect on the outcome of any proposal of a given percentage change in each of the critical variables.)

Since all three forecasts cannot have the same probability of being fulfilled, a weight must be given to each. If the forecast derived from 'reasonable' assumptions were thought to be twice as likely to be accurate as the one derived from pessimistic assumptions, which in turn were thought half as likely again to be right as the optimistic one, the weights would be 6:3:2. The net cash flow for each forecast is then multiplied by its weight, and the sum of these weighted forecasts is divided by the total of the weights to give the forecast which will go forward for appraisal.

The main practical difficulty likely to arise with such a procedure is simply that of getting more than one forecast; arriving at one set of figures will be hard enough, and asking the same people to work out two more sets on different assumptions may mean paying too much, in terms of present strain and effort, for an uncertain future benefit.

17.73 AT THE APPRAISAL STAGE

Assuming, as is probable, that the choice between competing proposals is going to be made on the basis of their n.p.v.s., uncertainty may be dealt with through the rate of interest chosen for discounting purposes. Since the uncertainty which worries people is always that things may go wrong, not that they may go right, the present values of the expected proceeds must be under- rather than over-estimated to compensate. This can be done by deliberately discounting them at a rate of interest higher than the business's cost of capital. Proposals which still manage to produce positive n.p.v.s. may then be undertaken in the knowledge that they have a built-in reserve to cushion the investing business against some unforeseen deterioration in their performance.

17.8 SUMMARY

Two investment appraisal techniques are considered: the pay-back period and the use of discounted cash flows. The simplicity of the former does not compensate for its inability to take proper account of the timing of cash flows within and after the pay-back period, and it is best used as a screen to sort out proposals worthy of evaluation by d.c.f. methods. The latter recognize the existence of time in cash flow forecasts and, by discounting, remove the distortions due to it. Thus, despite their heavier demand on calculating facilities, d.c.f. techniques (especially the practically more-useful net present values) provide in principle a more satisfactory basis for ranking investment proposals. Investing on the strength of forecasts which have been weighted to take account of future uncertainties, or discounted more heavily than strictly necessary, helps to reduce disappointment.

18 Preparation and Insurance

18.1 INTRODUCTION

Having obtained assets of various kinds, the businessman is in the same position as anyone else with possessions – i.e. at risk. Risk is inseparable from business, irrespective of the form or size of the organization engaged in it. Resources may not be available when, where, in the quantities, or at the prices required; once acquired, they may fail in some way to perform as expected; the market(s) aimed at may prove inaccessible or, if accessible, unable to absorb the planned output; earnings may prove lower than has been reckoned, or taxed higher; etc. Businessmen may not know any more than ordinary mortals – or be any better than them at guessing – what the future holds; so the plans of both large and small enterprises often go awry. This chapter identifies the different types of risk and the means available to minimize their impact on both the assets themselves and their performance. No distinction is made, incidentally, between 'risks' and 'uncertainties' – the former statistically predictable and therefore insurable by conventional means, the latter not.

18.2 ATTITUDE TO RISK

The underlying principle where asset protection is concerned is simply stated: never carry an avoidable risk. This does not mean that operations are brought to a virtual standstill, paralysed by fear of the consequences of taking any action; nor does it mean that so much is spent on insurance of one sort or another that insufficient resources are left over for activities in the chosen field. What it does mean is this: In any line of production there are uncertainties which the businessman himself will have to cope with: re-arrangements of work schedules because of sickness or disputes in his plant or a supplier's; breakdowns and accidents; specification changes to meet customers' requirements or legal standards at home or abroad; changes in the availability of funds; and a whole host of others. Given this as a normal situation, it would be an act of sheer irresponsibility for him to bear any risk which he could hive off on reasonable terms. The risk-bearing entrepreneur of the economics textbooks is not some manic gambler, deliberately exposing his business to all the hazards he can find. He is, on the contrary, much concerned to minimize those which he must take.

18.3 TYPES OF RISK

The risks which may affect a business can be classified under four headings: human, physical, technical, and economic. They are interrelated, and the distinction between the types is not always clear-cut, but the classification is helpful and will be followed here.

18.31 HUMAN RISKS

Obviously these arise from some error, weakness, or malice of people, whether employed by the firm affected or not. Some detriment may derive from one or other of the various kinds of perverse behaviour, of which the most extreme is sabotage. In general, however, an undertaking is more likely to suffer serious damage as a result of dishonest acts such as fraud or theft, or just plain carelessness – the latter probably most of all (although there seem to be no figures on losses arising under each of these headings). For example, a high proportion of the fires both in the United Kingdom and abroad may be attributed to carelessness.

One of the most dramatic illustrations of the cost to a business of carelessness was the blaze which, in seventy-five minutes on 12 August 1953, destroyed the General Motors Corporation's Hydra-Matic transmission plant of $1\frac{1}{4}$ million square feet at Livonia, Michigan [1]. This fire, which until that date was the largest loss in a single plant ever to have occurred in the United States, seems to have cost the company about $20 million (net of insurance recovery), plus a loss of production of about 100,000 cars [2, 3]. The fire started because an outside contractor's welding crew was working without the protective fireproofing tarpaulins specified by General Motors' regulations, and a spark fell into some flammable rust-proofing compound.

18.32 PHYSICAL RISKS

These, if they materialize, affect adversely the physical condition or existence of the assets involved. They comprise such things as fire (when not due to human agency), flood, drought, earthquake, and hurricane. Their common characteristic is some natural phenomenon which damages or destroys assets.

18.33 TECHNICAL RISKS

These are inherent in productive assets as made, installed, and operated at any one time. When they materialize, they push operating costs above, and/or operating revenues below, those forecast. Assets' performance is therefore worse than expected, although their physical condition or existence may not be affected (unless, for example, an attempt is made to run defective plant at its rated capacity). This lowered performance may be confined to the period when production is just starting or develop after the asset has been running satisfactorily for a while; it may persist throughout the asset's life or emerge only towards the end of it. The common feature of such risks seems to be ignorance – lack of know-how or experience in making and/or operating the assets, wholly or in part, in the form or the particular process in which they are employed. In some cases, 'ignorance' may be too hard a word; the real fault may be more correctly described as recklessness, undue haste or overconfidence. After all, one can scarcely be ignorant of something which is not known at the time; if developments in technology are at the margin of knowledge, malfunction of assets incorporating such developments can hardly be ascribed to ignorance.

(a) West Midlands Gas Board example

Just before local natural gas made its presence felt, the U.K. gas industry was replacing the old retorts needed to make town gas with completely new plant; this new plant was to produce gas from naphtha, using a process worked out by I.C.I. The West Midlands Gas Board (which, with its massive industrial off-take, was one of the most important suppliers in the country) was heavily committed to the new process. On two occasions during the winter of 1965/6, it found itself in deep trouble, so much so that on the worst day, 20 January 1966, 30% of its total gas-making capacity was out of commission [4]. The report of the inevitable official inquiry, after commenting on the interruption of gas supplies to scores of firms because of commissioning delays and breakdowns of newly commissioned plant, referred to the new plant as employing 'process conditions which are on the threshold of present knowledge and experience; and involve an element of pioneering in techniques, materials and methods of construction' [5]. This then was a classic case of technical risk. The new assets failed to perform as the Gas Board had hoped and gave rise to both higher costs and lower revenues than had been forecast – basically because of what were later seen to be design faults and lack of operating experience.

(b) Other examples

Wilmot Breeden's experience in establishing production facilities for car fittings in France in the early 1960s is also relevant – though the technical problems there seemed to be more in the field of personnel selection.

Cunard's difficulties with the maiden voyage of the *Queen Elizabeth 2* provide another and more recent illustration of the same type of problem. There is no shortage of examples – in the United Kingdom or abroad, in the private or in the public sectors. (In looking for examples of technical risk, however, it is probably wise to exclude the aircraft industry everywhere, because this is so closely linked with defence requirements that ordinary commercial criteria of performance may not apply. Shipbuilding also must be regarded with care, as the financing of a large part of it makes it look – not only in the United Kingdom – like an extension of social security arrangements.)

18.34 ECONOMIC RISKS

Economic risks are those arising from a partial or total failure of demand or supply, or both. They are often the most difficult to deal with, as well as being the most damaging. Demand may be less than expected because, for example, of the emergence of competition, changes in tastes, or new government fiscal and monetary measures to deal with a balance of payments crisis – cutting either home sales or, if the government concerned is overseas, exports. Wars, revolutions, and similar disturbances may close markets or cut off supplies; unfortunately they are so common as to make examples otiose. Strikes – in a firm's own plant or in that of a supplier of some component or subassembly – trade embargoes, boycotts, and sanctions all may influence supply.

Of course, the same event will present itself as a different kind of risk to different producers, depending on where they are in the production sequence. Thus, the interruptions of gas supplies referred to earlier were a technical risk for the West Midlands Gas Board, but they were an economic risk for car plants and other gas users. Furthermore, the impact of any damage caused does not stop at this first stage. A drought in an agricultural economy may well lower its ability to export its crop(s). To the extent that such exports are raw material inputs for some later productive operation, the latter will suffer a partial failure of supply – but the original economy may also experience a fall in export earnings. This may lead to a fall in its imports, which in turn may mean a reduction in the demand for someone else's output.

18.4 DEALING WITH RISK

The owners of assets may take various preventive measures to try to avert or reduce the different types of risk mentioned above.

18.41 PREPARATION

(a) Good management

To the extent that there is a business answer to human failings, it lies in good management. This shows itself in such things as the establishment and maintenance of proper procedures for the acquisition, storage, and issue of stocks, and for the carrying out and recording of financial transactions. Such procedures may greatly reduce temptations to dishonesty and probably go as far as is practicable in this field, when allied with effective arrangements for the recruitment and training of staff generally, and for the supervision of risky operations in particular.

(b) Factory design and structure

Among the physical risks, fire hazards, for example, may be reduced by the design and lay-out of plant and machinery, the use of fire-resistant or fireproof materials in structures and products, and the installation of sprinklers and other control devices. The G.M.C. Livonia fire referred to earlier occurred in a single-storey building which was undivided by fire walls and had over 2,000 tons of tar, asphalt, and pitch in the roof [8]; sprinklers were installed in only about 20 % of the area [6], and the heat was so intense that most of the sprinkler heads fused and were thus ineffective anyway [7].

(c) Prototypes and pilot plants

Where the risks involved are technical, and are linked with a finished product which emerges as a discrete unit, the construction and testing of a small number of prototypes (full-scale working models) enable forecast and actual performance to be compared. Any resulting modifications and improvements called for can then be embodied in the final design before commercial production begins; expensive mistakes can thus be avoided. If the technical risk is linked not to a product but to a process – as with the gas-making plant mentioned earlier – the equivalent risk-cutting exercise is the construction and testing of a pilot plant. This is intermediate in size between the laboratory apparatus in which the process was first proved to work and the full-scale production facility in which it will, hopefully, justify itself commercially. As with prototypes, the object of pilot plants is to enable technical 'bugs' to be identified and dealt with before resources are heavily committed; they thus minimize the chance that, when large-scale production begins, costs will go up and/or revenues down because of undetected defects. Either type of investigation may show that the product or process concerned should be scrapped. For obvious reasons, decisions to do so are not widely publicized.

(d) Economic measures

With economic risks, the range of hazard is wider and the range of preparations to deal with it equally so. To forestall or minimize supply interruptions, producers may resort to backward integration or research into substitutes, or they may, as a matter of deliberate policy and despite the possible scale economies forgone, resort to 'multi-sourcing' – i.e. spreading orders for materials and parts over several suppliers rather than relying on just one. To protect themselves from demand uncertainties, they may engage in forward integration or diversification, or may use market research in one or other of its many forms to ensure that, as far as possible, the products they propose to try to sell are those that customers are prepared to buy.

18.42 INSURANCE

If a risk still exists despite all the appropriate preventive measures, it may be dealt with by insurance of one kind or another – i.e. by paying some specialist institution, outside the general production network, to bear the damage which may arise from the risk.

Obviously, such specialist insurers are not able to help where technical risks are involved. If the likelihood of the event to be insured against is unknown, they will probably react by quoting a premium which is so large a fraction of the sum at risk that the owner of the asset concerned will be forced, at least for a time, to be his own insurer.

(a) Fidelity bond insurance

Insurers provide protection from part of the human risk linked with dishonesty, via fidelity bond insurance. With this, the employer of a selected, named person employed in a position of particular financial responsibility is covered if that employee should steal or abscond with the firm's funds.

(b) Physical risks insurance

The most familiar aspect of insurance is probably the policy designed to provide cover in the event of fire, flood, or physical risk generally. (Those who hire their assets instead of buying them may not see the policy or

arrange the cover, but their premiums will be included in the hire charges.)
Two things need to be borne in mind in this connection.

1 However well drafted and suitable the policy providing cover against such
risks is, and however rapidly and fully the insuring body settles claims
arising under it, the asset owner will still suffer damage as a result of the
event insured against if he has not provided himself with cover against
consequential losses and loss of profits. The best insurance company in the
world cannot immediately restore to full operating efficiency buildings,
plant, machinery, and equipment which have been damaged or destroyed –
even if, directly or through subsidiaries, the insurance company itself
makes the assets at risk. For the whole of the interval which must elapse
before the business is back to normal, sales will not be made and profits
will not be earned. Full protection against the physical risks affecting
assets must therefore include protection against any loss or interruption
of the income the assets produce (which, after all, is why they are wanted).
2 In some cases the most important asset of a business is *human*. Where the
continued success of an enterprise rests on the services of someone of
proved gifts, the person in question should not only be retained by a
service contract, but also be covered by generous insurance so that the
business he benefits will have a lump sum to cushion it against the shock
of his injury or untimely departure. Beatles fans, for example, may be
relieved to know that Northern Songs Ltd insured the lives of Messrs
Lennon and McCartney for £500,000 each [9].

(c) Broken contracts insurance

Insurance is also obtainable against some important elements of economic
risk – partly from ordinary commercial firms, partly through the government. The commercially available insurance was referred to in Chapter 5,
where it was noted that a firm may insure its invoices against bad debts. By
so doing, it greatly reduces the economic risk of a partial failure of demand –
failure arising not because people refuse or are unable to take up the
product on offer, but because having bought it they fail to pay for it.

The government department which is concerned with providing insurance
against this particular aspect of economic risk – when it arises in foreign
trade – is the Export Credits Guarantee Department of the Department of
Trade. It will insure anyone who sells goods (and, increasingly, services) on
credit to overseas buyers against the risk that he will not have received
payment for them within six months of the due date. Policies which, in
general, provide cover for 90–95% of the loss involved, protect the seller
from – amongst other things – the risk of the buyer's insolvency, failure to

take up goods which have been sent to him, and failure to pay for them when he has taken them up (which may, of course, be due to reasons rather more sinister than insolvency). They also protect the seller from harm arising from changes in the importer's foreign exchange regulations, if such changes make it impossible for him to discharge the contract originally entered into.

18.5 SUMMARY

Risks of various kinds (human, physical, technical, and economic), affecting the material condition of assets and/or their performance, are inseparable from business operations. Many of them may be reduced by preventive or exploratory measures of different kinds or may be hived off on to specialist insurers. Where these options are open on reasonable terms, common sense dictates that they should be exercised.

19 Hedging

19.1 INTRODUCTION

One particularly damaging form of economic risk is that of a change in the value of certain types of assets due to rapid and unpredictable changes in their prices. In order to deal with this a specialized form of insurance called 'hedging' has developed, based on the use of futures contracts (i.e. those providing for sales or purchases at prices agreed now, but with delivery and settlement deliberately postponed to some specified future date). With these, cover may be obtained in two distinct markets:

1 The commodities market, when the asset at risk is a stock of one or more of the raw materials traded in such markets.
2 The foreign exchange market, when what is at risk is any asset denominated in 'foreign' currency.

This chapter outlines the operation of futures in each of these markets in turn, and indicates some of the peculiar features of the foreign exchange market in them.

19.2 PRECONDITIONS FOR COMMODITIES FUTURES MARKETS

The commodities markets – they are real places – are those in which trading in commodities takes place, for either 'spot' (i.e. immediate) or future payment. The *Financial Times* lists fourteen commodities for which future contracts may be made: copper, lead, tin, zinc, barley (foreign and home-grown), cocoa, coffee, maize, sugar, wheat, jute, wool, and rubber.
   Certain conditions must be met before futures contracts in a commodity, and the hedging they make possible, can work satisfactorily:

1 The product concerned must be capable of being described in some standard form, so that trading in it can proceed, by description only, in terms of this standard.
2 It must be capable of being stored for long periods without deterioration,

so that carrying it physically through time presents no serious problems.

3 Its cost must represent a significant part of the price of finished goods into which it enters, so that a movement of its price will, other things being equal, have a proportionately significant effect on the price of such finished goods.

4 There must be reasonably competitive conditions as to both the supply of the commodity and the demand for the product(s) into which it is made.

Conditions (1) and (2) are more important from the viewpoint of the organizers of the market concerned and of the professional dealers in it; (3) and (4) are those which make commodity processors interested in hedging operations. When they are all met, a market can develop, and a producer whose business consists of processing one or more of the traded commodities into finished or semi-finished products will be able to protect himself against the effect of changes in commodity prices by making the appropriate futures contract. The following much-simplified example illustrates this.

19.3 EXAMPLE OF COMMODITY HEDGING

19.31 THE RISK

Assume that a business processes each month, without waste, fifty tonnes of copper bars into tubing. (This may imply batch production, whereas continuous operations are much more likely in fact; whichever is the case, the hedging requirement and arrangements are unaffected.) Initially, the cost of these bars represents half the selling price (£2,000 per tonne) of the finished goods, but during the month under consideration the cost of copper falls to £900 per tonne and stays there.

Suppose, then, that on 1 November the processor buys fifty tonnes of copper bars. These are delivered physically to his premises and his employees start to fabricate some of them into tube, the remainder being stored until required. This purchase constitutes a spot transaction, based on a primary contract with a seller of copper bars, without which he could not continue to produce. He has either paid or undertaken to pay £50,000 for this consignment, and he expects to be able to sell the tubing made from it for £100,000 on 1 December.

On 3 November the price of copper bars falls by 10%. This cannot affect the price of the copper going through his works – he can hardly go to the seller and ask for some of his money back – but, on the assumptions given, it will have an immediate effect on the price at which he will be able to sell his output. Buyers of tubes know what has happened to the price of the main raw material used in them, and they know that this change will quickly be reflected in lower finished-product prices. (Other processors, replenishing stocks on or after 3 November, will be doing so at the lower price, and will be selling their output in a few weeks at a price based on this.) Such buyers will therefore delay their purchases of tube as much as they can, until the expected price fall occurs. Producers, meanwhile, will find sales dropping at the old price level, and the lock-up of working capital in stocks of tube will soon give them little choice but to lower prices. (Since no one of them is in a monopoly position, or has any degree of market control, any attempt to insist on the old price because that is what is required to cover raw material costs will simply mean that the producer concerned will make no sales at all.) The finished product price will thus fairly quickly fall to a level based on the new, lower level of raw material costs (i.e. to £1,900 per tonne – made up of raw materials: £900, plus other costs (unchanged) and profit: £1,000). At this price, the producer in the example will, on selling his next output of tube on 1 December, make profits of £100 per tonne less than he has expected. (He will not necessarily make a loss, but he will certainly receive less revenue.) This will be due to a change, over which he has no control and for which he is in no way responsible, in the price of his main raw material.

19.32 THE PROTECTION

But he can protect himself against this shortfall by hedging, in the following manner. On 1 November, when he takes delivery of the fifty tonnes of copper bars covered by the primary contract, he can make another, secondary contract (so-called because, unlike the primary one, it is not essential for production actually to occur). The other party to this secondary contract is a 'speculator' or dealer in copper futures. Under its terms, the processor agrees to sell fifty tonnes of copper bars, at roughly the price ruling on that day (e.g. £998 per tonne), for delivery to the dealer in one month. (This period is used here because the production cycle in the example takes a month; there may well be standard contract periods for a commodity.) This secondary or futures contract is the hedge which protects the processor against any significant loss arising from fluctuations in the price of copper; having made it, he can devote his whole attention to the job he specializes in – the running of a plant fabricating copper tube – without having to worry any more about the effect on his business of possible changes in the price of his main raw material.

Suppose, as before, that the price of copper bars falls by 10% shortly after he has taken delivery of a fifty-tonne consignment. As before, when he comes to sell his output the processor will find that he has to accept a lower price for it than he has expected, and that his fabricating operation is therefore less profitable than he has reckoned. But, on 1 December he also has to discharge his 'futures' contract. This requires him to deliver fifty tonnes of copper bars to the dealer concerned, in exchange for which he will receive £998 per tonne. This copper he can now buy, spot, for only £900 per tonne – so under this contract he gains £98 per tonne which practically offsets the shortfall of revenue from his output. The difference between the spot and futures prices of £2 per tonne is analogous to the premium on an insurance policy to cover some other type of risk.

19.4 CHARACTERISTICS OF THE FUTURES CONTRACT

19.41 ITS VOLUNTARY NATURE

As already indicated, the futures contract is quite separate from the physical aspects of production and, like most other business insurance contracts, is an optional commitment. The law, it is true, requires some assets and operations to be insured, e.g. those involving road vehicles or pressure vessels. Generally speaking, however, businesses do not have to insure their assets; it is simply imprudence verging on recklessness not to do so – and the same is true of commodity hedging.

19.42 NO DELIVERY INVOLVED

There is not, nor is there intended to be, any actual physical delivery of the commodity specified in the secondary contract. The dealer's main asset is knowledge; his prime instruments are the telex and telephone. Should delivery of even a fraction of the materials covered by the hedges he enters into be made to him, he would probably have an embarrassing storage problem. The hedge is there to protect a value, and discharge of the contract embodying it calls merely for a transfer of value between the two parties concerned. The dealer will know what has happened to the price of the commodity in which he trades before the processor does. If the price has fallen by the date the future has to be discharged, he will in principle send the processor a cheque for the difference between the contract price and the price actually ruling on the day the contract falls due for discharge; if it has risen, he will expect to receive payment, similarly calculated.

19.43 IRRELEVANCE OF THE DIRECTION OF PRICE MOVEMENTS

Prices may go up as well as down. If the price of copper in the example had risen, the hedge would have worked to offset the processor's windfall gain; he would have been able to sell his output for more than he had expected, but this would have been largely cancelled by the loss made on the future. As already stated, the processor is not obliged to hedge, but if he decides not to do so because he wants to collect a windfall gain he is, in fact, speculating – taking a view about price movements – and thus stepping outside the area of his chosen speciality. He should make up his mind what he wants to do, and stick to it. (The penalties for 'playing the market' were highlighted by the results of some dealings (not all authorized) in cocoa futures in 1973. Rowntree Mackintosh, for example, were reported to have lost about £20 million in this way [1].)

19.44 COST

Although the processor would like the price in the futures contract to be as close as possible to the spot price he has paid, it would be unreasonable to expect it to be exactly the same. The explanation for this can be seen if the situation of price stability is considered. When the commodity price remains stable, the processor will sell his output for the amount he has expected and, when the futures contract is discharged, will neither make a payment to the dealer nor receive one from him. This means, however, that the dealer – who has stood ready to cover the processor against the damage he would suffer if the raw material price fell – will receive no reward for his services. As an insurer of a quite genuine risk he is entitled to some minimum income, and this is most easily provided by quoting future prices for processors' selling contracts at a discount on spot ones. As already pointed out, the processor would regard this difference as an insurance cost, just like any other premium. By the same token, just as he will shop around when he is seeking cover for other risks, so, the processor may be able to choose from a range of prices quoted by speculators at any one time, when he is looking for forward cover in a commodity market; even if dealers all have the same view about the direction in which prices will move, they may easily differ as to how great and when they think the move will be.

19.45 CONTRAST WITH THE PRIMARY CONTRACT

The futures contract must not be confused with an ordinary contract made between one type of producer and another, under which delivery of and/or payment for some specified goods or services are to be made in the future. If, for example, the processor of copper bars makes an agreement with the owners of a copper refinery to buy a stated amount of copper at a fixed price, and/or with an engineering firm to sell the latter an agreed amount of copper tube at a fixed price, these undertakings will not be futures contracts.

It is true that they may call for delivery or payment – on one or more occasions – in the future; contracts very often do. It is also true that, by the first contract, the processor will stabilize for himself, for the term of the agreement, the price at which he will get supplies of copper, and, by the second, the price at which he will be able to sell tube. Combining these will enable him to insulate himself from the effect of fluctuations in the price of his main raw material.

But this is really to miss the point of the whole exercise. The contracts entered into, however long they may last, merely move vulnerability to the hazard of price changes from one stage of the production sequence to another; the risk the processor no longer has to carry is now borne instead by the refiner at an earlier stage and by the engineering firm at a later stage. (The former may push it back, via another contract, to the owner of a copper mine; the latter may try to push it on to his customers – but this does not affect the argument.) Insurance, as a commercial activity, is not concerned with the reallocation of risk among producers; it is concerned with taking as much risk as possible off the shoulders of producers completely and putting it, instead, on those of specialist businesses which are quite distinct from any productive activity (apart, of course, from that of providing the service of insurance!).

19.46 THE SPECULATOR'S REWARD

The speculator makes his money partly, as already indicated, from the spread between spot and future prices and partly by assessing correctly (and sufficiently frequently) the way prices will move. As already mentioned, there must be some minimum spread or dealing margin between spot and future prices if dealers are to be rewarded for their services in periods when prices are expected to be stable. Obviously, the narrower this margin is, the cheaper the cover will be for processors; the wider it is, the less attractive the cover will be to them.

19.47 UNAVAILABILITY OF FORWARD COVER

The dealing margin may widen so much that cover becomes effectively unobtainable. Putting this situation in its most extreme form, suppose that dealers generally thought that the price of copper bars in a month's time might be only half the present £1,000 per tonne, so that none of them was prepared to contract with a processor for future delivery by him at a price above £500 per tonne. (After all, the futures contract of the kind considered here entitles the dealer to receive a stated amount of copper bars on some specified future date. How much he is prepared to pay for this entitlement must depend on how much he reckons he will be able to sell them for.) If this were so, the processor in the example above would face the interesting prospect of a shortfall of £500 per tonne of tube, which he could offset fully via a future only if the price of copper bars fell to zero. He could be forgiven for thinking this improbable, and for concluding that forward cover had dried up.

19.5 FOREIGN EXCHANGE HEDGING

19.51 THE NEED FOR COVER

The other major use of futures as a means of insuring assets against the risk of a loss of value emerges when the assets concerned are denominated in a foreign currency. Two distinct needs exist: one where only some of the current assets of a business are at risk; the other where the whole collection of assets which a business owns in a foreign country is in jeopardy.

Typically, the former need arises when a firm exports to, and invoices in their own currencies customers in, countries the currencies of which are liable to lose some of their foreign exchange value. (This loss might be due to a formal devaluation, if a par value had previously been maintained, or to a 'sink', if the currency were one of those euphemistically described as 'floating'.) The position will then be that the seller, having incurred production costs in his own currency, stands to receive some time in the future foreign currency for that part of his output sold overseas. Whether he is interested in discounting such debts or not, he will certainly wish to safeguard their value against the risk of loss arising from a fall in the relevant exchange rate. In the same way, of course, an importer invoiced in his supplier's currency will suffer an increase in domestic-currency costs if that foreign currency appreciates before the debt is settled. He will be able to avoid this by using the facility outlined in 19.52 – but buying, naturally, where the exporter is selling.

The other situation in which cover is required is one where much more is at stake: a firm with a subsidiary in a country whose currency is vulnerable is looking for protection for the value of fixed as well as circulating assets.

In both cases, the damage arising from the materialization of the exchange rate risk may be less severe and rapid when rates are floating than when they are fixed but, in principle, the risk exists just the same and, as long as it does, it needs to be dealt with.

19.52 THE FACILITY

The exporter above will be able to get the protection he seeks by selling 'forward', through his bank, the foreign currency which he expects to receive.

This means selling for delivery, not at once, when he makes the contract (he cannot deliver what he has not got), but on the day when he reckons the currency concerned will actually reach him. The rate at which he sells will be the future rate ruling in the foreign exchange market at the time of the transaction; in the circumstances specified, it will be below the spot rate. Having made such a contract, the exporter can relax in the knowledge that, no matter how much (if at all) the currency he is to receive falls in value on the foreign exchange market, he will be able to change his sales' proceeds into domestic currency at a rate he already knows. He will thus have safe-guarded himself against finishing up with domestic currency receipts lower than he had expected – or, indeed, had needed to cover production costs.

The firm owning assets overseas can protect itself in the same way – i.e. by selling forward (for delivery in, say, three months' time) an amount of the suspect currency equal to the value of its assets in the country con-cerned. If the currency is not devalued during that three months, the firm will have incurred a cost – the discount on the forward currency – which it can regard as an insurance premium for securing itself against a devaluation loss. At the end of the period it can renew the cover, if it thinks the risk is still present, and do so as often as it likes. It is improbable that the firm will maintain such cover for very long, however, as its cost will outweigh the loss likely to be suffered from any eventual devaluation. If devaluation does occur within the period covered by the futures contract, the firm will reap a 'profit' on the latter to offset the reduction, in terms of its own currency, in the value of its overseas assets.

(It can be argued that this exchange loss is only a paper one – that all the assets are still there in full working order and that, especially if the sub-sidiary is engaged in exporting or is in direct competition with imports, their profitability will rise following the devaluation and their value thus soon be enhanced. This may be so, but it will take some time for such effects to work through the economy. If, in the meantime, the whole overseas concern were to be sold to another, domestically-based business, this sale could quite easily be at a domestic price determined by the new exchange rate. In that case, the paper loss would be realized.)

19.6 FOREIGN EXCHANGE AND COMMODITY FUTURES COMPARED

19.61 MARKET ORGANIZATION

Unlike commodity markets, the foreign exchange market is not a place but a worldwide communications network plus the organizations, mainly banks, which have access to it. The 'speculator' – the other party to the hedge – is not a private dealer but, ultimately, the authority responsible for managing the foreign exchange reserves of the country whose currency is involved (usually the central bank). If that currency has a par value, the central bank uses these reserves, and also any other foreign exchange to which it has access to maintain it. If the currency is floating, it will use them to prevent the market price fluctuating too much, too quickly. The central bank will be under strong pressure to support both the forward and the spot markets – partly because doing so eases the immediate strain on the reserves, and partly because the profits on futures contracts are attractive (as long as the exchange rate does not change). It if does change, however, the losses may be correspondingly spectacular; the 1967 devaluation of sterling cost the Bank of England £356 million [2].

19.62 MARKET SIZE

The markets also differ greatly in sheer size of turnover. Although in both there are minimum trading quantities (e.g. ten tonnes for cocoa futures and $50,000 or its equivalent for foreign exchange), for a variety of reasons the value of foreign exchange transactions greatly exceeds that of commodities, reaching on occasions $1,000 million-worth per hour; among these reasons are the resources of the users of the market and the speed of dealing.

19.63 DELIVERY

It was emphasized earlier that, with commodity futures, discharge of the contract is by transfer of values, not by physical delivery of the commodity concerned. With foreign exchange futures, however, actual delivery of the currencies involved is required. This is to make life a little harder for those who trade in currencies solely because they hope their values will change; as 19·64 below indicates, they otherwise have things pretty much their own way.

19.64 PRICE MOVEMENTS

The nature of the price change which is hedged in the two markets also differs. With a commodity, on any given occasion a genuine possibility may exist that its price will either rise or fall in the next few weeks or months. Where foreign exchange values are concerned, however, the situation is different. If par values are being maintained, it is unrealistic to suppose that a given currency will either appreciate or depreciate in the near future. If currencies under pressure change their values, some will go up (and there will be no chance at all of their going down instead) and others will go down (and there will be no chance at all of their going up instead). When currencies are floating, the day-to-day movements of exchange rates become less predictable, but even then the general direction of these movements is usually clear. (However, it obviously could not have been completely so to the two men in Lloyds Bank Ltd's Lugano branch who, in unauthorized forward dealings, lost their employer about £33 million gross [3].) The much greater frequency of these movements makes no less pressing the need to insure against losses arising from them.

19.7 OTHER FINANCIAL MANOEUVRES

19.71 INTRODUCTION

A business owning overseas assets the value of which is threatened by devaluation may take other steps to minimize the damage, or maximize the benefit, following any change in exchange rates.

19.72 MINIMIZED CASH HOLDINGS

An obvious step is to keep to a minimum any cash and bank balances denominated in the suspect currency. Their value in terms of other currencies would be immediately reduced by a depreciation or devaluation, with no offsetting gain, and the business will try to keep this potential loss as small as possible.

19.73 USE OF LOCAL DEBT ISSUES

If any expansion or development is to be undertaken in the country whose currency is under suspicion, efforts will be made to finance it by borrowings of that currency. Servicing and eventual repayment of such debts will be unchanged in terms of that currency if a devaluation of it occurs, but both will be less expensive in terms of other currencies.

19.74 CREDITOR STATUS IN WEAK CURRENCY

Similarly, if trading takes place between the subsidiary and the parent, or between the subsidiary and one or more other subsidiaries in countries whose currencies are thought not to be weak, dealings with the former will, as far as possible, be so arranged that it has a balance of claims on the other(s). Then, after a devaluation, if invoicing has been in the seller's currency, it will be possible to settle the seller's claims with smaller outlays of the buyers' currencies without reducing the domestic currency receipts of

the selling subsidiary; if billing has been in the buyer's currencies, an
unchanged outlay of these will generate larger amounts of local funds for the
subsidiary in the erstwhile weak currency country. Either way, the group
gains overall.

19.8 SUMMARY

Businessmen have enough to worry about without having speculation in
commodities and/or foreign exchange forced on them. Providing certain
market conditions are met, they may largely insulate their profits from the
effects of price changes in commodities by dealing in the appropriate futures
contracts. The foreign exchange market – a more 'official' one than markets
in commodities, and differing from these in several important respects –
offers protection by similar means against loss of value of current and/or
fixed assets arising from exchange rate changes, whether such rates are fixed
or floating. The damage caused by exchange rate fluctuations can be further
limited by suitable financing and trading arrangements.

References

Bolton Report: Bolton Committee, *Report of the Committee of Inquiry on Small Firms*, Cmnd 4811 (London: H.M.S.O., 1971)

Gower: Gower, L. C. B., *Principles of Modern Company Law*, 3rd edn (London: Stevens, 1969)

Take-over Code: *The City Code on Take-overs and Mergers* (London Issuing Houses Association, 1974)

Yellow Book: *Admission of Securities to Listing*, revised edn (London issued by authority of the Stock Exchange, 1973)

CHAPTER 1

1 *Trade and Industry*, 1974, vol. 14, no. 10, p. 420

2 Bolton Report, 13. 15

3 Statutory Instruments 1968: 1222; 1970: 835, 992 and 1319; 1971: 78 respectively

4 Bolton Report, 13. 16

CHAPTER 2

1 Finance Act 1972, s. 95

2 Jenkins Committee, *Report of the Committee on Company Law*, Cmnd 1749 (London: H.M.S.O., 1962) ss. 67 and 63 respectively

3 *Company Law Reform* Cmnd 5391 (London: H.M.S.O., 1973) ss.. 30–

4 *Companies in 1973* (London: Dept of Trade) table 5. The figures quoted here are from the two registers covering Great Britain; separate registers cover Ulster, the Isle of Man, and the Channel Isles

5 op. cit., table 6a

6 Gower summarizes the advantages on pp. 250–1

7 Income and Corporation Tax Act 1970, ss. 282–3

8 Finance Act 1922, s. 21

9 Bolton Report, 13.19

10 *Companies in 1971* (London: Dept of Trade and Industry) p. 2; *Companies in 1973* (London: Dept of Trade) table 3

11 Bolton Report, 17.23
12 *The Stock Exchange Fact Book*, 31 December 1973, table 2, part A
13 Yellow Book; *see*, for example, p. 133
14 op. cit., p. 161, s. 128
15 *Companies in 1973* (London: Dept of Trade) table 2
16 *Economic Trends* (London: H.M.S.O., November 1967); *Annual Abstract of Statistics* (London: H.M.S.O., 1964) no. 101, table 368
17 *Company Law Reform*, Cmnd 5391 (London: H.M.S.O., 1973) s. 38
18 Sears Holdings Ltd, *Annual Report 1973/4*, pp. 6, 16
19 Monopolies Commission, *Report on the Supply of Certain Industrial and Medical Gases* (London: H.M.S.O., 1956) s. 251
20 *Who owns Whom*, 17th edn (London: Roskill, 1974)

CHAPTER 3

1 Bolton Report, 12.4
2 *See*, for example, Maddison, A., *Economic Growth in the West* (London: George Allen & Unwin, 1964) p. 76
3 Faith, N., 'Companies and their taxes', *The Listener*, 22 April 1965, pp. 583–5
4 Richardson Committee, *Report of the Committee on Turnover Taxation* Cmnd 2300 (London: H.M.S.O., 1964) s. 282
5 Business Monitor Series M3, *Company Finance*, 2nd issue (London: H.M.S.O., 1970) tables 5 and 11

CHAPTER 4

1 ED6 of the Institute of Chartered Accountants is concerned with valuation problems
2 Bolton Report, 13.46–8
3 Page Committee, *Report of the Committee to Review National Savings*, Cmnd 5273 (London: H.M.S.O., 1973) s. 584
4 Reed International Ltd, *Annual Report for year ended 31 March 1974*, p. 13

CHAPTER 5

1 Bolton Report, 12.76
2 Bank of England, *Quarterly Bulletin*, March 1965, table 9(i). Up to May 1972, bank holdings of commercial bills included amounts lent under re-financeable export credits. This figure has therefore been adjusted to exclude £59 million-worth of such credits shown in the *Quarterly Bulletin*, December 1969, p. 434

3 op. cit., June 1974, table 11/1
4 *See* the *Annual Abstract of Statistics* (London: H.M.S.O., 1971) table 394, and the *Monthly Digest of Statistics* (London: H.M.S.O., August 1974) table 171
5 Bolton Report, 12.26
6 op. cit., 12.28
7 Trade Indemnity Co. Ltd, *Annual Report 1973*, p. 17
8 Trade Indemnity Co. Ltd, *Annual Report 1970, 1971* and *1973*, p. 16 in each case
9 Fridman, G. H. L., *Law of Agency*, 3rd edn (London: Butterworths, 1971) pp. 27–8
10 *See*, for example, Griffin Factors Ltd, *Factoring* (1974)
11 Alex Lawrie Factors Ltd, *Factoring*, p. 7
12 Gooding, K., 'Inter-company loans gain in popularity', *Financial Times*, 11 January 1971
13 Raw, C., and Vincent, L., 'Money market loans to M.T.: the vital question'. *The Guardian*, 5 April 1972
14 Gayler, J. L., Richards, I., and Morris, J. A., *A Sketch-Map Economic History of Britain* (London: Harrap, 1957) p. 87

APPENDIX TO CHAPTER 5

1 *Documentary Credits*, 6th edn (London: Waterlow, 1972) appendix 'B', para. b of General Provisions and Definitions
2 op. cit., article 1b

CHAPTER 6

1 *Occupational Pension Schemes 1971*, Fourth Survey by the Government Actuary (London: H.M.S.O., 1972) ss. 6.2 and 3.1 respectively
2 Fleming, S., 'Pay in – lose later', *The Guardian*, 20 November 1972
3 *The Guardian*, 1 March 1973
4 Powell Duffryn Ltd, *Report and Accounts 1972*, p. 8
5 *The Guardian*, 3 October 1974
6 *Financial Statistics* (London: H.M.S.O., 1974) no. 146, p. 88
7 op. cit., p. 90
8 Bolton Report, 12.45

CHAPTER 7

1 Personal communication, 27 July 1973
2 Gower, pp. 347–8

3 Offer for sale document, 18 March 1965; De Vere Hotels and Restaurants Ltd, *Annual Report 1972*, p. 9; and *1973*, p. 5

4 Imperial Chemical Industries Ltd, *Annual Report 1973*, pp. 34 and 33 respectively

5 Offer for Sale document, 7 May 1973

6 Industrial Reorganisation Corporation, *Report and Accounts 1967/8*, pp. 19, 21, and 8 respectively

7 Yellow Book, p. 41, s. 16

8 Letter to stockholders, 3 May 1974

CHAPTER 8

1 Gower, p. 344

2 Associated Hotels Ltd, *Annual Report 1959*

3 Reed International Ltd, *Annual Report for year ended 31 March 1974*, p. 18

4 The Savoy Hotel Ltd, Articles of Association, clause 73

5 *Company Law Reform*, Cmnd 5391 (London: H.M.S.O., 1973) s. 48

6 Yellow Book, p. 164, ss. 149 and 150

7 The Rank Organization Ltd, *Annual Report and Accounts 1973*, p. 48

8 J. Lyons & Co. Ltd, *Annual Report and Statement of Accounts 29 March 1974*, p. 34

9 The Great Universal Stores, *Annual Report for year ended 31 March 1973*, p. 12

10 Letter to ordinary shareholders, 10 January 1969; *Report and Accounts for year ended 30 June 1969*, p. 18

11 Companies Act 1948, table A, s. 118

12 Gedge Committee, *Report of the Committee on Shares of No Par Value*, Cmnd 9112 (London: H.M.S.O., 1954)

13 Jenkins Committee, *Report of the Committee on Company Law*, Cmnd 1749 (London: H.M.S.O., 1962) ss. 32–4

14 Yellow Book, p. 18(6)

15 *Company Law Reform*, Cmnd 5391 (London: H.M.S.O., 1973) s. 49

16 Yellow Book, p. 20(9)

17 op. cit., pp. 154–6

CHAPTER 9

1 Treasury Information Division, *Economic Progress Report* (London: H.M.S.O., 1974) no. 51, p. 2

2 Labour Party notes for speakers, *Industrial Policy No. 13* (London, 1974) p. 8

3 Prest, A. R., *How Much Subsidy?*, Research Monograph 32 (London: Institute of Economic Affairs, 1974) p. 29

4 National Research Development Corporation, *Annual Report and Accounts 1973/4*, pp. 10 and 5; and *1972/3*, p. 7

5 F.F.I., *First Report and Accounts 1973/4*, p. 7

6 *Financial Times*, 15 January 1975

7 *Financial Times*, 18 July 1974

8 I.C.F.C., *Annual Report 1973/4*, pp. 9, 20, 4, 15, and 21 respectively

9 Ship Mortgage Finance Co. Ltd, *Annual Report 1973/4*, p. 5

10 EDITH, *Annual Report and Accounts 31 March 1974*, pp. 4 and 5

11 Agricultural Mortgage Corporation Ltd, *Annual Report 1974*

CHAPTER 10

1 Yellow Book, p. 1, s. 2

2 op. cit., p. 1, s. 4

3 op. cit., p. 2, s. 7

4 op. cit., p. 2, s. 8(a)

5 op. cit., p. 115, s. 111(a)

6 *The Guardian*, 19 September 1966

7 Yellow Book, p. 2, s. 8(b)

8 Offer for Sale document, 7 May 1973

9 *The Guardian*, 10 December 1971

10 Gower, p. 286

11 Yellow Book, p. 4, s. 10

12 Richardson, M. J., *Going Public* (London: I.C.F.C., undated); p. 18 gives a specimen timetable, occupying about four months.

13 Newbould, G., *Business Finance* (London: Harrap, 1970) p. 195

14 Yellow Book, p. 2, s. 8(c)

15 op. cit., p. 115, s. 111(b)

16 *The Guardian*, 16 January 1975

17 Yellow Book, pp. 4–7

APPENDIX TO CHAPTER 10

1 Yellow Book, p. 3, s. 8(i)

2 op. cit., p. 3, s. 8(j)

3 Companies Act 1948, s. 54(b)

4 J. Lyons & Co. Ltd, Appendix to Notice of Extraordinary General Meeting, 2 July 1973

5 Yellow Book, p. 3, s. 8(h)

6 op. cit., p. 2, s. 8(d)
7 op. cit., p. 8a, s. 19
8 *Financial Times*, 17 January 1973
9 Yellow Book, p. 115, s. 111(b)
10 *Financial Times*, 16 January 1973

CHAPTER 11

1 Yellow Book, p. 3, s. 8(e)
2 op. cit., p. 9, s. 22
3 op. cit., p. 10, s. 25
4 Finance Act 1963, s. 59
5 *The Guardian*, 22 June 1972
6 Yellow Book, p. 140, s. 8(b)
7 op. cit., p. 10, s. 25
8 op. cit., p. 120, 1st footnote
9 *The Guardian*, 24 September 1971
10 Yellow Book, p. 3, s. 8(f)
11 op. cit., p. 3, s. 8(g)
12 Gestetner Holdings Ltd, *Report and Accounts 1972*, p. 17
13 Personal communication, 5 July 1974

APPENDIX TO CHAPTER 11

1 Companies Act 1948, s. 56
2 Sears Holdings Ltd, *Annual Report 1972/3*, p. 13
3 Sears Holdings Ltd, *Annual Report 1973/4*, p. 13
4 The Savoy Hotel Ltd, *Annual Report 1972*, p. 3
5 *The Guardian*, 27 September 1972

CHAPTER 13

1 Kleinwort Benson Ltd, *Financial Productivity* (London 1971)
2 Bolton Report, 12.43
3 Association of Certified and Corporate Accountants, *Sources of Capital*, 1st edn (London, 1965) p. 33
4 Business Monitor Series M3, *Company Finance*, 5th issue (London: H.M.S.O., 1974) tables 3, 5, and 6
5 Hire Purchase Act 1938, ss. 11 and 12
6 Sheldon, H. P., and Drover, C. B., *Practice and Law of Banking*, 9th edn (London: MacDonald and Evans, 1962) p. 338

7 Wood, F., *Business Accounting*, 2nd edn (London: Longman, 1973) p. 599
8 Bolton Report, ss. 12.40–1
9 ibid.
10 *Reform of the Law on Consumer Credit*, Cmnd 5427 (London: H.M.S.O., 1973) pp. 11 and 39 respectively

CHAPTER 14

1 *The Guardian*, 4 October 1972
2 Take-over Code, Rule 18
3 op. cit., p. 8
4 op. cit., Rule 33
5 op. cit., Rule 34
6 Reed International Ltd, *Annual Report for year ended 31 March 1974*, p. 14
7 op. cit., p. 15
8 Turner, H. A., Clack, G., and Roberts, G., *Labour Relations in the Motor Industry* (London: George Allen & Unwin, 1967) pp. 49–50
9 Take-over Code, Rule 15
10 Reddaway, Prof. W. B., 'An analysis of take-overs', *Lloyds Bank Review*, April 1972, p. 19
11 *The Economist*, 12, 19, 26 September and 10 October 1964
12 Take-over Code, Rule 21
13 *The Guardian*, 4 May 1974

APPENDIX TO CHAPTER 14

1 Beveridge, Sir W., *Full Employment in a Free Society* (London: George Allen & Unwin, 1944) p. 47
2 National and Commercial Banking Group Ltd, *Monthly Summary of Business Conditions in the U.K.*, February 1975 table 7

CHAPTER 15

1 Slater, G., *The Growth of Modern England*, 2nd edn (London: Constable, 1939) p. 74

CHAPTER 16

1 Board of Inland Revenue, *Capital Allowances for Machinery or Plant (New System)*, Leaflet C.A.1 (May 1973)

CHAPTER 17

1 *See*, for example, National Economic Development Council, *Investment Appraisal* (London: H.M.S.O., 1965), and *Nationalized Industries: A Review of Economic and Financial Objectives*, Cmnd 3437 (London: H.M.S.O., 1967) s. 8

CHAPTER 18

1 Factory Insurance Association, *Report on General Motors Corporation Fire* (Hartford, Connecticut, U.S.A., 1953) p. 11
2 Jones, J. C., 'G.M.'s war against fire', *Factory Management and Maintenance* (U.S.A.), July 1954
3 General Motors Corporation Inc., *Annual Report 1953*, p. 20
4 West Midlands Gas Board, *Annual Report 1965/6*, s. 35
5 Wynn-Edwards Report: *Report on Shortages of Gas Supplies in the West Midlands during the Winter of 1965–6* (London: Minister of Power, 1966) s. 52
6 Factory Insurance Association, *Report on General Motors Corporation Fire* (Hartford, Connecticut, U.S.A., 1953) p. 5
7 op. cit., p. 8
8 op. cit., p. 3
9 Offer for Sale document, 11 February 1965

CHAPTER 19

1 *The Guardian*, 13 July 1973
2 *Annual Abstract of Statistics* (London H.M.S.O., 1970) no. 107, table 275
3 *The Guardian*, 3 September 1974

Additional Reading

Apart from the material already referred to, the following books will be found useful – either generally or in connection with a particular chapter as indicated in brackets:

AYDON, C. *Financing Your Company* (London: Management Publications Ltd, 1972). A very good, succinct analysis of the financial options open to a company, designed for businessmen – but others may benefit, too.

BIERMAN, H., and SMIDT, S. *The Capital Budgeting Decision* 1st edn (New York: Macmillan, 1960). One of the clearest and most thorough treatments of the whole procedure for the appraisal of conventional-type investments (i.e. those with outflows followed by inflows of funds). (Chapters 16 and 17.)

BRITISH OVERSEAS TRADE BOARD, *Export Handbook*, 7th edn (London: H.M.S.O., 1974). This brings together, in one free practical manual, all the essential information required by those contemplating or actually engaged in exporting.

CENTRE FOR INTERFIRM COMPARISON LTD (London). The basic pamphlet shows how, by comparing certain critical operating ratios, a firm can check its performance with that of its peers. (Chapter 15.)

CONFEDERATION OF BRITISH INDUSTRY, *Sources of finance for industry and commerce* (London), 1974. A very useful (though rather dear at £1·50 for fifty-six pages) critical review of the whole range of financial facilities available to firms, designed both to make them aware of what is on offer and to encourage them to use it with discrimination.

HIRSCH, F. *Money International* (London: Penguin, 1969). A slightly dated but still masterly exposition of the origin, purpose, institutions, and operations of the international monetary system. (Chapter 19.)

HUTCHINSON, H. H. *Interpretation of Balance Sheets*, 4th edn (London: Institute of Bankers, 1972). An excellent pamphlet, giving the banker's assessment of the balance sheets which potential borrowers put before him. (Chapter 15.)

INDUSTRIAL AND COMMERCIAL FINANCE CORPORATION
LTD (London). An excellent range of free booklets, giving expert treatment of a variety of practical issues (e.g. the valuation of shares in
unquoted companies, and the procedure for going public).

INSTITUTE OF COST AND MANAGEMENT ACCOUNTANTS,
The Profitable Use of Capital in Industry, 2nd edn (London, 1974).
A valuable compact guide to the principles to be followed and the
techniques employed by managers concerned with the most efficient use of
the resources under their control.

MIDGLEY, K., and BURNS, R. G. *Business Finance and the Capital
Market*, 2nd edn (London: Macmillan, 1972). A good general treatment
of the subject, within the framework of the various markets for funds.

PAISH, F. *Business Finance*, 4th edn (London: Pitman, 1968). One of the
earlier classics, but still useful in certain areas, e.g. sources of funds.

PENIAKOFF, V. *Popski's Private Army* (London: Corgi Books, 1965).
The author ('Popski'), in writing about adventuring generally and the
private army which he formed in World War II in particular, urges a
business-like approach to risk. (Chapter 18.)

RUBNER, A. *The Ensnared Shareholder* (London: Macmillan, 1965). The
stimulating original presentation of the argument that directors, in not
distributing as dividends all disposable corporate income, not only
weaken the economy but also deprive shareholders of an important part
of their freedom. (Chapter 3.)

SAMUELS, J. M., and WILKES, F. M. *Management of Company Finance*
(London: Nelson, 1971). Although written for financial managers, this is
undoubtedly the next step for those who want to go more deeply into the
subject.

SYRETT, W. W. *Finance of Oversea Trade*, 5th edn (London: Pitman,
1971). A first-class and comprehensive exposition of the practical and
technical aspects of documenting and financing foreign trade. (Appendix
to Chapter 5.)

Examination Questions

All questions are from past H.N.C./D. Business Finance papers unless otherwise acknowledged.

1 Explain the *financial* advantages which a business may gain by becoming incorporated.

2 In recent years, a significant number of companies have changed from limited to unlimited status. Explain the meaning of this step, the financial reasons for it, and the potential disadvantages arising from it.

3 How does depreciation differ from other economic costs of production? What effect does providing for it have on the resources at the disposal of the business concerned?

4 'The U.K. arrangements for taxing corporate profits are again neutral.' Explain this, and argue the case either for or against such neutrality.

5 According to a leading journal, the factoring of commercial debts is a fast-growing significant service to the world business community. A client has asked you for an explanation of this statement and whether factoring would be helpful in his business. Draft a letter replying to your client's inquiry. (You may assume such facts concerning his business as you need. The letter should be written as from a firm, using a fictitious name and address.) (From Institute of Chartered Accountants, Final, Part II, General Paper.)

6 Consider the significance of credit insurance from the viewpoint of an individual business, and of the economy as a whole.

7 Discuss the effectiveness of the ways by which, in a period of inflation, long-term lending may be made more attractive.

8 The financial problems facing a business may be solved by changing the composition of its assets rather than by increasing their total. Consider the ways by which this change may be made.

9 Cash & Carry Ltd is a quoted company operating a fast-growing retail chain, and its balance sheet as at 31 December 19.. showed:

Assets:	£
Freehold premises	1,300,000
Furniture and fittings	150,000
Stock	500,000
Cash	50,000
	2,000,000

Financed by:	
1 million fully paid £1 ordinary shares	1,000,000
Revenue reserves	1,000,000
	2,000,000

Further expansion is planned, but internally generated funds alone will not suffice to finance it. Assuming that £250,000 in permanent capital is needed in two to three months' time, and an additional £750,000 within twelve months, describe and justify the methods you would recommend to obtain these sums.

10 Describe the main features of the 'Offer for Sale by Tender', and explain the reasons for its decline in popularity. (*From* Association of Certified Accountants, Certified Diploma in Finance and Accounting, Illustrative Paper 4 – Finance.)

11 Critically examine the proposition that it would be in the national interest, as well as that of individual shareholders, if the general level of gearing in British companies were raised.

12 What is meant by the term 'asset stripping'? Explain why it has been so severely criticized and consider if there is any justification for this activity. (*From* Institute of Chartered Accountants, Final, Part II, General Paper.)

13 The directors of a company are considering the acquisition of equity shares in C.R.W. Ltd. They are divided in their opinions in regard to an appropriate method of valuing the shares to be acquired. The following bases have been suggested:

Net assets.
Price/earnings ratio.
Gross dividend yield.

Required:

(a) A brief explanation of each of these bases with a concise description of the method of calculation.

(b) A short report on the relevance of each method, having regard to the circumstances of the acquisition and distinguishing between the acquisition of a minority holding and the acquisition of the whole issued equity share capital of C.R.W. Ltd.

Note: Ignore taxation. (*From* Institute of Chartered Secretaries and Administrators, Final, Part II, Advanced Accountancy.)

14 The simplest and quickest way for a firm to expand may be for it to take over an existing business. What financial calculations will affect the consideration offered?

15 What is meant by 'overtrading'? In what circumstances is it likely to arise, and what indications of the condition would be provided by the balance sheet of the business affected?

16 The term 'cash flow' is commonly used to refer to a firm's net profit (after tax) plus depreciation. These amounts for Barker Ltd in 1971 were:

Net profit (after tax)	£10,000
plus Depreciation	£15,000
'Cash flow'	£25,000

The following comments arose in a discussion of the implications of the £25,000:

(*a*) The £25,000 is the amount by which the firm's bank balance would have increased (or its overdraft decreased) if the firm had not paid any dividends.

(*b*) The £25,000 is identical with the cash flow which would be used for *discounted cash flow* calculations.

(*c*) An increase in the company's rate of depreciation would increase the amount of its cash flow and consequently increase the working capital available to the company.

(*d*) The depreciation provisions of companies are decided on such arbitrary bases that they may as well be ignored in analysing accounts.

You are required to:
State, with reasons, whether you agree or disagree with each of the four comments. (*From* Institute of Bankers, Banking Diploma, Part II, Accountancy.)

17 Goldsmith requires some equipment for his firm. The following methods of acquisition are available:

(*a*) Purchase of the equipment for cash.

(*b*) Purchase of the equipment under a hire purchase contract, involving an initial deposit and two annual payments.

(*c*) Hire of the equipment.

You are given the following information:

Cash price of equipment	£10,000
Period of use in Goldsmith's firm	5 years
Sale value at end of use	£1,000
Initial deposit under hire purchase contract	£4,000
Two subsequent payments under hire purchase contract, one year and two years after initial deposit	£4,000 per year
Annual rental under hire contract, payable at the end of each year of (five years) service	£2,500 per year

In all cases maintenance and running expenses would be borne by Goldsmith.

Goldsmith's estimated cost of capital over the five-year period is 10% per annum.

Required:

(*a*) Calculate which is the best method of acquisition, on the basis of the available information. (*Ignore taxation.*)

(*b*) Comment *very briefly* on any further aspects which may be relevant to the decision.

(*From* Institute of Bankers, Banking Diploma, Part II, Accountancy.)

Table of factors for $r = 10\%$

Years	Future value of £1 $(1 + r)^n$	Present value of £1 $(1 + r)^{-n}$	Present value of £1 received per year $\dfrac{1 - (1 + r)^{-n}}{r}$	Annual value of £1 received now $\dfrac{r}{1 - (1 + r)^{-n}}$
1	1·100	0·909	0·909	1·100
2	1·210	0·826	1·736	0·576
3	1·331	0·751	2·487	0·402
4	1·464	0·683	3·170	0·315
5	1·611	0·621	3·791	0·264
6	1·772	0·564	4·355	0·230
7	1·949	0·513	4·868	0·205
8	2·144	0·467	5·335	0·187
9	2·358	0·424	5·759	0·174
10	2·594	0·386	6·145	0·163

18 What steps might an international company take, in a period of exchange rate uncertainty, to protect the value of its overseas assets? What problems must be borne in mind in connection with the action taken?

Index